Insights into the world of astrology for everyone. In
reveal why they do it, how they began, why they
researchers, who explain their methods and detail their doubts. I couldn't put it down—
fascinating reading.

Shelley von Strunckel, The Sunday Times astrologer

Phillipson's innovative technique of interviewing professional astrologers reveals the
infinitely rich interconnections between astrology and other fields of inquiry as diverse as
medicine, music, law, politics, mythology, literature and design. It is an essential source
book for a new approach to the tradition of astrology.

Dr. Morine Krissdóttir, psychologist and literary biographer
Books include 'John Cowper Powys and the Magical Quest';
'Shielding: Man and Shelter'; and 'The Dorset Year'

Phillipson's book draws skilfully on interviews with a range of leading specialist
astrologers to create a snapshot of astrological practice at the dawning of a new
millennium. Unlike many books on the subject it sets out to reveal what astrologers
actually do rather than confine itself to generality. Written in an accessible style and even-
handed in its treatment of diverse opinion, this is an important and commendable
contribution to the field.

Dr. Peter Case, Senior Research Fellow, Oxford Brookes University

In this thought-provoking collection, Garry has produced the kind of book that one argues
with and reflects upon, to the benefit of a greater clarity in one's own approach to the craft.

Reviewed in '**The Astrologer's Apprentice**' by John Frawley

A book which has been long overdue... What was needed was a clear, analytical mind
reviewing both positions in an unbiased way and taking stock of the situation. Who better
to do this than a philosopher with a Libra Ascendant, able to weigh the pros and cons in a
spirit of fairness? What better time than a Jupiter–Saturn conjunction to bring together
Saturnian doubt and need for proof with Jupiterian faith in a meaningful universe?... This,
however, is not a dry philosophical book. It is a greatly enjoyable book. For a start, its
layout makes it very readable... Reading the book is like watching a very informative TV
documentary based on solid research, which is presented grouped around clear themes
[and] there are unforgettable little vignettes... The book has a Hegelian dialectic feel about
it, but with a dramatic quality. The *Thesis* having been presented, i.e. the case for astrology,
with its buoyant, inspiring mood, then comes the *Antithesis*, the case against astrology, with
its sobering and even dispiriting tone. Astrologers are shown as having doubts as to what
astrology can and cannot do and the scientific community is brought in with researchers
offering proofs against the validity of astrology. The final chapters, however, offer a
Synthesis in which the latest views of modern science and philosophy are presented... This
book, which makes captivating reading, invites astrologers to reflect upon the nature of
their art in a spirit of genuine inquiry. It also provides a thorough introduction to the subject
for non-astrologers [and] will be a rich source of information for future historians about the
state of astrology and about the attitude of science at the present time.

Reviewed in '**The Astrological Journal**' by **Hélène Haw**,
Agrégée de l'Université (La Sorbonne), DF.Astrol.S, R.C.Astrol,
Tutor of the Faculty of Astrological Studies

Flare Publications

Flare *Astrology Now* Series

www.flareuk.com

ASTROLOGY
IN THE YEAR
ZERO

GARRY PHILLIPSON

First published in 2000 by Flare Publications.

A catalogue record for this book is available from the British Library.

ISBN 0-9530261-9-1

Cover Design: Douglas Mullen
Series Editor: Xen Andreas

Astrological charts generated using Io Edition

Printed by Biddles, Woodbridge Park Estate, Woodbridge Road, Guildford, Surrey GUI IDA

Please Note:
The opinions expressed by the interviewees and the author in this work
are not necessarily a reflection of the opinions of the Publisher or its staff.

About the Designer:
Douglas Mullen lives and works in Scotland. He studied illustration, design and photography at Duncan of Jordanstone College of Art and Design, where he subsequently returned to enrol in the Master of Design programme. He also works as a part-time lecturer. Douglas' work consists mainly of work for print and one-off pieces for exhibition. He has won numerous awards for exhibited work and for multimedia presentations. He welcomes new opportunities and is always on the lookout for new challenges. Douglas Mullen can be contacted on 07974 704860. His website address is **www.d-10.co.uk**

To Write to the Author
To contact Garry Phillipson please write c/o Flare Publications, 29 Dolben Street, London SE1 0UQ, England
He can also be contacted on email: astrozero@btinternet.com
His website address is www.astrozero.btinternet.co.uk

Visit our website at: **www.flareuk.com**

Flare Publications
Head Office: 29 Dolben Street, London SE1 0UQ, England
tel: (020) 7 922 1123; fax: (020) 8 3814169

Dedication

This book is dedicated, with grateful thanks, to everyone who talked to me about their experiences of astrology.

Thanks

In addition to my gratitude to the contributors,
I should like to express particular thanks to Dr Brigitte Friedrich,
Pat Harris and Dr Peter Case for reading and commenting on parts of the text;
to Brigitte again, for being there; to Angela Voss for introducing me to
Iamblichus; to Ray Fury for Mac wizardry; to Frank Clifford and Jenni Harte of
Flare Publications for their support and encouragement; and to Christeen
Skinner for suggesting the idea in the first place.

Contents

Note

Where text comes from an interview it is in Palatino font; my links and additional comments are in GillSans.

Chapter I
Two Kinds of Amazement

Astrology amazes everyone who thinks about it. Some see a universe in which the stars signal the quality and course of their lives, and find this amazing. Others see a superstitious pseudo-science, mired in beliefs from a medieval world, and find it amazing how gullible people can be.

These two kinds of amazement both suggest reasons why astrology is worth thinking about. If it really works as astrologers claim, there are (obviously enough) good reasons to study it. But if all the astrological work ever done has been pure fantasy, there are still compelling reasons to learn more about the subject and the motivations of its practitioners.

If astrology grew entirely from imagination, then it is a collective myth that has been formed, sustained and developed by us in an attempt to make sense of the world; an intellectual fossil whose form shows what we do when we try to understand the world and our place in it. This, together with the fact that a belief in the power of the stars has influenced humanity and its institutions through much of recorded history, means that the study of astrology—*even if astrology itself is not considered objectively valid*—can disclose new perspectives on this world and the way we relate to it. If we can decide what we are looking at, it will be worth looking—but, given the range of misconceptions about the subject, this seems to be easier said than done.

Astrology tends to polarise opinion. Skeptics frequently argue that astrologers are at best delusional, at worst frauds; many astrologers insist that their craft works so clearly, so reliably, that only prejudice keeps critics from accepting it. Such simplistic views commonly lead to intellectual deadlock between the two camps, with neither willing to concede an inch. This is in the interests of no-one: those who seriously investigate the subject and believe they have substantial evidence—either that astrology works or does not work—are denied a fair hearing because of a common assumption that the case is already closed. And those who have no axe to grind, but might simply be interested to know the facts, find it difficult to penetrate through a fusillade of propaganda from both sides.

This Book's Method and Structure

In an attempt to get away from misconception, and instead to examine the core of astrology, this book presents what astrologers do, and why they do it, in their own words. The text has largely been assembled from thirty-three interviews recorded between 1996 and 2000 with some of the most eminent, and/or interesting, figures in the field. Amongst the contributors are people who believe completely in astrology's validity and accuracy, some of whom present compelling evidence for their subject's scope and power. There are also scientific researchers who present evidence to show that nothing has been proved, that all conclusions are either partial or just plain wrong.

I have tried to present the issues, and the range of opinion, accurately—so that readers may draw their own conclusions. It would be artless to pretend that I do not have opinions of my own; but I have tried to set those to one side, so as to present the strengths of each of the views I encountered. In fact I found that the more I probed astrology's status—true or false, science or myth—the more complex and refractory the issues became. So if this book appears fragmented and contradictory, I claim that as a virtue—if it were otherwise, it would not be a faithful account.

To present each interview in its entirety would have made the book both huge and tedious to read, so the approach taken has been to assemble excerpts theme by theme. The chapters develop in what is hopefully a natural progression, beginning with a look at the ways in which people get interested in astrology in the first place. This introduces the question of what, exactly, astrology is. Several chapters are therefore devoted to different applications of the subject, beginning with the most high-profile variant—the star-sign column in newspapers and magazines—and moving on through astrology in business, therapy, football, and many other areas of life.

Having defined the subject in this way, the focus shifts to broader issues, taking in different ideas about what astrology actually is; how it works; and *if* it works.

The whole book has been written so that it can be understood by those with no prior knowledge of astrology. Inevitably, some astrological terms appear, but these can be translated by recourse to the glossary in Appendix 4—where a very brief introduction to the basics of the astrological chart will also be found. Anyone interested in pursuing one or another of the avenues of thought referred to in the book will find references to people, organisations, books, and so on in Appendices 1, 2 and 4.

Better Questions

When Percival Lowell heard that there were canals on Mars, he decided to devote his life to finding out more about them. It eventually turned out that there were no canals on Mars, but the process of looking for them led Lowell to discover that there was a planet beyond Neptune. The existence of this planet, Pluto, was finally confirmed eighteen years after Lowell's death. Perhaps in looking at astrology we will find ourselves in a similar position to that of Lowell—the questions we started out with no longer relevant, but supplanted by new and better questions.

For there are questions lurking behind the very idea of astrology; perhaps they may turn out to be more significant than astrology itself. Is life driven by blind impulse, or drawn toward vision by intelligent design? Is it possible to know? How can thought approach such a question? Should we trust scientific methodology to determine what is real, or is there latent in humanity a way of understanding that surpasses reason?

If the different ideas and perspectives contained in this book lead to such questions being asked then it will have found, and served, its purpose.

Chapter II

Getting Interested in Astrology

Beginning with a Mystery

Astrology's origins are, appropriately, shrouded in mystery. Archaeological discoveries show astrologers serving the courts of Mesopotamia around 2100 BCE (Barton 1994, p.11), but there is no evidence to suggest whether it originated there, or was a migrant from yet earlier cultures. The perception of mystery, coupled with a desire to do something about it—embrace it, destroy it, or understand it—is often what attracts an individual to the subject:

> **Christeen Skinner:** I was brought up in Scotland. My father used to walk me back from Brownies when it was dark. One night, he pointed out the planet Mars; he explained that 'planet' meant 'wanderer', and told me about the planets and constellations. Then he said, rather coyly, "Some people think that they influence life on earth." There was a long silence, because I didn't have a clue what he meant. We walked on, and as we were walking down our garden path, he said, "Don't say anything to your mother about that."
>
> It was almost like some great sexual secret. I'd been told something, but I didn't know what the next question was. The following week my father was very reluctant to talk about it. Eventually, I got a book on astronomy from the library and realised that that was the wrong thing, it didn't have the answers. I asked about astrology at school. The teacher went bananas: "Don't use that word in this place," and so on. Then I really knew that it was something I needed to know about!

Christeen Skinner now provides astrological advice to a range of major businesses; the tale of how she got there will be picked up in Chapter IV. Another who was attracted by the prospect of mysteries being revealed was Dennis Elwell:

> **Dennis Elwell:** The way I became interested in astrology set the path I was to follow. When I was sixteen, there were a lot fewer books available and their tone was different. In the public library I came across 'Secret Service of the Sky' by Louis de Wohl... Imagine—the planets as spies in the sky, leaking secret information! It appealed to my Scorpio ascendant.

Geoffrey Cornelius was another hunter after secret knowledge:

> **Geoffrey Cornelius:** I think that a certain type of male consciousness, at a certain age, gets very interested in the symbolic, in occult and spooky things. I did; I made little symbol systems for myself, and did all sorts of things—I tried scrying, and all sorts of magicky, telepathy, weirdy things. I discovered the Tarot quite early, and I made my own Tarot symbols, tried my own

systems—I was into that trip very early. I can detect it in someone immediately; that thought-form, that state of mind. That thought-form actually develops into full-blown occult systems.

So I was always into that type of symbolic world. I did quite a bit of Tarot-reading—whilst other people were going out being normal teenagers, I was into this sort of thing! I got interested then in kabbalah through Tarot, and that's when I read Dion Fortune and such things.

So, like many earnest young people, I was seeking the meaning of life—I really was! That's when, around 19-20, Jung came in. I was totally blown away by Jung, who seemed to encompass all of this area completely. I'd come across astrological symbolism, and realised that there was such a thing, but it made no impact on me. I then encountered the I Ching, and got interested in all the surrounding philosophy of the I Ching, tried to read up a bit of Chinese philosophy. That's the background, before I ever got involved in astrology.

Then I was on holiday in Wales... and there was a girl there who did astrology; she had an ephemeris, and asked for my date and time of birth. She said, "Oh yes, your Moon's in Capricorn as well as your Sun," and began to say a few things about my Moon, and something else in my chart. I was quite surprised at what she said, it seemed perceptive (very simple, the things she was doing). My response was absolutely dreadful, actually. I remember thinking, "Hmm... that's interesting, if she can do that, I certainly can..."

That really was the moment. I thought, "Yes, I must look at this astrology." And then I did what a certain type of intense young man does — I plunged in, consumed everything. Within six months I was studying Indian astrology, I was studying house systems, the astronomy of it, techniques... just totally wrapped up in it.

I'm Going to Earn a Million Bucks...

A frequent theme of interviews was of having, at some point, an experience of astrology giving impressively accurate information. Another theme was that of feeling skepticism towards the whole idea of connection between the stars and life on earth; yet another was dismay at the ineptitude of many who consider themselves astrologers. All three themes come together in the following excerpt:

Noel Tyl: How I first heard of astrology is different from how I first became interested in astrology. While I was at Harvard I did a lot of study of comparative religions. I had the great fortune of studying under the lectureship of Paul Tillich—the great Protestant theologian. And in the readings of ancient histories and archaeological backgrounds of civilisations, with particular regard to the spirit—which preceded formalised religion, of course—we found always a reference to 'the firmament'; to the skies, to apparent natural order in the sky. Of course the old thesis of the gods with their influencing earth, and the way gods were then brought down to earth within communities: the polytheistic approach of the heavens related to nature below, was a seed for every one of these civilisations and religions. And astrology kept appearing in beautiful, cogent, meaningful ways. So that is really the first time I heard about it in a *serious* way. I guess I was familiar beforehand with newspaper astrology, and thought it a bunch of fol-de-rol, and playthings and gamesmanship, and I never read a column that I can remember. But of course, I had a general awareness.

But it was a serious, nice beginning. An awareness that looked *antique* to me at first learning.

Q: And when did you actually begin practising astrology?

Noel Tyl: Well… some years after leaving college, I continued my studies of archaeology and ancient history as a hobby. At that time I was pursuing a music career, studying to become an opera singer, and at the same time I was working as a promoter on Madison Avenue, New York City. So I was exerting a lot of energy to find my place in the world. I subsequently became an opera singer for twenty-some years. And also, as I transitioned out of that I went back to promotion and started my own advertising agency in Washington D.C. Very early on, as both these careers started to develop, I was watching television one evening. And the television programme was monitored by a very famous American producer and television personality of that era, which was 1965-67, a man named David Susskind, a very well-known man then. He had a talk-show, in which he crucified guests routinely. I turned it on to watch, and there were three women there with grey hair, and what I recognised to be old ways of presenting astrology. Even then it sounded arcane, the way they talked about astrology. And Susskind was just ripping them apart.

Something like a bolt of lightning hit me—seriously! And I *exploded*. I remember calling my wife into the room. She came in, and I said, "*Look* at this! What these people are saying is *valid*. It's *got* to be *real*. But they're saying it so *poorly*! And they're getting butchered." We watched it a little bit, and I exploded. It wasn't just a comment—it deafened the room! I said, "I'm going to learn how to do this, and earn a million bucks!" Those were my exact words. And so we calmed down, and the programme ended. The next weekend, when we were free, we went to the Yellow Pages, and looked up 'astrology', and we found a book store. Now there's a very well-known book-store just above Bloomingdale's in New York City (on Lexington Avenue). It was on the second floor. We climbed up these rickety steps, and we walked into an astrology book store, which was run by a prominent little Hungarian astrologer named Zoltan Mason. We started talking. I said all the arrogant things which novices still say about astrology—"How can it be true that everybody's horoscope is destined for death when a plane goes down?"—things like that. Naïve speculation without any information at all. And I was really trying to assert my intellect in a field that I was basically, probably, afraid of, although I had this early beginning of respect.

I think it's everybody's way. When they are confronted by astrology at the beginning, it is threatening—because we don't know about it. Yet we hear, and presume, that it is going to manipulate us somehow. My wife was very patient, standing there. And Mr Mason said to me, "Don't be afraid of what you don't know." He sounded like Bela Lugosi, you know? He said to me, "You must be a Capricorn." I looked at my wife, and she said, "You are!" And immediately my analytical mind asks, "Now, how did he know?" It was obvious from the shape of my head, the way I was talking, I was dressed totally in black... not a hard guess!

Then he looked at my wife, and said, "You, madam; you must be a Pisces!" She said, "I am!" I was *stunned*. I looked at him and said, "Mr Mason, how do you know that?" He looked at me, and the classic, wonderful line which I'll never forget was: "Capricorns always victimise Pisces!"

He was putting me down while displaying his skill.

A Natural Talent

Noel Tyl's comment, "From the very beginning, astrology was a natural thing for me. It was so natural I couldn't believe it," was echoed by a number of astrologers. Two examples follow:

Maurice McCann: I gave up music to go into astrology. Astrology just took me over—I couldn't resist it. And at that time, to me, astrology was really very easy. All my life, everything had been very very difficult. Anything I attempted to do, anything I tried to learn—even just in life in general, everything was an uphill slog. It was a typical Saturn opposing the ascendant, with double Capricorn, thing*.

But when I got into astrology, I just couldn't believe it. I got this little paperback book ['Astrology'] by Ron Davison. It showed how to draw up a horoscope, and said that you had to buy an ephemeris. So I went out and got the ephemeris, and that night I looked at the instructions and drew up my

---

* A good example of the way an astrologer will use symbolism as shorthand. The planet Saturn signifies (amongst other things) difficulty and seriousness. These qualities are reckoned to feature significantly in the life if Saturn forms an opposition aspect to the ascendant, as in McCann's case (see Appendix 4 for definitions of terms). 'Double Capricorn' means, in this instance, having both the Sun and Moon in Capricorn; Capricorn has a similar quality to Saturn, hence it suggests more of the same.

horoscope. I didn't realise until years afterwards that people couldn't normally do that.

I practically learned the symbols in one night. I don't remember learning them, I just seemed to do it. You can imagine—I was struggling with the music, playing guitar in some really terrible bands. And the astrology was so easy, so I decided to go down that path, and eventually gave up music for astrology.

Christeen Skinner: Looking back now, I don't remember learning astrology; I honestly don't think I did. It's as if it was just a language that was already there, lying dormant.

The recurrence of that phrase, "I don't remember learning [the basics of] astrology" calls for some comment. How do you teach people something if they know it already? Two people who have considerable experience of teaching astrology, and who work on the basis that the necessary knowledge is largely innate, are Adrian Duncan and Warren Kenton:

Q: If you were going to set up a school to teach people astrology, how would you go about it? What would you emphasise?

Adrian Duncan: I did have a school for seven years. I wouldn't set up another one today, because I feel that I've gained all the experience I can cope with. I would be repeating experiences if I carried on. It was wonderfully enriching, and I would do it the same way today—which was totally experiential. Not teaching the way planets work in theory, but evoking the experience of the planets in the living testimony of the people who are present. Obviously, that's the most interesting way of doing it; people never get bored that way, you don't get tired, everybody gets inspired, you learn something all the time as a teacher. The idea of just saying what you know—you have to do that to a certain extent, but it would be very tiring in the long-run, for me.

So you want this incredible process of discovery all the time, and I do that through interview techniques. For instance, you describe the effect of Mars in aspect to Saturn, then anyone who has that aspect evokes the experience of it through their own words. It's crystal clear for everybody present, and couldn't possibly be something anyone's invented.

I like to see astrology proved every moment, through people's testimony. So that's the basic thing about how I would teach—experientially.

Q: So it's important for the individual to re-invent astrology within themselves?

Adrian Duncan: Yes, otherwise they are never going to be any good. Even some people studying astrology don't really believe it works. They don't realise how much it works; and I like to show them that it is working all the time, and never takes a rest. It's really there all the time.

Adrian's comment about doubt in astrology—even amongst astrologers—raises a theme that will be examined further in later chapters. His comments on learning astrology, meanwhile, were echoed by Warren Kenton. It needs to be mentioned, by way of introduction to the following excerpt, that Warren uses and teaches both astrology and kabbalah. (Kabbalah is an ancient system of esoteric knowledge, with many parallels to astrology.)

Q: Whose books did you study in the first place?

Warren Kenton: Well, the interesting thing is that I didn't learn from books. We had a kabbalistic-astrological study group, and we learned by doing a series of exercises such as bringing in a poem or a picture which described one of the planets. Then we would spend weeks working through the zodiacal signs. We had a wonderful arrangement of inviting someone who was desperate to have their chart done to cook us a supper, on the basis that we did their chart. After a slap-up dinner, we would do the cook's chart, influenced, no doubt, by the standard of their cooking. After doing many charts, we began to recognise archetypal patterns and the way they affected temperament or fate. One could see the way the planets would harmonise, or generate discord and strife.

The question arises of how it could be possible that a knowledge of astrology might be "already there, lying dormant" as Christeen Skinner put it, so that the task of the astrological teacher is not so much to give out information as to awaken a way of thinking about the world within their students. Two possible explanations came from Bernadette Brady and Pat Harris:

Bernadette Brady: I really do believe that each human mind is its own starry sky—we do have our circumpolar stars, we do have the centre of our mind, and we seek it just like the Pole Star; we seek the place that everything else orbits around. In other words, inside here is exactly the same as outside there.

I personally believe that this is so because, when the human mind was forming, we were very much devoted to the starry sky; and as we came into awareness (whenever that was) we did so with the sky as our guide. So we built our mind, collectively, mirroring the sacred pole and everything moving around it. That's my personal philosophy on the construction of the human mind.

There are whole slabs of philosophy in various tribes which say that, if you go out at night and look at the pole, this is very healing. You can actually heal diseases that way. Really, this is just a form of meditation—it's going back to that centre.

Pat Harris: Because we haven't traced [astrology's] origin, we don't know where it comes from—yet. And until we do that, we won't be fully confident that we know what there is to know about it. And when I say 'it' I mean astrology in its developments through different cultures. It may have originated at different points in different cultures.

Or, again, it may have originated (as Cayce implies in his work) from one point, which predates what has become known as the Atlantean civilisation. Cayce, an American mystic of the first half of the 20th Century, living in Virginia, talked of the beginnings where [he said] we were not solid beings, we were elemental rather than flesh and blood. But we were attracted to the earth as it evolved, because we became fascinated by the different kinds of experience that could be had by entering into the developing species on the Earth itself. And the more that spiritual consciousness entered into flesh, the more trapped it became by it, and the less it remembered of its spiritual life to help it get out again. It would be an interesting point for discussion to consider that astrology may have been developed by these beings, so that they would have a language to reclaim their spiritual consciousness again, once they had become firmly trapped in this incarnating cycle. Well, it's just an idea!

A Will to Power

This description of astrology's origins can (as I think Pat implies) be taken as literal truth or metaphor. In either case, astrology is seen as a reminder from ourselves, to ourselves, of who and what we actually are; a tool, therefore, for self-knowledge and wisdom. To draw a broad generalisation, it could be said that this is one of the two things which attract people to astrology; the other being the desire for power:

Robert Zoller: I am certainly one of those people who came into astrology driven by egotistical impulses. I was interested in astrology because I was interested in magic; I was interested in magic because I wanted power for myself. I was willing to cut a deal with God (or whatever powers might exist) to get a little bit of power, because I was such a powerless wretch that I needed something to make myself feel as though I were doing something significant in the world. I'd been systematically frustrated, teased, the butt of many cosmic jokes; constantly confronted by my own impotence and at the same time having intuitions of glory, which always seemed to be like Tantalus, a little bit out of reach.

Adrian Duncan and Warren Kenton put forward the merits of learning astrology 'from the ground up'—starting with a few basic principles, trying to apply them, and learning in the attempt. It is interesting to contrast this with Robert Zoller's approach. Zoller is one of a small band of contemporary astrologers who, in order to reach a level of astrological knowledge with which they could feel satisfied, has shouldered the burden of learning archaic languages in order to translate medieval texts. I don't want to portray Robert Zoller's approach as a polar opposite to that of Adrian Duncan and Warren Kenton, but it certainly exemplifies a different slant on the business of learning astrology, where more emphasis is placed on academic research and precision in mobilising the resources which astrologers from ages and cultures long gone have bequeathed us.

Robert Zoller: I started studying astrology systematically in 1970 or '71, with Zoltan Mason in New York City—he had a bookstore in Lexington Avenue. He was teaching what you would call modern astrology, a mixture of psychological and predictive astrology. In his case, his origins being central European (he was Hungarian) it had a very strong central European flavour to it. It was demanding, rigorous, not terribly optimistic (in fact he's been accused of being a doom-sayer in the United States, where they like people to speak very optimistically, regardless of the circumstances). His style of astrology appealed to me, because I saw him as a no-nonsense, down-to-earth sort of fellow. Nevertheless, I could see that he was teaching—again and again—fairly modern stuff. When I found, in his bookstore, 'The Astrologer's Guide' (Bonatus, 1986), including the 146 considerations of Guido Bonatti, I knew that I had found the real astrology.

Ultimately I asked him, "Why do you trouble us with all these theories of psychology and all this incomplete theosophical mysticism? How can I get to the good stuff?" And he told me, "You have to learn classical languages— Greek, Latin, Hebrew, Arabic, maybe German and French as well—in order to get to the real material." So I went back to school and learned Latin. In the process, before I stopped studying with Zoltan, he began to instruct me in the 21st book of 'Astrologia Gallica' by Jean-Baptiste Morin de Villefranche. I've since come to see that Morinus was a reformer of the older material I encountered with Bonatti in the 'Astrologer's Guide'. Nevertheless, one of the things that appealed to me about Morinus's work was his rationality, his rigour, his discipline, his Aristotelean philosophy (which he has in common with Bonatti and medieval astrologers generally).

That was 1973 or so, when I began to get interested in medieval astrology. It wasn't until I got finished with the Summer Latin Institute at City College Graduate Center, 42nd Street New York in 1974, that I began to have any facility in Latin. In 1975, when I was at the Institute for Medieval and Renaissance Studies at City College 138th Street in Compton Avenue, New York, I began to translate Marsilio Ficino's 'De Vita Coelitus Comparanda' and some of Agrippa, and was able—through the good graces of my teacher in palaeography at City College, who was also a professor at Colombia University—to get an actual microfilm of Bonatti's 'Liber Astronomiae' from Columbia University.

So I began to translate from Bonatti's work back then. I got through the

Institute for Medieval and Renaissance Studies; I was able to get hold of Bonatti's 'Liber Astronomiae' and John Baptiste Morin de Villefranche's 'Astrologia Gallica'. Those two works have basically dominated my astrological endeavours since that time. Of late, I have gone in the direction of the medieval.

Q: You mentioned having worked as a dynamiter and in a bar at different times. Presumably your studies were going on at the same time?

Robert Zoller: Yes. I left Pratt Institute in 1968—a year short of graduation: there was too much revolution, too much sex, drugs and rock 'n roll going on, and I was too closely involved with it. So I went back upstate to where my family was living (in Putnam County, New York State—a fairly rural area) and very quickly ran foul of my old man. The two of us had to live in the same house for a while, which neither one of us particularly featured! I had already begun to entertain my interest in the occult by reading cards (mostly poker cards at that point, but I was starting to get into Tarot cards). I was getting far too weird for my old man, who was a German engineer. I wish I could have learned more from him, but things being the way they are, that wasn't the way it worked out.

I left the house and got a place of my own, so was free to do whatever I wanted. I began buying books on astrology, working in the meantime for the electrical utility company as a labourer. That was where the blasting and drilling came in—working on a pneumatic drill all day long, blasting holes, setting poles, things of that sort. I eventually got into climbing, became a lineman... that was 1969/70. By 1971 I was tired of freezing my tail off (as a lineman I was outdoors all winter long, 10 degrees below zero, with the wind blowing round my ears. I couldn't feel my feet when I came down off the pole). I began asking myself questions like, "What the hell am I doing here? Frostbite! who am I trying to impress?" So I went back down to New York City, and that afforded me the opportunity to study with Zoltan Mason, and so to continue my astrological studies. But I had to support myself while I was doing this, so I was working in an electrical business, in a machine shop for a while, as a bartender for a while. Then I would go in and out of the construction business—working in it for a year, getting out, working as an astrologer for a year or so, getting out and going back into construction. I did that for a number of years.

In 1992 the bottom fell out of the construction business in New York City, and this tremor in my left arm began in 1991, so I was sort of forced into the direction of going into astrology full time and staying there. I've been very productive since I did that, so it's serendipitous.

Robert Zoller added, "Maybe it's true when they say that the disempowered feel as if they need magic." The sentiment might be echoed by Adam Fronteras:

Adam Fronteras: I was fairly ill as a child, with asthma. I watched a lot of horror films, because often I was so ill that my last medication wouldn't be until twelve o'clock at night. And the only thing that would keep me quiet was horror films. So even as a six or eight year old, I was watching Hammer horror films from the late '60s. I think that started an interest in the occult in general.

Because I was a very ill child, confined to bed (I was basically at Great Ormond Street continuously until I was eight years old, then I went to a hospital school until I was sixteen) I did a lot of reading—often things like 'Dracula' and 'Dr Jekyll and Mr Hyde'. Through my teen years I read a lot about the occult, and took a basic interest in astrology. When I was twelve or thirteen, 'Live and Let Die' came out; Tarot cards were very much at the front of the sales drive for the film, and my parents bought me a pack. After that, I was reading the Tarot for all the nurses and cleaners in Eastbourne Hospital, where I was at the time...

Science Meets Astrology

Christeen Skinner was attracted to astrology by an urge to explore a mystery; a motivation for Robert Zoller and Adam Fronteras was the urge to overcome dissatisfaction with their lives by gaining magical powers. In the case of Bernadette Brady the initial motivation was intense irritation with astrology, and a desire to disprove it once and for all:

Q: How did you get interested in astrology in the first place?

Bernadette Brady: God, I hate that question!

Q: Sorry, but it has to be asked.

Bernadette Brady: The Parkers got me into astrology—they have a lot to answer for, for many people. I've told them this! I think the Parkers do a tremendous job for astrology, because they act as that bridge between the Sun-sign and the serious astrologer. They are the doorway that so many people pass through.

What happened was, I was very interested in the positions of planets, so I needed an ephemeris. I had no idea where to get one, so I wandered into a bookshop and they had the Parkers' book ['The Compleat Astrologer']. What interested me was, at the back of it they had that simple Moon ephemeris. So I bought it for the ephemeris, to be aware of where things were, and then I read the book! That afternoon, I sat down and taught myself how to draw up a chart. I can remember the distinct Saturday afternoon, I've even backtracked the date and roughly the time, because obviously this is important!

I had a blank piece of foolscap paper, used a plate to draw the circle, and I drew up my own chart. I can remember looking at it, thinking the whole thing was a load of garbage. I was just doing it for interest. And then of course the ego kicks in and thinks, "Well, what does it mean?" So it was back to the Parker book, obviously really cookbook* stuff. I thought, "Well, that's an interesting fluke"—because it was quite accurate.

My siblings and I had grown up knowing our birth times—you know, "You're not really nine until eleven fifteen..." That was part of our birthday ritual. So I knew the birth times for my three siblings, and immediately plotted them up and used the Parker book to look at these charts. What really amazed me was that... you know every family has a black sheep. I don't mean this negatively, maybe it's better to say "one who is different." Well, in our family, that one is a Sun-Uranus conjunction in Gemini, with Aquarius rising. Well, *of course* they are different!

The Parker astrology picked that one up, and that really amazed me—that I had these four charts, and this had picked up that this one was different; this was the one marching to a different beat. And it annoyed the hell out of me, because if astrology worked then what I had devoted my life to was in tatters. It was a personal experience that was very important to go through, and I think if more astrologers had to go through that they would really understand the anger that science has against astrology—because if astrology's right, they are in trouble.

Q: You were a microbiologist at this time?

Bernadette Brady: Yes. So, I took the attitude of, "I'm going to disprove this." So I started to simply collect up the birth data from all my friends, you know the way you do these things. It was *not* a Gauquelin approach†, let me make that quite clear! I kept drawing up these charts by hand on scraps of paper, and using the Parker book.

The damned stuff kept working—that's what really annoyed me. So I started doing more and more (this was in 1976). I'd spend a weekend drawing up charts; I went and got more books, started writing things up... I started getting very angry. Then I had a very bad car accident where a Volkswagen doing 40 mph hit me on the back of the head. Of course they carted me off to hospital and x-rayed the head. They found that my head had an inch-thick

---

* 'Cookbook astrology'—compiling a character profile by putting together sections from an introductory astrology book.
† That is, it was not a statistical/scientific approach. The work of Michel and Françoise Gauquelin is described briefly later in the book.

plate of bone—so actually I don't have much room here for a brain... it's official! [laughing] Apparently my father had it as well, and he had a bad accident (obviously, with my strong Saturn I have a lot of my father in me). Anyway, I had bad concussion and had to just lie in a dark room. I could listen to a radio but couldn't do anything else. Couldn't watch TV, couldn't read a book.

That accident was 1st June 1976 at nine in the morning. Whereas some people have a gentle tap on the head to tell them, "Let's get metaphysical here," I had to be belted by a Volkswagen doing forty! But that did it. I thought about astrology. By the time I came out of that, I had moved from Philosophy A to Philosophy B!

So then I just started studying astrology. I'd gone through the anger and the rage at having wasted my life studying science, and I just started studying astrology very seriously. Kept working as a microbiologist, but eventually I just quit the whole thing and became an astrologer—I did that in 1980. I was driving to work one day thinking, "When I retire I'm going to really be able to study astrology..." I hit the brakes, and thought, "My God, why wait until I retire? What a stupid thing to do—to wait until you're sixty before you do what you want to do with your life!"

Although I didn't quit then and there, I decided that I *would* quit. It was a bit of a decision to work out the financial side of the process, but within six months of that decision I had quit and was becoming an astrologer.

A Miscellany of Introductions

Another person who was persuaded to trade in a conventional career for life as a full-time astrologer was Robin Heath:

Robin Heath: In Spring 1973, I was travelling back from the Far East after a three month business trip. It was the Arab-Israeli war and the TWA707 was 'diverted' to Bahrain, where we passengers spent 24 hours in fear and 100+ temperatures. A Bulgarian man offered to 'read my stars' in order to pass the time. I was a little skeptical but he was very good. However, what perhaps impressed me more was his ability to draw up a chart from scratch, working out the positions of all the planets using just a calculator—he got them all to within a degree I think! I was hooked thenceforth and after my eventual return to the UK, I found Jeff Mayo's little 'Teach Yourself Astrology' book. I learned it off by heart within a month and I still think it's the best beginner's book.

It's interesting that what struck Robin particularly was the astronomical accuracy demonstrated by his fellow passenger. Robin's own astrological career has been characterised by his fascination with the way humanity has observed and related to the astronomical patterns of nature—Chapter VII has more details.

Another astrologer was hooked by a (quite misleadingly literal) answer to a question which astrology gave him. Maggie Hyde recalls the story:

Maggie Hyde: I always remember Derek Appleby (who was a great mentor for me), who said that his first horary—when he'd just found a book on horary in a secondhand shop—was for his next-door neighbour, who had lost her wedding ring. She said, "Can astrology find it?" So he did his first horary question. It was, "Where is the lost ring?", and it had Libra rising. He said to her, "Have you looked in your kitchen scales?"* Lo and behold, she'd been baking, had taken her ring off, and the ring was left in the scales. So she thought astrology was amazing, and Derek thought, "Wow! This horary astrology is really something!" But there was a ridiculously simple judgement that turned out to be amazingly true. You can bet it would never happen [that way] again. It's a thing that happens at the beginning. So the simplest piece of symbolism can be amazingly trite but extraordinarily true— at any level. You start reading Sun signs, and it begins to work for you—and it doesn't stop.

Whilst some people can discover astrology in the kitchen, Adrian Duncan had to travel to India to find it. Given his comments earlier in the chapter, about learning astrology experientially, it makes sense that his own initiation into the subject was experiential (and how!):

Adrian Duncan: It was in India, when I was a part of the drug culture of 1970 and everybody was travelling to India. As a result of taking drugs I had an experience of the influence of the outer planets—Uranus, Neptune and Pluto. The experience was so strong I actually stopped taking drugs, and haven't indulged since. It was an incredibly strong perception of the Aquarian age.

The first planet I discovered in my consciousness was Pluto, and then I discovered Neptune, and then Uranus—as living, tangible forces in material things today. It was a stunning experience.

So then I started trying to learn astrology! It went very slowly. I learned, but I wasn't very good. Then, after ten years, I moved to Denmark. An odd thing happened: it's difficult to find property in Denmark, but in a newspaper we found a house to rent. I got the house, and it happened that the person who had just vacated it was the President of the Danish Astrological Society— which I eventually became President of, five years later. So there was a fated sense in every stage of the astrological journey for me. It was encouraging to know that one was being ushered along!

---

* Astrologers will recognise that this judgement did not even begin to follow the (conventional) rules.

Q: This experience of Pluto… were you consciously thinking in terms of Pluto whilst you were having the experience? Or is that a subsequent interpretation?

Adrian Duncan: What had actually happened was: I was in Delhi and came across the book 'Astrology for All' by Alan Leo. I'm not sure whether I didn't actually steal it from one of these piles of books on the street—can't remember if I bought it or stole it. But it was a poisoned gift, because I was riveted by the book. I read it ravenously, and every night I used to sit on the roof of the house in Delhi and see the wonderful stars.

One night, I experienced what can only be described as a Pluto sunrise. This is a ridiculous story and it probably won't come [across well] in interview, but what happened was that I had a blocked nose. Pluto is actually really related to the nose, and blockages. By concentrating on this blockage in my nose, it changed the whole landscape around me. I had had this block for a couple of years, and a noise in my ear. It all disappeared—it was like Pluto's presence. I said out loud that night, "Pluto!" That's how it started—a bit crazy! A very powerful transcendental experience. Later I realised that my progressed Sun was exactly conjunct Pluto, and as my natal Sun is on the Uranus/Pluto midpoint, Solar Arc Uranus was simultaneously conjunct my Sun. It was an Aquarian baptism.

A note for any young persons reading: *do not try this at home!* Generally speaking, the adoption of astrology is not such a mind-boggling or strange affair; and in the case of a few interviewees, astrology was something that was familiar from the beginning:

Robert Hand: My father was using it to forecast the stock market. And I was interested. But it wasn't that he taught me astrology, exactly—he'd been studying only a little while himself. He created an environment that I could learn in. I think it was like the junkie's first dose of heroin. My first reaction was, "Holy Cow! The universe isn't the way they taught me it was in school, it's totally different!" Basically, my fascination with astrology is as a form of natural philosophy. I respect all the things you can do with it, but fundamentally I'm into it for what it teaches me about nature, cosmos and psyche.

Even for someone like Robert Hand who finds early support for astrological leanings in their immediate circle, the career of an astrologer in the West cannot go far before they run into the profound skepticism with which much of society views the subject. It is worth remembering, however, that this is not the case in all cultures:

Komilla Sutton: I was not born into a jyotish* family at all. I was born just post-independence in India, so we were—I would say—confused. We were

---

* 'Jyotish' means 'astrology'—specifically, that form of astrology indigenous to India.

learning about our own Indian roots again, but still had a major western influence. My father was in the army, which had a very powerful western influence. The Indian tradition was taught to us by our grandparents and at school; and jyotish is part of tradition in India, very different from what it is here. Everybody accepts the astrologer (the jyotishi) as having their own place, almost everybody knows lots of jyotish laws, and all the mythological gods are part of our daily life. So subconsciously, we all get information, which makes it much easier for people from India to understand the myths and the symbolic meaning of Jyotish.

I am not a Hindu, I was born a Sikh. Sikhism is a relatively modern religion (four hundred years old—not that modern!), and in it knowledge is very important rather than deities and gods. So we had that kind of upbringing as well. My own birth chart was drawn up by the family astrologer, but my parents were not necessarily interested in it. It was part of the tradition. Then I went to an astrologer in 1979 (aged 25 or 26) and I was just amazed at the information available to the Jyotishi from my birth chart. I was going through a period of change, there were lots of problems—things that I was dealing with in life—and here was this field of knowledge giving me a way to understand the purpose of my life, how to deal with the energies that were given to me at birth. My first Jyotishi became my first teacher. He was a very spiritual person himself, and was a Sanskrit scholar, and therefore his whole way of looking at jyotish was at a very high intellectual level. I feel that I got some really good knowledge and information from him. But when I was learning from him, it wasn't for the sake of becoming an astrologer—it was just something that was of great interest. I always had another career.

So I studied my family's charts and the new-born additions to my family at that time. Following jyotish to its natural level, I did everything... a lot of remedial measures, like wearing proper stones, doing prayers and mantras. Like a late developer suddenly getting involved, I practised everything, so I've done all that—as a client and astrologer.

Of course, something in my chart suggests that I have lots of change in my life, and I moved to England at that stage. I followed my interest, and had two other teachers here in England. One of them was a very successful Vedic astrologer, who has since died. But most of my work is really self-taught, so I can't say that I had that one specific guru who taught me everything. But I look back at '79 and the Jupiter cycle—I am ruled by Jupiter myself, and the Jupiter cycles have had major meaning in my life for change—[at that time] I started paying more attention to jyotish and less to my other career; and now I am a full-time professional astrologer.

It is interesting to compare Komilla's comments on her introduction to astrology in India with the experience of westerners. Many of the people with whom I spoke had their first introduction to astrology through the astrology columns that appear in newspapers, commonly known as 'star sign' or 'Sun-sign' columns.

These columns present a simplified—not to say simplistic—version of astrology for mass consumption. The streamlined form in which astrology is often first encountered provokes an ambiguous response amongst astrologers. If their first contact was through Sun-sign astrology they may find it difficult to disown it totally; yet at the same time, they may feel doubtful as to whether their initial impressions were based on anything more substantial than a simple desire to be impressed, and to find oneself reflected in the words and suggestions of others. Maurice McCann underscores this dilemma:

> **Maurice McCann:** I watched a television programme, where they were interviewing Patric Walker*. I didn't know who he was. He was describing Sun-signs, because that was what he did. He described a Capricorn, and I thought, "My God, that's incredible, because he's just described me." You know how you are always fooled into this thought.

Could there be something more to Sun-sign astrology than merely fooling people? In the next chapter we consider this popular form, beginning with an account from Shelley von Strunckel, one of today's leading writers of Sun-sign columns, of how she came to work in this field.

---

* Famous Sun-sign astrologer—see the following chapter for more on him.

Chapter III

Sun-Sign Astrology

On 24th December 1999, the story broke that Jonathan Cainer was about to become the most highly-paid journalist in Britain for his astrological columns in the 'Daily Express'. The 'star-sign' or 'Sun-sign' column is the most well-known type of astrology in the West today, and the astrologers at the top of this particular tree are the discipline's top earners.

In any discussion of Sun-sign astrology, the first point to be made is that there is a good deal more to astrology than Sun-sign columns. The second is that many astrologers regard Sun-sign work as not proper astrology at all because it simplifies the subject to an unacceptable extent.

Although there have been cases of harassed sub-editors making up predictions for the day, newspaper columns are nearly all written by people who have studied 'proper' astrology. One of the most well-established of the newspaper astrologers is Shelley von Strunckel.

A Route into Sun-Sign Astrology

Q: How did you first get interested in astrology?

Shelley von Strunckel: My jocular answer is, "I grew up in California!" But the fact is, when I was a kid in Los Angeles, I was surrounded by numerous studies of a metaphysical nature; it was just part of life there. So as a teenager I might go to a lecture on Buddhism and go out for a hamburger afterwards. It was very normal in California at that time to be interested in everything from EST to eastern thought.

I encountered astrology as part of that exploration, and a friend took me to my first class. At that time I was working as an assistant buyer in the fashion business, and certainly never thought that astrology would become central to my existence. But I was fascinated, primarily because I had always been interested in what makes people tick. That was part of the reason why retailing was so rewarding to me; I continued to be intrigued by what would motivate people to buy one thing over another. As I consider it in retrospect, however, I realise that it was all about the cycles—in this case, of course, the cycles were those of fashion.

So even though it was retailing I was involved in, what interested me in it wasn't really a million miles apart from one element of astrology. Intriguingly, when I was studying astrology—still just because I thought it interesting—I was also attending night school at UCLA (the University of California), and was studying the psychology of dress and the history of costume. Here, again, it was back to cycles, back to what motivates people. That's actually one of the first things that interested me about astrology— linking cycles of costume, and people's style, their appearance. As I learned more about the twelve star signs I realised that they were nothing but points of view, an individual perspective that, as a buyer, I could almost see as the choices a customer could make.

For me, astrology was part of an extensive study of eastern and western philosophical thought, not something that I identified as being particularly special—and certainly not as my future career.

Q: When did it start to become special?

Shelley von Strunckel: Well, when else? The Saturn return*! As with so many people who study astrology, I had done people's charts, and had looked a bit at my own—but not much. But when I was 28, I was working for a company in California. I called the people I was working for (not entirely jocularly) Attila the Hun and Simon Legree (the villain from 'Uncle Tom's Cabin'). They were pretty unsympathetic employers, and although I'd enjoyed the fashion business, my experience with them acted almost like aversion therapy. They were very unpleasant to work for.

In September 1975, my brother and my boyfriend died on the same day. I have four planets in the eighth house, so things tend to happen that way; it's not the only time in my life that there have been multiple deaths. Anyway, I took the week off from work; they wanted to deduct that from my vacation pay. We disagreed about that, and a month later I found myself unemployed.

At that point it crossed my mind, for the very first time, that I could actually work as an astrologer. The thought that followed it was a decisive one; I said to myself, "If I don't try this now, when I'm 65 and I look back on my life I will regret not having given it a go." That's one of the most motivating factors possible—the potential for later regret.

By this time it was Halloween. I went to a Halloween party, and when people asked "What do you do?", I told them, "I'm an astrologer." At that point a lawyer said, "Oh, good! Maybe you can tell me how a case I'm working on is going to come out..." I noted the time, did a horary chart. I told him that one of his clients was suppressing important evidence, what it was and why. He said, "Tell the client, if you will." So the next day, at the lawyer's request, I called the client (who was in New Jersey; I was in California). I said "This is your lawyer's astrologer. Don't ask me to explain, but he has consulted me and as a result there are certain facts I have to tell you, which are X, Y and Z..." There was a long silence, then he said, "How do you know that? No-one knows that!"

Intriguingly, the client was himself a PhD chemist. He was so fascinated by how I had come to know this quite specific information, that he came and

---

* Around age 29, Saturn returns to the position it had at a person's birth; this transit is said to indicate inner and outer events that are usually difficult at the time, but can be seen as new beginnings in retrospect.

studied with me. So I went from a standing start to working with an attorney *and* having students. In fact, during the early years of my practice I taught a great deal.

I have no doubt that in the early days of my career as an astrologer, the marketing background I acquired as a buyer helped. Having been a buyer, I was particularly conscious of presentation. The marketing that I'd been trained in just shifted!

Meanwhile, as part of my studies in eastern and western philosophy, I had been studying and working with someone who was involved with the Theosophical Society. When I began my practice, I also was working with him, and was invited (two years later) to go to India—where, at the Theosophical Society in Madras, they asked me to lecture on astrology. That was an enriching experience. Of course, most of the audience were Indian, and having been exposed to the very destiny-focussed Indian astrology, found a more free-will orientated 'Western approach' fascinating. However broad the scope of our dialogue here [in the West], we take an approach to free-will that is ever so much more liberal than Indians.

While there were early successes, as with anyone starting their own business, I spent years being really poor—poor enough that I'd look at a copy of 'Vogue' (which, ironically, I write for now) and have to think carefully whether I could afford to buy it. I learned a lot about my priorities that way, which was great—maybe not fun, but illuminating…

Q: What happened next?

Shelley von Strunckel: I enjoyed working as an astrologer; loved seeing people. But what I found tiring was dealing with the field's dreadful image. It very quickly stopped being amusing that people were surprised that I, who looked like a 'normal' person, could be an astrologer. Being by nature someone who changes what I don't like, rather than accepting the status quo, I eventually got around to the idea that instead of complaining about the image of my field, I would do what I could to change it. I thought about how I could accomplish that. The answer seemed to be through the media. Then I considered, "How do you get into media?" You start talking to editors, and you write.

At that time I was living primarily in LA, but began going to New York frequently to see clients. When I was there, I made it my business to get to know magazine editors. At this point in the story, I have to back up a little: for some time, private clients had been coming to me because they had read Patric Walker's columns, which then appeared in the States in a monthly magazine called 'Town and Country'. They were affected by his magic touch, so I studied how Patric wrote, analysing what about his star-sign column could be that poignant. I became very familiar with his writing. Consequently, when I was having lunch with the editor of a magazine called 'Mirabella', who was quite a fan of astrology, and we were talking about the impact of Patric, I said to her, "I think I know how he does it." She said to me, "Well, if you know how he does it, do it for us."

I said—in shocked tones—"Me?!" I was really surprised. Getting a column really wasn't my objective in that conversation; I was just talking with her about Patric's remarkable style. The ironic thing is that I had thought of writing for magazines in terms of articles; I hadn't thought about writing a star-sign column, because (I have to confess) I had the same bias as many other astrologers do—that they misrepresent the field. So I told her I'd like to think about it. And then I called someone I knew, an individual who had done for the field of psychology what I wanted to do for astrology. The name is one you may remember from radio in London: Philip Hudson. Philip is a psychologist, who started doing phone-in programmes on LBC, London radio. People would call in with all sorts of problems, and he'd talk them through their dilemmas. Over a ten year span of daily broadcasting, he substantially changed the general attitude towards counselling. When he began all problems were being buried, ignored, held in. Discussing concerns openly was viewed as weak. Now, it's fine, it's quite a normal thing—even the police get counselled if they've faced something dreadful.

So I called Philip up, explained that I had an offer to write a column, and told him about my reservations about this star-sign business versus what I regarded at that time as 'pure astrology'. He said, "Well, if you don't like it, do the column and change the way the industry is from within." It was one of those crystalline moments of 'getting it'; of understanding. Of course, that was the problem; everyone was standing around on the outside whingeing. So I called the editor back, and said, "Yes, I'll do it." I wrote a trial column, it was accepted, and was printed in June 1990. At that time the magazine 'Mirabella' was owned by Murdoch's News International; Patric was published in Murdoch newspapers in the States. The executives at News International knew that Patric was looking for a successor and they spotted my column. Not surprisingly, it was similar in style to Patric's! This certainly showed how successful my efforts to learn from his style were. I am still grateful for all that I learned from studying his writing.

Out of the blue I received a call asking whether I would be interested in writing a daily column. I said, "Sure!" They asked, "Would you write a sample?" "OK." Then I got another call saying, "Would you like to meet Patric Walker?" I was incredibly excited, so of course I said, "OK!" A meeting was then set up. Noting that Mercury would soon be retrograde, I set it up in early August, in London, just before Mercury went retrograde. That was my first meeting with Patric. It was like seeing an old friend. I had read his writings so thoroughly that I'd figured out most of his chart already. When I told him my observations, I guess it impressed him. We talked about a lot of things—everything from religion to sailing. At the end of that meeting, there was a scene that could have come straight from the cinema—he walked across the room to the phone, picked it up, called 'The Evening Standard', and said, "I've found her!" In October, I was announced as Patric's heir.

So it was a very swift journey—from one magazine, to working with Patric worldwide, within five months.

Q: What was the secret of his style that you figured out?

Shelley von Strunckel: The secret is that each sign is written from an entirely different point of view, and has its own unique language and syntax. Most astrologers write in the same way for all twelve signs. But of course, it's got to be different if you are writing for an eternally frustrated Aries; a Taurus who is afraid you are going to tell him he'll have to make a change yet again; a bored Gemini; a Cancer who just wants to know it'll be all right; a Leo who wants to know whether their talents will finally be recognised... the approach shifts from sign to sign. It's not just the aspects or the signs planets are in, it was the way he would write for the individual signs. For one—say a Scorpio— a full Moon in Taurus might reveal welcome information about money and sex. For a Libra, that same full Moon might upset the emotional apple cart that they have just worked so hard to get sorted. That is what he did, superbly.

Q: What happened next?

Shelley von Strunckel: Less than a year later, 'The Sunday Times' called. A lot happens through the phone in my life! There was a message on the answering machine: "Please call the Sunday Times." Again, out of the blue. It was Robin Morgan, editor of 'The Sunday Times Magazine', asking me if I would like to do a column—one that would start in a week and a half. That was, of course, the first ever astrology column in a quality broadsheet. It literally made history, to the extent that we had news crews from Europe covering the story. Now we think it's normal, but then it took tremendous courage—and Robin and the then 'Sunday Times' editor, Andrew Neil, understood that. Robin was sweet. He said that in terms of consumers, those regarded as being at the top, what marketers call the 'A and B readers', deserved their own column. At that time astrology columns appeared only in tabloids, which were considered to reach a less upmarket readership. In the world of journalism this was a very real breakthrough.

What the column was then, and still is now, is a good long read. It's enough words that you can think about the week. When I began, I started with the [agreement] that my words could not be changed without my permission. This is not done in journalism, there are very few journalists who have the final edit. From a practical point of view, I pointed out that no sub-editor knows astrology well enough to make a change; they could turn something into an astrological nonsense. But also, I know the intensity with which people read those columns, and I use words very carefully. I remember my lessons from Patric. I wasn't going to have someone else thinking, "Oh— I've got a better word…" So they literally can't change a comma without my permission.

Leaving Patric wasn't easy. When I went to 'The Sunday Times' I talked it over with him. While it was exciting for me, it proved to do wonders for the field as well. And when we discussed the change, I gave him thanks and credit for the fact that it's the dignity that he brought to the field that led to a world-class newspaper running an astrology column. He gave me his blessings. And the first day the column ran, he rang up and said, "So what's the number?" [He was] asking about the premium rate phoneline number so he could ring his! He then rang me back, which was incredibly sweet and supportive, telling me, "It's just fine, really good."

So I went from being Patric Walker's heir and being syndicated world-wide to one newspaper, but that one newspaper was the 'The Sunday Times'. And then I had to build the rest of it up all over again, on my own. Of course, when Patric died a great deal of the columns in the rest of the world came back to me. But I'm not 'the new Patric Walker.' As the years have passed, I have, quite naturally, gone in different directions than he would have. For example, Patric loathed the press, loathed television and radio; I quite enjoy it.

I'm now poised at the next level. Patric brought the field dignity; my objective has been to mainstream it. Now I hope to take that out further, as well. Not merely with books, but products, television and radio…

Q: What kind of products?

Shelley von Strunckel: I'm still discussing them, so I'll wait to comment on that!

What do People Get from Sun-Sign Columns?

Q: How much of the creation of one of those columns is astrological technique, and how much is about introducing a kind of cosmic 'feel-good factor' into people's lives?

Shelley von Strunckel: It's *all* pure astrology. First of all, I focus on the sign I'm dealing with, so it's absolutely astrologically conditioned. I am speaking to a Virgo; I am speaking to a Scorpio and so on. Sometimes I think of someone I know who is that sign, and imagine how I would explain what I'm trying to get across to them. The philosophical perspective is fundamental, for a reason I'll explain in a second. But because astrology portrays life's cycles, the foundation for the information that's given is completely astrological. I am describing to someone their life experience at that time.

The second part of this—the philosophical perspective—took me a while to figure out. Bear in mind that I write daily columns as well. When I was writing for 'The Evening Standard' and would be on the Underground, I'd watch readers just *tear* open the Standard, to read about their sign. I saw this frequently and thought about it. Finally I realised that the intensity with which these people are looking at the star-sign columns is not about whether they are going to get a letter in the post tomorrow; there is something else going on here. I meditated long and hard on what engendered such an intense need to look at the stars.

I realised that it's such compulsive reading because, for most people, those few moments when they look at their stars is about the only time during the day that is for them, 100% personal, quiet and reflective. Most people's minds are buffeted by external stimuli all day. And very few make the conscious choice to be still. The world just gets up, turns on the radio, turns on the television; people around constantly making demands; you go to work, you talk, you eat… But being still is a discipline we aren't taught.

The other part of it is that, in what we are pleased to call 'education' today, what might be called 'living philosophy' is excluded. Sure, we study what philosophers said. But a here-and-now, use-it-today, life-philosophy isn't part of the usual curriculum. So again, most people have no access to any kind of tool that will give them perspective, something that helps rationalise life's crises, its ups and downs. Therefore, those who aren't given other opportunities in their lives to reflect are drawn to the perspective that newspaper astrology offers, and they savour that moment of stillness whilst reading—even if it is only just a moment.

If they also get information about the specific day, or the specific week, I imagine they find that useful, too. But I actually think that that dose of perspective, which for many people comes from nothing else in their life, is terribly important. This phenomenon would simply never have occurred to me had I not started writing star-sign columns—and started looking at people's reactions. I've also become conscious of it because I'm aware of how deified media astrologers can become. But it makes sense. If as a writer your words bring readers a moment of peace, a glimpse of a clear perspective, then they're bound to see you as special. In that sense, it's both an honour and a responsibility, and I take it as such.

Q: If I understand what you're saying, it is that modern humanity's need for experience of meaningfulness (spiritual experience if you will) is generally denied an outlet by the prevailing worldview, and that Sun-sign columns help by offering people an opportunity to be still and reflect for a few moments. Is that what you are saying?

Shelley von Strunckel: Yes. In general print media today (newspapers, magazines) with the exception of one column on a Saturday (in 'The Telegraph') there is absolutely nothing—that I know of, anyway—that's of a spiritual or reflective nature—full stop. That isn't the way I think it should be, but it's the way it is.

Q: Given all of that, how would you like to see this developing? Do you think that Sun-sign columns in newspapers can become bigger and more philosophical, for example? Do you think that there's room to start using Sun-sign columns to start encouraging people to have their charts read by an astrologer?

Shelley von Strunckel: Actually that is happening now, in my column. Associated with most Sun-sign columns there are phone-lines, three to four minute tape-recorded messages, usually voiced by the astrologer him or herself, which describe in greater length than is possible in print what's going on during the week. Again, this is an opportunity for the public to be exposed to a little deeper thinking about the nature of the individual's experience, sign by sign.

There are companies that specialise in the technological end of the phone-line business; it was someone from one of the companies I work with who came up with the idea of having live astrologers on-line billed the same way. The person who created it went to all the astrological faculties in the UK, seeking astrologers who would like to work in this way. That means that now, through my page in the paper, the public can actually speak to real astrologers—real, proper, trained astrologers. To me this is brilliant. The other Sunday, at church—of all places—someone I'd seen before but don't know personally sat down beside me and said, "I called one of your astrologers the other day." I said, "Oh, was it good? How long did you talk?" He said, "Oh, we talked for about twenty minutes, it was tremendous, very useful."

I think that it's just wonderful. It's the first time it's been possible techno-logically. What's also lovely—and I really like it when business works this way—is that it's a win-win for everyone. Astrologers who might be too shy to push themselves, or can't get out of the house, are still able to work at home. They get exposure and experience with all kinds of people. And the public, who might not know where to go to find an astrologer, are exposed to individuals—astrologers—who are vetted. So they are speaking to qualified people. And the astrologers make an income from it, which is wonderful.

Q: So people phone up, give their birth data and get a reading on the spot?

Shelley von Strunckel: Yes, exactly. The astrologer is there with their computer on, and of course now you can get a chart done in seconds. They will also often phone back. From 'The Sunday Times', it's often businessmen who are calling—and they make notes about important business decisions.

Criticisms of Sun-Sign Work

Shelley mentioned, in passing, some doubts she experienced in the early days of her career about the value of Sun-sign columns. Whilst she was able to resolve these doubts to her own satisfaction, this is still a live issue in the world of astrology, as suggested by some of the following excerpts. It is perhaps worth emphasising that each of the interviews quoted was recorded in isolation, so (despite the way it may sometimes appear) there is nothing personal in the comments from those opposed to Sun-sign astrology.

Q: What is your attitude to Sun-sign columns?

Mike Harding: I have a very negative attitude to Sun-sign columns, primarily because that's the only thing one reads in newspapers. If there were more serious articles on astrology I don't think I would bother about the Sun-sign columns at all, but because they are basically the only thing that the ordinary member of the public will see in newspapers about astrology, I think it's a continual form of trivialisation.

   I don't think it's done for anything other than money. I think astrologers kid themselves if they think, "Well—I'm keeping astrology alive." I think that statement is demonstrably false. You only have to look at what has happened recently in the former Soviet Union—astrology was banned for fifty years, there were no Sun-sign columns. With the collapse of the last part of the Soviet empire, astrology has absolutely taken off in Russia. The idea that some arcane knowledge is filtered in through Sun-sign columns is, I think, nonsense. I think people do it purely for the money, and it doesn't help at all in keeping astrology alive. I think it constantly gives a negative spin to the subject. It's the very first thing the critics of astrology pick up on. It's a way into the criticism.

Do Sun-sign columns deter potential clients by giving the impression that this is all astrologers are capable of? Maggie Hyde thinks not:

Maggie Hyde: They know it's not real astrology, don't they? Don't they know the difference? Aren't we all grown up now? Can't they tell the difference between a Sun-sign column and getting their birth-chart done for £60? I think they know the difference!

Back to the case for the prosecution again, this time with Dennis Elwell:

Q: Would you ever write a Sun-sign column?

Dennis Elwell: Astrologers are the custodians of a knowledge that can change the world, and the hope for the future has to be that they will work with a more conscientious attitude towards this awesome responsibility. Part of it involves educating the public to recognise the value of the treasure that astrologers hold in their hands. Progress here would certainly sound the death knell of the Sun-sign columns, because people would realise what nonsense they are. No, I would never write a Sun-sign column. For one thing it must be mind-numbingly boring, having to churn out such drivel day after day. More important, I would fear for my immortal soul. I think a special place in hell is being warmed over for those who cynically trivialise a great truth...

If the odious Sun-sign columns have a value, it is to persuade everybody that astrology is just a bit of fun. They serve as a smoke screen. In fact astrology is dangerous knowledge, which could be devastating in the wrong hands. Perhaps it is better for people to be kept in ignorance.

It has been said that you can only earn real money from astrology by pandering to this market. I hope that will not remain the case for long. There ought to be at least as many astrologers as there are medical practitioners, and remunerated at the same level. The reason astrologers are not in hot demand is that what they offer nowadays is not seen as relevant to the burning issues of life. The tendency to use astrology as the back door to a psychotherapy practice has distracted attention from its real power.

Nicholas Campion, on the other hand, sees much that is positive in Sun-sign columns:

Nicholas Campion: A lot of astrologers will say, "Well, there's Sun-sign astrology, then there's real astrology," which is what Russell Grant said when he was on 'Newsnight', being interviewed by Jeremy Paxman in 1996 at the time of the Richard Dawkins affair*, which was a weakness, because he immediately conceded that some astrology wasn't 'real astrology'. That's nonsense. Sun-sign astrology is no less real than any other application of judicial astrology. It's daily mundane astrology applied to the twelve zodiac character types rather than to countries or stock markets, and if I could compare a decent Sun-sign column to anything then it would be to an I-Ching

---

* In a lengthy newspaper article (Dawkins, 1995), Richard Dawkins—holder of the Chair of Public Understanding of Science at Oxford University—had suggested that "we should fight [astrology] seriously as an enemy of truth." This was met with outrage in the astrological community, and resulted in some media coverage—including the 'Newsnight' interview.

hexagram. At their best, Sun-sign columns encourage people to pause for a moment and reflect on their lives, circumstances and feelings. The closest parallel I've seen has been in the Taoist temples in Hong Kong, which are always bustling with people consulting the I-Ching.

I love Sun-sign astrology. It was my introduction to astrology, and it's become my main way of consulting other astrologers. In moments of confusion or crisis I'll consult Shelley von Strunckel's column, or whoever else happens to be handy. I was writing my column for 'Harper's Bazaar' this morning and thinking, "I really like doing this; I really like this way of using astrology to communicate with people." I have no sympathy at all for the idea that some astrology is 'serious' and some not, or that astrology should be just for people in small clubs and societies and not available to the public at large.

Q: What is the method for Sun-sign work? Do different writers use different methods?

Nicholas Campion: You can use whatever techniques you want. Michel Gauquelin wrote about the increase in the metabolic rate when the Moon rises and culminates, so you can look at the times of day when that happens if you like. The basic idea, though, is that you look at the planetary aspects for the day, particularly lunar ones, or any sort of planetary relationship, and look at how it might relate to the different character types. For example, if there's a Venus-Pluto conjunction, it might indicate emotional volatility, and hence a real chance of unexpected arguments as hidden resentments emerge without warning. One might look at how a Sun-Scorpio might relate to it (they might be in their element), or a Sun-Capricorn (they might be more uncomfortable). Then you might consider what sign the conjunction is in. If it's in Scorpio then it's trine Pisces, for example, but if it's in Sagittarius then it's square Pisces.

Such considerations are obvious, and all astrologers works in this way when they look at the daily ephemeris. Solar charts also rely totally on techniques that are part of astrological tradition, such as whole sign aspects and houses, and house systems, set according to symbolic principles (as in the twelve Athla). Using these principles, the cusp of the sign containing the Sun becomes the cusp of the first house.

I've never been entirely sure what the objections to Sun-sign astrology are, except that they seem to be bound up with issues of image and public presentation or, in other words, taste. The most misleading criticism levelled at it is that to provide accurate information from a reading one needs an exact time of birth. I think this criticism comes only from astrologers who have no experience of anything outside natal horoscopy. Coming from a background in mundane astrology, and with a deep interest in horary astrology, I have no problem with applications of astrology which do not rely on birth charts. In fact I prefer them!

Q: If you were to do a chart reading for someone now, would you find it useful to see what was going on for them in terms of this Sun-sign column approach?

Nicholas Campion: Yes. It's fast and simple. The first time I spoke to Patric Walker I had been going through my Uranus opposition, my Pluto square and a range of other major outer planet transits, and I felt pretty emotionally exhausted. He asked me what my Sun-sign was and, on hearing it was Pisces, he gave me a complete reading based on the presence of transiting Saturn in my solar twelfth house. He did as much with that as any other astrologer would have done with Pluto, Uranus and the rest of the cast. I actually spoke about this way of doing things before I became a professional Sun-sign astrologer. It was in a lecture titled 'The Astrologer as Artist' at an Astrological Association conference around 1985.

Q: What is it that you like about Sun-sign work? What do you think it has to offer people?

Nicholas Campion: Quite simply, it's fast, available, accessible. Actually, I was talking to Bernard Eccles the other day. He also writes Sun-sign columns and he said that we're like chefs who end up working in fast food restaurants. It is a little like that. But then sometimes fast food is just what you need. I get a different sort of satisfaction from my writing and academic work, which can feel more like creating a six-course banquet.

Q: Do the Sun-sign columns generate much correspondence?

Nicholas Campion: It's variable. You get a lot from a national newspaper, virtually none from regional papers. I get a lot of correspondence from India, but I actually don't answer it—I don't solicit correspondence as it becomes much too time-consuming. If people just want the simple recommendation of a local astrologer, I give them one. When I was at 'The Daily Mail' I used to get quite a few letters, and I used to answer them because I didn't want them complaining to the Editor that I hadn't answered their letters! Quite a substantial proportion were from people who seemed to be in a difficult situation, and were desperate for some kind of help. I was really unable to give them what they wanted, except by writing something vaguely reassuring in reply.

Q: Have there been any Sun-sign column entries which have hit the spot remarkably?

Nicholas Campion: A great many, but they all depend on people's personal appreciation—you write a Sun-sign column in a very general manner, obviously. I've had hundreds of letters from people saying, "Your accuracy astonishes me." But I'm aware of the fact that, like astrological consultancy, Sun-sign astrology works with the reader making an *active step* to participate in the reading; saying, "Yes, that reflects my life, it's amazing." If you come to a Sun-sign column as a total skeptic, in your eyes it will be flat and one-dimensional and won't mean anything. If you come with that wish to participate, the words become three-dimensional. Which is exactly the same as in a consultation, where the client will very often be hearing very different things to what the astrologer is saying. The client will be editing, not hearing some things, distorting others, making them fit what they already know or are anticipating. The same processes hold with Sun-sign astrology.

I began to understand Sun-sign astrology in around 1981. My 'Daily Mirror' column warned that a friend would have a 'bright' idea for saving money, but that I should resist. What actually happened was that a friend persuaded me to buy a car with him. After many twists and turns of fate I finally had one drive in the car, as a passenger for about a hundred yards on London's Harrow Road. The car gave up the ghost and we abandoned it! My friend's name was Bright! I relate this story because it shows how astrology depends partly on selecting the right words at the right moment. My example is from a Sun-sign column, but the same process underpins counselling, in which the goal is effective communication between astrologer and client.

Q: How do people get to write Sun-sign columns in the first place?

Nicholas Campion: Such jobs aren't publicly advertised, so there's usually some sort of personal connection. With me, when I joined 'The Daily Mail' I took over from John Naylor, whom I had been in contact with over historical matters, and who was the son of R.H. Naylor (who wrote the first newspaper astrology column in 1930). Marjorie Orr on 'The Express' has a background in journalism; as for Jonathan Cainer—when he started with 'Today', it was because the Features Editor had gone there from 'Woman' magazine and knew him. Personal connection counts for most. Peter Watson, who is now doing 'The Evening Standard', was working with Patric Walker, as was Sally Brompton (on 'The Mail on Sunday') and Shelley von Strunckel ('The Sunday Times'). Patric Walker himself was introduced to astrology by the writer of the Celeste column in 'Harpers and Queens'.

I encountered at least one opponent of Sun-sign astrology whose attitude had been softened by discourse with Nicholas Campion... and his cat:

Robin Heath: I have drunk several cups of tea with Katy, Nick Campion's cat, whilst discussing with Nick the morality of Sun-sign work. As a result, I have moderated my views on its practitioners, though not on its usefulness. We remain good friends, and I still like Nick! Sun-sign columns are here to stay, part of our modern pop culture. Much of the material in magazines and papers is total drivel whilst at least the 'stars column' suggests a non-materialistic causality. As editor of 'The Astrological Journal', I had the misfortune to read some outrageous and downright fascist letters about expelling Sun-sign astrologers from the AA or the APA*. It was the single issue that attracted the most letters! Adrian Duncan thinks that astrologers should be paid for doing astrology—any astrology—rather than be stacking shelves in Tesco. Maybe he's right, but pop astrology seems so trivial to me.

In the Marketplace

Nicholas Campion observes above that many of the objections to Sun-sign astrology are "bound up with issues of image and public presentation." The kind of thing that astrologers object to can be seen in 'The Independent on Sunday' for 26 December 1999. The article 'Shares in Line for a Savaging by Saturn' presents some astrologically-based comments on likely trends in the money markets for the year 2000 from Arch Crawford and Christeen Skinner—exactly the type of serious coverage that the subject is often denied. The article that follows it leads off with the comment, "If gazing at the stars is not your style when it comes to money management, an industry expert or financial adviser might be a better person to consult than Mystic Meg." Just as it seems that astrology is being presented in a serious light, the image of a Sun-sign astrologer is casually dropped in, to remind everyone that astrology really belongs on the cartoon page, not in the business section.

Unfortunately Mystic Meg herself—possibly the most famous astrologer in the UK today—did not take up my invitation to be interviewed. Some discussion of her approach did, however, crop up in my interview with Adam Fronteras, who was involved in setting up the Mystic Meg astrological phone lines.

Adam Fronteras: It was interesting when they were setting up the Mystic Meg line; they would phone up astrologers with the Astrological Association, and they'd go, "Mystic Meg? No!" They didn't want to be associated with it at all.

The argument has always been, do people such as Mystic Meg and Russell Grant help astrology's image or not? My own opinion is that Meg may provide a caricature of what people imagine astrology to be; but if you pull an interest in, that can only be to the good. A lot of people coming for readings do so because they've watched a TV programme with Russell on, turned to the teletext page and seen, 'For more information write to BAPS†.' I've done star

* The Astrological Association, and Association of Professional Astrologers.
† British Astrological and Psychic Society.
Please see Appendix 1 for details of these and other groups.

columns where you have lineage for BAPS at the bottom, and it does attract interest; it starts some people off. And this Mystic Meg thing: OK, they are using professional clairvoyants and psychics, and the astrologers all come from approved lists, so they are getting proper astrology readings.

Q: Do the astrologers have time to prepare the charts?

Adam Fronteras: No, you sit by the computer; someone phones in and you say, "Hi, could I take your date, time and place of birth?" You put it up on the computer and give them a reading for twenty minutes.

Q: Do you think most people are happy with what they get?

Adam Fronteras: Yes, I think there's been an extremely positive response from this, because this is the first one where the people doing the readings have been vetted or come from an approved list. They aren't people who have been trained up in fifteen minutes. I don't know if you saw a documentary, a year or so ago, on a place in Scotland where they were literally given fifteen minutes' training in Tarot and then were all sitting together doing readings over the phone. This way [with the Mystic Meg line] the calls are being routed through to people's homes, so it's actually costing the operator more, they are doubling up on the phone costs. It was very much Mystic Meg who said, "If we're to do it, we'll only want the best." Because, at the end of the day, she has her name to protect. Obviously, I can't know how successful the whole thing is from the individual astrologer's point of view, but it is a way of them getting readings; they aren't having to advertise.

Q: I'm interested in what you say about Mystic Meg wanting to protect her name—I'm sure that a lot of astrologers would think that her reputation couldn't get any worse! I don't know anything about her actual qualities, but I don't think there's any argument that the way she presents herself on TV caricatures astrology.

Adam Fronteras: I'd agree with you. But then again, I think the reason Russell Grant is so successful is that he's seen as a fairly flamboyant person. I think it's hard for an astrologer to attack that market if they're not a bit over the top.

Mystic Meg... well, she doesn't even really use her own name; and she's a recluse in many respects. But she does give that image, and she almost is that image in a way. So I don't think it's necessarily projecting an image that she isn't, just as Russell is very much like he is on TV.

The question is, does it open doors? I think you're right in that it can make it difficult for a serious astrologer to be booked. I know there are some things that work against it... but I don't think you could say that it's wrong, any more than you could say that a children's presenter gives a worse image of presenters than someone who presents a political show; it's a different thing.

Whilst some astrologers regard Sun-sign work with embarrassment, others can't wait to talk about it.

Maggie Hyde: I do Sun-signs as well. Did you know that? I'm quite strong on Sun-signs. Are you going to get to that?

Q: I think we just did! What do you do?

Maggie Hyde: I used to write for 'Cosmopolitan' magazine and several teenage magazines.

There's something of Geoffrey's [Cornelius]—it's in the beginner's book (Cornelius, Hyde & Webster, 1995)—which I took up, which is that the Sun-signs are like totems. I think that's a fascinating idea. It's like they are someone's identification—so if you're a Leo, and your sign is the Lion, it gives you an image or a totem to identify with. I think Sun-signs are fabulous, they're amazing. This circle of animals has just survived the centuries, and is still the way in to more spiritual paths for people. They're great fun, and they generally work, which amazes me. I can't believe they do, but they do. You meet these people, who are exactly like their sign. They just seem to exemplify their Sun-sign. The columns are the best format you can come up with, I think.

I've had editors giving immense support, and showing real interest in astrology. Most of the editors and journalists in the women's magazines love astrology. They want their own charts doing, and their boyfriends. And they'll say, "If you have any ideas for features, let us know, because our readers love it and it makes magazines sell." But I can never think of anything. Jonathan Cainer's probably the best at thinking of formats that people can play about with for themes. I think he's very good at that.

So we can't blame the journalists and the press, saying "They just want Sun-sign columns, they don't want serious astrology." They'd have serious astrology, if we could find a way to convey it. But how do you do it, other than Sun-signs? I can't see how you can make astrology any more serious in the popular press than it is; what do you do?

Q: Do you know the column in 'The Observer' that Neil Spencer* used to do?

---

* Neil Spencer now writes a Sun-sign column for 'The Observer'; the column referred to was a more adventurous one, focussing on a different astrological theme each week. His book, 'True as the Stars Above—Adventures in Modern Astrology' is due for publication by Gollancz in 2000.

Maggie Hyde: Lovely column! Yes, I do, that was a nice column. But that column would mean nothing if it wasn't for the fact that everyone knows about their Sun-signs.

It is about 'If the cap fits wear it', Garry. People read Sun-signs, and it doesn't matter whether it works or not. They don't read it for it to be true or not; they read it because they've got something in mind that they're thinking of doing, and they think, "Ah!" They read this little script, and if it turns out to fit with what they want to do, they think, "Brilliant!" Otherwise, they'll say, "Oh, it's all a load of rubbish"—that's it. And they'll read it the next month. They aren't stupid people, but they aren't reading it for a rational purpose; they're reading it because they want that little moment of engagement in something bigger than them—I think.

I just think it's alright—besides which, it pays me. I wouldn't have the freedom to do all my other astrology if I wasn't supported by the Sun-sign columns. And I don't know how to improve them any more (but I'm open to suggestions from all your readers).

There are, as this chapter has hopefully served to illustrate, a variety of attitudes toward Sun-sign work amongst astrologers, and doubtless the issues will continue to be discussed for a long time yet. Here is a final contribution on the validity and importance of such columns.

Q: What's your attitude towards Sun-sign columns?

Lee Lehman: I write one. There, that was simple, wasn't it! I look at it this way: there's science, there's science-fiction; there's astrology, there's astrology-fiction. Sun-sign columns are astrology-fiction. But like science-fiction, there is an element of realism there. And I think potentially, a good Sun-sign column can bring someone into our community. A bad Sun-sign column is random access.

Q: Quite a few of the people I've interviewed were introduced by Sun-sign columns.

Lee Lehman: Sure. That's the point. I think there are times when we take ourselves way too seriously.

Chapter IV
Turning Stars into Money

Business Astrology

As a counterpoint to Sun-sign work (often accused of dispensing vague aphorisms that could fit anyone), this chapter considers the work of astrologers who compete with experts and pundits in environments where exact information is critical. I asked Christeen Skinner to explain how astrology is used in business and finance.

Christeen Skinner: Those are two distinct things; you have a business astrologer or a financial one, and, in this country, I don't think you can actually call yourself a financial astrologer. The Financial Services Act (1986) means that, if you say to me, "I've got £10,000—what shall I invest in?" I can't help. So I wouldn't say that I was a financial astrologer.

The work I do *is* sometimes financially geared, though. I might have someone who asks me to study a particular commodity—gold or silver, say. They will want to know whether I can predict the moments when there will be fluctuations in that market. Clearly, if I was really good at that, I wouldn't be sitting here still working as an astrologer! But those of us [astrologers] practising this actually have as reasonable a track record as the economists or financial analysts.

I have two commodities that I specialise in: gold and one other. If somebody asks me to look at, say, sugar, I will do it, but there is a huge amount of research required in order to do that. My shipping owner might be very interested to know: (1) how much it will cost when he is picking up his sugar in Cuba (he's not, by the way, this is a made-up example!) and (2) if it takes three months to get the sugar here, what the prices will be like when he drops it on the market. That kind of work is financial.

Q: Why is the Financial Services Act a problem? What do you do about it?

Christeen Skinner: The Act says that nobody should offer you any kind of financial advice unless they have been taught and have a proven understanding of what the markets are about. And I am not registered. On the other hand, the kind of people who come to me tend to be very wealthy, and don't give a monkey's about the Act. When I say, "I can't do that because of the Financial Services Act," they say, "OK—how do I need to ask the question in order for you to do the job?" And it's quite easy; they just have to pick ten companies, then I tell them what I think each will do next year. But I can't say, "These are ten companies you should invest in."

Q: How does what we've been talking about so far differ from business astrology?

Christeen Skinner: Business astrology is quite different. For instance, someone says to me, "I've got shares in Rolls-Royce, what do you think they are going to do?" That means looking at the chart for Rolls-Royce. A company I was working for recently had gone from being a quiet company to being floated on the stock exchange. We didn't really have any say about the date of the flotation, unfortunately. But they wanted to know what their turnover of shares was likely to be, who would they attract, and so on. They were already having difficulties, and that was quite obvious from the Pisces-Sagittarius mix that they had at the time.

Then (this is one from earlier today) I might be asked to choose a date for a chain of shops to start their sales.

Q: How do clients get in touch initially?

Christeen Skinner: It's all done by referral. Every client I've ever had has come that way, I've never had an advert anywhere. People phone up and say, "I hear that you did some work for so and so—he gave me your card..."

Q: And then what? Do they visit you?

Christeen Skinner: Occasionally, but more often I visit their offices. I prefer the variety and like to get out and about. I also have clients in Hong Kong, Singapore, Tokyo, Los Angeles, New York—obviously I don't go to them! Their work is sent by fax and email. I think business astrology lends itself very well to tele-working.

I next asked Christeen if she could describe what happens when a business client first approaches her. The first steps involve her asking questions to ascertain the client's position in the company, whether they were involved in founding it, and the type of services or products they provide.

Christeen Skinner: Given that information, this is how the conversation would go. I'd thank you for making contact and would then write to you. This is a security test for me, because then I know that your address is genuine. What I say in that initial letter is that I'll be happy to do some work for you, and explain a few things about how I work.

I'd explain that, in order to do the job, I'll need as much information as possible. So you shouldn't ever worry about swamping me with information. What I require to start with is your date, time and place of birth. I then need to know when your company was formed. This is going to trigger a lot of questions; you have to ask me what I mean by the company's formation. You may have decided in the pub one night that it would be a jolly good idea to sell hard drives for computers—but you can't remember which night it was.

Maybe we can narrow it down to the month. That will help me, looking at your natal chart, to understand what mood you were in when it all happened. That's important; in the whole behavioural pattern of the company, your attitude is going to play a very strong role.

It will be worthwhile to go to the bank and ask them for the date when the company's first account was opened. The company's cheque book would have come legally into force as of midnight that night, even if you didn't pick it up until three in the afternoon. That would also give me a date. There may be a date when you actually registered the company; you might have bought it off the shelf, and then it had a company name-change. So I'm going to have a whole series of dates. Think of them all as tunes; there ought to be some chord structure that is similar with all of them, and that is for me to find out. Then I need you to tell me what the company is going through at the moment. I then go back to that little pool of charts and determine which one is singing loudest right now. I'll then take that as my working chart—banking on my experience, my nose for the job, to make sure that I don't choose the wrong one out of the four.

What I will then do is suggest to you what the company may be experiencing over the next six to eight weeks. What I want you to do is come back to me and report on whether that is correct or not, before I go on any further. In our contract with one another, you have to feed me information, and you have to allow me time to process that as best I can. Then I'll meet you for about an hour and a half; at that point I say, "Let's see how it works for six weeks," because sometimes you just don't work with somebody. So we agree a base fee, and see where we go to from there. But my experience is that generally, people do convert to some sort of retainer scheme.

Q: So what might happen next? What kinds of things would you get involved in for the client?

Christeen Skinner: Let me take a real live instance. This is a new client from last year [i.e. 1995]. He knew a little bit about astrology, but he didn't know how it could apply in business. He was just setting out with his own business; he'd had it for about a year, and was wondering where it was going. We went through the process I just described, and it's been absolutely right for him.

What he asked initially was, "I think I'm going broke, should I take on another director? Should I get some new funding? Should I pack it up, because if I put it on the open market I think I'd be picked up by any of a number of companies?" So they were personal questions, but they also required me to look at the actual business charts. He had a further question, which was, if he did continue, how long might it be before the thing turned around?

All this switched round completely in six weeks. He is now on target, and we are now picking the best dates for him to have meetings with people, choosing the dates for him to do his research for a new product—and we have got a very nice timetable going. It looks like he is going to hit a financial problem later in the year, but we've got a contingency plan for that.

Q: How is the problem shown?

Christeen Skinner: He's got a rough Saturn transit to both his chart and the company chart—he's moving into a different area which is quite uncharted, so those transits may be foreign governments saying, "We don't like this way of working." But until I look at which countries he is working with—and there are eighteen—I can't say where the problem might come from.

Q: Has it ever gone disastrously wrong for you?

Christeen Skinner: The only time I've been in trouble was with a company who wanted me to choose a date for them to run adverts in the papers; and picking advertising dates is a very straightforward job. I picked some dates, and a while later the advertising manager called me to say that one of the Sunday papers was offering them a slot at a big discount, but it wasn't on one of the dates I had picked, what did I think? So I said, "It has to be your decision; but my opinion is no, the date looks lousy." In the end, they decided to go with the date I had given; when I heard that they were going ahead, I said, "Make sure you have enough staff. It says '24-hour answering', but I think you'll need two telephone operators for the first day."

Something extraordinary happened. Whereas normally they increase their mailing base by 10,000 with one of these campaigns, it had gone up by more than 20,000. Naively, I thought I had done wonderfully well. They were furious, because the extra 10,000 people needed brochures which were about £2 a time—I had blown their marketing budget!

This is where we can go wrong. Whilst I'm not being paid to do the chief executive's job for them and plan for every contingency, it would have been very helpful for me to have thought more about what the numbers would actually mean. Because I cost them a lot of money! They didn't fire me, though.

The remarks above come from an interview recorded with Christeen in 1996. I caught up with her in 1999, when she mentioned a couple of projects that were on her mind then:

Christeen Skinner: One particular organisation has got a top management structure (four or five individuals who are constituted almost like the board), and below it they have a much larger pool of twenty to thirty people. There's a certain overlap between the two. What they want me to do is assist them in choosing from the pool of twenty to thirty people, the people to form a management planning team to oversee their strategy and make sure it happens. That means trying to develop a working team, because we can't afford too many mistakes here. Now that's almost personnel management, and it's very different.

Q: Does that involve looking at individual (natal) charts?

Christeen Skinner: I will only have charts for the day [i.e. the date the person was born, but not the time]. It's going to be a hard job, because we don't want the people who are not chosen to go on to feel resentful. So it's really an analysis of each of those charts, suggesting who is best qualified, who will be in the right mood for doing it, and who will work well with others. It's a very, very big job and I don't know how we are going to do it in the time.

The other job, which came in last night, is a nightmare. We've got an international company that went through a management buy-out, and is now going through another big financial whammy. Because of the way the company is spread across the world, there is going to be a point where £X million are going to be sitting somewhere, in the form of shares, over a fortnight period which happens to be right across the two eclipses. [Christeen and I were talking on 13 July 1999: a lunar eclipse was due on 28 July, and a solar eclipse on 11 August.] They now want an urgent analysis of where that [money] should be.

Another job, which came in just this morning, is that I have to write a company report making statements of trends for the next year, when there will be peaks in demand and so on. The problem is that it's impossible to generalise about the work, because every single job is so different. Of course, that's the stimulating thing. I think the important thing to say in this, is that no matter what I deliver, nobody will be able to say, "The astrologer chose these people." That's not how it is set up; I am one part of their toolbox. As it happens they find it a valuable tool, but I am not the only thing.

One of the problems in researching what astrologers do resides in the issue of client confidentiality.

Noel Tyl: I have done some secret work (that I can't talk about) that has been *extremely* rewarding. For several years, at a very high level of social awareness—but behind the scenes. I was proud to be involved, super-challenged to do well, and both astrology and I performed well. We were given a high rating for it.

All we can do is wonder. This kind of secrecy—whilst obviously necessary and admirable from a professional point of view—is problematic when it comes to revealing details of particular astrological methods. Hence the particular interest of the next case:

A Case of Fraud

Q: Do you have another episode from your case-book that you could talk about?

Christeen Skinner: Fraud is worth mentioning; astrology is very good for picking up fraud. If you see a company chart that is being zapped by Neptune, you can bet anything you like that fraud or loss will be an issue. Astrologers have an edge on other professional pundits here, because our understanding of *time* is usually good… I don't think there's any security firm in the country that can do what we do, at the speed we can do it.

Q: Have you ever pinpointed who was perpetrating fraud in a company?

Christeen Skinner: Yes…

In the following discussion we established that (by an extreme coincidence) I knew the Managing Director of the company in question, whom I'll call Ms A. Since Ms A had already talked to me about her use of business astrology, Christeen had no objection to me discussing this case with her. The upshot was that I was able to get a much more detailed account of the case than is normally allowed by the strict code of client confidentiality that most astrologers follow. I can vouch for this, having tried and failed to get details of specific cases out of Christeen and many of the other interviewees. She picks up the story:

Christeen Skinner: We were pretty certain that we'd uncovered something. We didn't have all the birth data, but we did have the birth dates for the people who might have been involved. With that, it was possible to identify who were the most likely suspects. It's not foolproof, but I think it's as good a measure as any. I think it was around £40,000 that had gone missing in that case.

Q: But if a company has shops all over the country, how do you know where to start looking?

Christeen Skinner: Astro*Carto*Graphy and Local Space can actually take you to the shops involved.

My next step was to interview the aforementioned Ms A—the Managing Director of an international retail chain. She begins by explaining her decision to remain anonymous:

Ms A: I'm half-thinking, "Well, couldn't it be good publicity?" I'm knocking myself out sending the press stories that they're not interested in, desperately trying to get them to publish something about the company. But I know that if I came out of the closet and said, "Hey! I use astrology," they all would be really interested. In fact I've already done various interviews on the theme of astrology—anonymously—for TV. You wonder, is there a moment when you can say that you use it and not be ridiculed? You know what the tabloids are like—it could easily be used negatively.

The last thought remains uppermost in her mind, so 'Ms A' she will remain. After discussing some other facets of Christeen's astrological work for the business, we got to the fraud case:

Ms A: The example which you were interested in, about the fraud, was based on astro-geography. Christeen identified Neptune lines and said to me, "You are more likely to find fraud along these lines." Now that is really interesting. You can draw it on a map, and that's where you would then look for it—that's also where you would be very wary about opening a new shop.

Q: Did you actually have a shop that was on a Neptune line?

Ms A: Yes, we had several. We focussed our investigations of losses on those shops and actually discovered fraud. Interestingly enough, we discovered it on specified dates. She had written a report and said, "Watch out for fraud on these dates..." And on those dates, things came up. So the shops were on Neptune lines, and the dates were for Neptune transits.

Q: So was this a case of you knowing that there was fraud going on and she told you where?

Ms A: She was the one who brought it up. In her report she said, "I think you are going to encounter problems with fraud." There was a major Neptune transit in play, I can't remember the details. But she picked that out and said that there would be fraud; and identified the 'fraud line' and said, "This is where you need to watch out"—which was absolutely right.

It was quite mind-blowing; [the report] actually said "16th May, *and* this day in June, *and* this day in July"—there was a series of dates, and things actually happened to the day. That's the most mind-blowing thing, I think—when somebody says to you that something is going to happen at ten o'clock in the morning on such and such a day, and it does.

Q: Having identified that there was something dodgy going on at a particular shop, was she able to help you any further?

Ms A: Yes, because then you can take the birth charts of people who might be involved. We subsequently fired members of staff in the branches that she had commented on.

A Businesswoman's Experience of Astrology

A Managing Director who uses astrology to help guide their business is a bit of a rarity, so I wanted to hear what effect this approach had had on Ms A's team:

Ms A: As a Managing Director, you cannot utilise astrology without your team being involved. After a little while they start thinking, "Hang on... why is this woman saying that she wants the sale to start at 9.35?" If you do it once you can get away with it, but as time goes by people do start to think, "What is going on here?" None of the team that I work with has any background in astrology or actually any belief in it. But because we started applying dates and they worked... afterwards, when things had happened, I would show them the report specifying that they would happen. They became convinced, and actually asked me to use it. In fact one guy now phones Christeen up directly when he has problems.

I asked Ms A whether, having used astrology for some time in the business world, she had any advice for other business people who might consider using it. She had:

Ms A: Within business you must be results-oriented. You cannot afford to pay an advisor who leads you astray. You cannot afford to lose money. Business, like it or not, is about profit. You would never do something unless you see what you are achieving with it. Therefore I would suggest that anyone who is interested in trying astrology should do it in a structured way, so that they can say, "Done this experiment, used astrology: here is the end result." And they should work out the profitability of working with and without astrology; probably they will end up convinced.

In the Film and Music Industries

Another case where it was possible to circumvent the confidentiality issue was the following case, where the client had gone public, in a radio interview, about his use of astrology:

Shelly von Strunckel: Pete Waterman thanked me on 'Desert Island Discs' for having completely changed his career. He was a mildly successful DJ when he first came to me in Los Angeles, and I did (as I do) a frank analysis of his character, including his shortcomings and how—by remedying some of those—he could perhaps do better in his work, and be happier and more fulfilled as a person. I tape-recorded the session, as I always do, and he took away the tape and listened. He acted upon the suggestions rather well—well enough that he could [eventually] buy his own railway! He used to be a trainspotter; now he owns the trains. Because of my business background, I've done that with a lot of people in business, which is very gratifying. When it comes to private clients, ironically, I've so trained myself to discretion that it's hard for me to remember what I've done.

Oh, but I know another interesting one. It dates from LA days. It being LA days, the landlord of the building I was living in was an executive of Columbia Pictures—he was what they called the Controller or Head Accountant. I did his chart, and told him, "You know, this is very peculiar; although you are clearly behind the scenes, you're going to be in front of the camera. There is something else strange here, something very peculiar about the accounting of the company that you are working for..." It was something to do with a very dodgy Uranus in the eighth house as I recall. I said, "I don't know if you are aware of anything wrong, but would certainly suggest that you look into things."

I merrily went off to India for a couple of months. On the way back, I remember reading on the aeroplane something in 'Time' magazine about there having been fraud in Columbia Pictures. When I got back he was particularly nice to me; but it wasn't until some time afterwards that I put two and two together; I realised that what—in Hollywood—proved to be the infamous David Begelman affair, in which the studio's president had put a little of the company's money in his own pocket, had just blown up. Of course, my landlord/client—as the Head Accountant—had been very much in front of the cameras. He told me later that he actually knew what was going on when I was reading his chart. But of course it hadn't come out in public at that point, so he couldn't acknowledge it. But it was chapter, verse and line of what I told him about from the start.

A Route into Business Astrology

On a very rough calculation, one in every 35,860 people in the UK is a competent astrologer*. In turn, the number of these astrologers who do business and/or financial work is very small. You might wonder how anyone ever gets into this line of work. Here is Christeen Skinner's story:

Christeen Skinner: I drew up my first chart when I was about seventeen and by the time I was twenty-one was doing readings. When I look back now, they were to an appallingly low standard. Then my daughter Claire came along, and I didn't have time to do very much. It wasn't until the kids were at school that I could do a bit more again. Now at that time, my friends were women of

---

* The basis of the calculation is the UK's Astrological Association having a membership of c. 1,600 in 1999, and the population of the UK being c. 57, 376, 000. An approximate figure indeed, but it should suggest the order of magnitude involved.

my age, so we were the Uranus in Cancer bunch! Quite a few of them were on their own, or about to be divorced, and several were thinking about starting their own businesses. So in looking at their charts, I started getting hooked into business astrology. I knew little about it at this stage, so I would go to the library and get books on different companies, then look at the charts for the companies. I'd try to work out whether you could actually see what was happening to the company by referring to its birth chart.

So it was not taught—it was [the result of my own] reading. As time went on, I got the Faculty Diploma*, and what became clear was that, amongst my contemporaries in astrology, nobody else was investing much time in this particular area [business work].

And so a career was born. Meanwhile, in the USA, Noel Tyl was doing similar work:

Noel Tyl: I have worked with many, many businessmen, including bank presidents [who had me prepare] robbery profiles of their banks over the years. Whenever we see the profile repeating [astrologically] we put on extra guards, and the robberies have decreased—so we must be doing something right over a fifteen year period.

I have done an enormous amount of high-level personnel evaluation. I've been on retainers by companies for a year at a time; inspecting employees that they would send me generalised birth data on with regard to a management analysis profile. That is not necessarily difficult to do. You just have to address their needs, and find out how to translate the horoscope into those needs. So you are helping the employee do his or her best work by being in the right position—or not being hired at all! And you are helping the company by pointing out what the employee needs to do a job best. That's what is important. It's not testing for criminality—that crops up so rarely in a bank. Where there was fraud, I've been able to do the same thing [as Christeen]: they had four suspects, and I suggested which one I thought was involved, and was right.

Don't Buy that Ship

A very few astrologers (of whom Christeen Skinner is one) spend the majority of their working life dealing with business issues. There is a greater number for whom business work is something which comes along periodically. Maggie Hyde gave this example of a question that involved her in judging a business investment:

---

* The Diploma from the Faculty of Astrological Studies is one of the best-known qualifications in the world of astrology. For more details on the Faculty, see Appendix 1.

Maggie Hyde: It was to do with this man who was buying a ship. He was a client of mine, and his job is basically buying and selling ships. He wanted to buy this particular ship that he'd heard he could get for a good price, but was worried that there was something wrong with it and it would need a lot of work. With ships, apparently (not that I know a lot about ships), if you want to really check them out, you have to do a dry-dock inspection. You actually have to get this huge ship out of the water—all of which has to be paid for. Obviously he didn't want to do this and waste all that money if the ship was all right.

So I did a horary for him on whether the ship was all right. It was extraordinary. It had a Moon-Pluto conjunction in Scorpio on the IC, with the Moon applying, and I just *knew* that the bottom of that ship was shot through. So I told him, "Don't buy that ship, because the bottom is completely rotted." Because he never listened to me, he went ahead and ordered his dry-dock inspection. It was true; the bottom was completely rotten. He phoned me up, very pleased that the astrology had worked—despite losing his money on the dry-dock inspection.

Millions of Pounds from Astrology

Mike Harding spoke of his experience with astrology in predicting movements on the Stock Market:

Mike Harding: I've done a lot of business work in the past, particularly research for market trading. I worked in California for several years, on and off, for private individuals in a small trading group. That was very interesting; it convinced me that there really is 'something' there—that astrology really can pick turning points in markets. But it also reminded me that life is far more complicated than we usually recognise, and that astrology has got something to contribute, but it is *part* of a way of looking at the markets. It is a tool one can use to make predictions with, but it is not the only one. But the fact that it can work at all underlines its extreme importance.

I don't do business work at the moment because it is very time-consuming. I would like to get back to it, for practical reasons—you really could, I think, earn your living at it. It would be nice to think that one used astrology to generate money for something useful. Also, it could be one of the best ways to demonstrate astrology, it could be one of the best research projects—because most people, when they hear of any new idea, will say, "Well, can you make money with it?" I wouldn't say that's the be-all and end-all of a particular idea, but it's not un-useful!

Mike gave this example from his business work:

Mike Harding: Someone came to see me: he was a property developer. That's putting it mildly—he owned a very large company that was concerned with property. It was in the year of the crash—'89—and it was a few months before that crash happened. He said he was getting slight doubts as to whether the property market would continue. I was looking at the Saturn-Neptune aspects that were coming up, and I also looked at what was happening in his own chart. I said very clearly that it was my honest opinion that we had seen the top of the market; that it would fall, and it would fall significantly. I must admit, when it did happen I was surprised at how far the property market went down. But he did sell, he got out—and that consultation must have saved him millions, even tens of millions.

Sports Astrology (1) – Australian Football

Another area in which a few astrologers are involved—very different from the business world, but equally public, and involving direct competition with conventional pundits—is the sports world. Bernadette Brady predicts the results of football games on Australian TV.

Bernadette Brady: It really blows their minds [at the TV channel] that I can tip a whole season—as any astrologer could. And they have all their experts who have to wait until two days before the match, to see who is playing and how somebody's knee injury is... I think they were quite jolted when I just sent in eight weeks [of predictions] in a hit!

So I now have broadcaster passes and things like that—they get me into matches whenever I want to, which is really nice of them. It's quite funny, I didn't use to like football until I started working with it just for battle astrology*. Now, I must admit I quite like it.

You can't kid yourself with sport. You lose your money or you win your money. And I am one of these astrologers who is prepared to put money on the line. And I'll go public with this stuff, because you've got to. I have this rather personal metaphysical theory—I am a Pisces—that you can only be confident in your predictions when you make them before the event; you go public and if possible put money on them. Then, if they work you have really done it, because it's very easy to make a prediction and get it right when there is no weight attached to the outcome. Predictions are very interesting, and to

---

* 'Battle astrology' is a system of astrological analysis developed by medieval astrologers, notably Bonatti, to predict the outcome of battles; see the article 'Twelfth Century Castle Besiegement in Sport' by Lee Lehman and Bernadette Brady in the Astrological Journal, May/June 1997, Vol 39 No.3.

know that you have confidence with the system, you have to put pressure on yourself. It has to work at the hard times, not the easy times.

Q: Could astrologers live from betting shops?

Bernadette Brady: Oh, yes! That's not a hard thing to do. That is something that I am moving towards quietly! [laughs] You see, you get the astrology worked out to give you 60% accuracy. That's enough to make money on. Now I don't know what others are doing, but I am reasonably confident of around 72 – 75% [accuracy]. But the next thing you have to learn as an astrologer is something which is not contained in astrology. You have to learn the art of betting, which is another whole body of knowledge. That's what I have been working on to try to learn. It is quite hard to get that information, but I have been slowly collecting it—I mean I understand odds etc., but the way to actually manage a betting pool is more complex.

You see, once an astrologer does that and gets all these pieces together, they are not really going to go totally public with it. I think you've probably got some people out there already making quite happy livings using some elements of astrology in their betting. But they are not going to be publishing articles on it!

Q: What kind of public response has there been to your TV work?

Bernadette Brady: I get small children stopping me in the street wanting me to sign their footballs; you know, it's really quite amazing. I get recognised in places, because occasionally they'll do a clip on me. So people really love it.

The interesting thing is, there are two avenues in which astrology is happily accepted without questions asked. One is financial and the other is sport. Because in both cases the individuals who want the information are financially driven, they don't care how it works; if it's making them money, they are happy. They don't care why it works, they just want good tipping.

I find it interesting that one can bump into many levels of prejudices or sniggering, but with sportspeople I don't get any of that whatsoever. When they first approached me to do it I said, "I'll only do it if you let me do the whole season." The scenario of an astrologer being approached to predict the outcome of a football match—well, it's a lose-lose situation. If they get it right, then they fluked it. If they get it wrong, then there is another nail in the coffin for astrology.

So I insisted I did the whole season. I knew that I could have a bad week, but over the whole season I would percentage out quite well. I knew that. And that is actually what happened. I had confidence in that. I also told them that if they didn't treat it with respect, then I would pull out. And they did treat it with respect.

What they expected to happen was that it would go quite badly. But halfway through the season they went public on their TV show and said, "We thought the astrology would really bomb out and it hasn't. We've got egg all over our face and we think this is fantastic." So that was a public announcement. I thought, "Score one for the team!"

Sports Astrology (2) – Horse Racing

Pat Harris described a system for predicting the outcomes of horse races, which she has evolved after looking at more than 600 races:

Pat Harris: You create a chart for the time a race begins. The planets and signs associated with the twelfth house and the fifth house will (in quite a lot of cases) describe the name of the horse and the colours of the jockey in the runners-up. And the Midheaven will describe the winner. Deborah Houlding said, and she's completely right, that in a trophy race—like the Grand National—the Midheaven will describe the winner, because it's the honour, the success, the outstanding individual, the king of the heap. Then I looked at the colours relating to signs, going back over a few astrologers (not just modern—Lilly and others, too) and worked out a system whereby you can work out the likely colours of the jockey. Then you can get the name of the horse from the signs on the 12th house or planets close to the cusp. There are drawbacks, however, when you come across foreign names for which there are no immediate translations. Also, it does take time to build up a glossary of names and to recognise them and the chart permutations for a race that will correctly identify them for you.

Last year, Taurus was on the Midheaven for the Grand National. I was thinking of various horses, because often two or three will fit the configuration, with the colours. I walked into the room, switched the telly on and there was 'Earth Summit'. I thought, "Hang on—this is symbolic; earth at the summit" [of the chart, i.e. the midheaven]. The blue colours fitted, too. Also 'Sunny Bay', who came second, was wearing the blue of Taurus on the midheaven. But Leo was on the twelfth house, which would describe the horse as well, Leo being linked with the sound of the first part of the name— "Sunny"—and "Bay" also being associated with the sign. And they came first and second. Not terribly scientific—but fun and intriguing!

I took a talk on this subject to Windsor, the home of Royal Ascot. I brought everyone photocopied race meet cards, split them up into four small groups, and taught them the system. Then I said, "OK—use my system to choose the winners." I had all the results, of course. They did *really* well. I was so pleased to see that they could use it, and they have used the system since with no complaints.

Sports Astrology (3) – Proper Football

An astrologer who has appeared on terrestrial TV in the UK in recent years is John Frawley.

Q: Could you explain a bit about what your TV appearances have involved?

John Frawley: My TV appearances have all involved my making specific predictions—I have no interest in confrontational debate. I had a regular spot on one sports programme making predictions for the coming week, and one-offs on various other shows, again making sporting predictions with astrology.

Q: What would you say TV people generally make of astrology?

John Frawley: Amused ignorance—and a strange fascination with the word 'Uranus'.

Q: Could you give some examples of predictions that you have made on these shows?

John Frawley: For a recent show I was taken to a sports bar and filmed watching the European Cup Final. With Manchester United trailing 1-0 and only 5 minutes left, I was recorded reassuring fans that there was still plenty of time and they would fulfil my pre-match prediction by winning 2-1. This they did, with two goals in the last minute.

I have a long series of correct forecasts in high-profile football matches, often predicting the most unexpected outcomes: France beat Brazil; Norway beat Brazil; Hearts beat Rangers; Dortmund and Real Madrid both beat Juventus; Denver Broncos won the Superbowl—all these teams had been written off by the 'experts', yet the astrology showed clearly that they would win. In many cases I have been able to predict the correct score-line as well. Other examples include forecasting that the hot favourite in the most reliable car would drop out of the San Marino Grand Prix with engine trouble, and predicting winners of the Grand National.

Q: What is your record like in terms of percentages?

John Frawley: The exigencies of TV mean that I am often required to come up with predictions when I frankly have no idea of what the outcome will be: I make no claims to omniscience! So a percentage measurement is meaningless—a heart surgeon will have far more of his patients die than a surgeon who mends broken legs, but it doesn't mean he is a bad doctor. On my own ground, my record is excellent: predicting the final matches in football tournaments, for instance, I have never been wrong—and this includes many quite unexpected results, as I've mentioned.

Q: How many finals have you made predictions for?

John Frawley: No idea. Including other sports, with the same reliability, dozens.

The question recurred of whether it is possible to live on one's earnings for astrological sports predictions:

John Frawley: Yes, if you want to devote yourself to it. I don't live by it myself, but I do make a profit out of [the betting chain] William Hill. I find, though, that the pursuit of lucre gets in the way of one's astrological judgement. It's certainly very possible. And it's a very good way of honing your astrology because you're predicting events and you get the results very quickly. It's not like predicting who is going to win the next general election in five years time. And you get a very clear, unarguable answer. If William Hill is going to pay you for doing the research, so much the better!

Q: So you would say that getting too caught up in earning money by doing astrology can get in the way of one's skill?

John Frawley: If you are pursuing greed, it's very easy to distort one's judgement. If you have a choice in, for example, a football match between the favourites going off at 2 to 1 on, or the underdogs going on at 3 to 1, it's very easy to convince yourself that it's worth backing the underdogs just because it's a much nicer price! So this is why the real money options tend to get in the way a bit. I also find that my knowledge of football, my interest in it apart from astrology, obscures the issue as well. I tend to look at astrological judgements and think, "Nah, that's not going to happen!"

Q: And do you find that the astrology tends to be vindicated rather than your football knowledge?

John Frawley: Definitely—my supposedly expert knowledge of football is evidently pretty patchy.

Q: Does appearing on TV bring you lots of work?

John Frawley: Less than I expected. It attracts a few loonies! I expected mass adulation.

A Gambler's Chart

I asked Bernadette Brady whether she had a system for winning the Lottery. Surprisingly, given the question, something interesting emerged:

Bernadette Brady: I don't actually buy lotto tickets, because the ruler of my eighth is in my twelfth, so I just don't have lotto wins in my chart. Why should I bother? The ruler of my eighth in the twelfth *could* do lottery, but it doesn't, I can tell you that now! It's the square to Saturn which stuffs it.

I have done a lot of work on when to gamble and when not to gamble. I've done that for clients as well, and it works quite well. Certain charts can win money. If you take those charts and collect five or six dates in their history when they have not necessarily won money at gambling but have had a really happy day—and pound them mathematically, analyse them harmonically, whack them through JigSaw* for the harmonic patterns, absolutely pull them apart and break them down into their atoms, you will find a common pattern that is unique to that individual. It's not a simple thing like a transit to one planet—quite often it's got to be a transit to that, and at the same time there has to be this, and at the same time there has to be that... you know, it's an algorithm. Once you find that for an individual you can run that quite successfully. It works!

Q: And then they go and buy their lottery ticket at that precise moment?

Bernadette Brady: Yes, but much better, take your chart to the casino. Darrelyn† has such a chart. If you take my chart to the casino it breaks even, rather than losing.

Usually an angular Pluto, a strong Pluto, is one of the key signatures for a chart that can win sums of money. It's nothing to do with Jupiter—absolutely nothing, I think. It's always the Pluto charts that work. Once I've worked out the patterns, they can take it to the casino, and you say, "You should gamble between this time and this time," and they gamble then and they can make a fortune. Then you've got to tell them, "Stop!" Which is another interesting little human thing.

That works for Darrelyn, as well. I have clients in America that I do this kind of work for—and they're happy little vegemites, as we say in Australia. But I don't do a lot of it, because it can be a bit boring—you know, my chart doesn't respond like that!

What I love about astrology is that it can go in any direction. If you've

---

* JigSaw 2 for Microsoft Windows (Astrolabe, 1998)—a program, designed by Bernadette Brady, which searches for meaningful patterns in astrological data.

† Darrelyn Gunzburg, co-principal with Bernadette Brady of the Astro Logos astrological school.

got something that you want to solve, you only have to go back and collect previous data, be prepared to put all your astrological beliefs, or theories, to one side, work the data, and *let it tell you* what is happening. Reproduce that in the future and nine out of ten times, it'll work.

Chapter V
Personal Work

The type of work covered in the previous chapter—dealing with companies and predicting sports results—is something with which only a minority of astrologers get seriously involved. Most astrologers, most of the time, focus on assisting clients at a personal level. This type of consultation takes three basic forms:

1) **Character analysis**, wherein the astrologer helps the client to see themselves as others see them (or as others would see them if they were sufficiently insightful) and helps the client gain more self-understanding.

2) **Forecasting**, which ranges from hard prediction ("You will be offered a new job on 15th June next year") to a more generalised discussion of trends ("Job issues may require your attention during June").

3) **Answering specific questions**—"Will Fulham win the FA Cup?", "When will I get married?", "Should I buy this car?" This is the domain of horary astrology, in which a chart drawn up for the moment a question is asked is considered to contain the answer to the question.

A Typical Chart Reading

What most astrologers mean by a 'chart reading' is a combination of character analysis and forecasting. Here is the basic format of such a reading:

> **Noel Tyl:** I try to convey a general understanding of the major developments, problems, potentials shown in the natal horoscope, and stimulate quite a good discussion about that—objectively, so it's not necessarily painful—in the first ten or fifteen minutes. In that period of time an awful lot can be covered. There are hundreds and hundreds of people who have said, "My God, it took my therapist six months (or a year) to get to that!" Many astrologers have that happen. It's a very reassuring thing about astrology, and rather a disparaging comment on psycho-analytic dialogue.
>
> Honesty of a client in astrology might be more forthcoming because of the *objectification* of the horoscope; you can always say it's not *you*—it's suggested in the horoscope. With the psychotherapist, the psychotherapist is talking about *you*—and there's a lot of tension about that. So often psychotherapists learn that there are delays in getting to the truth, and you can't rush the client, you have to wait until they are ready. A psychotherapist who uses astrology has got the best of both worlds.
>
> And then I try to test the timing of the horoscope by talking about developmental themes as they go through the life—so I am testing the reaction

levels of the client, ascertaining more detail about the life development. I like to ask what they are projecting for the next six months or year so that I determine the reality, what's feasible. Then I have done my homework, and I match the measurements [i.e. directions] to support that, or change it, or alter it, or suggest more. And then I encourage the client to call me up during [the projected period] and hopefully I have made a friend as well as a client.

And I can do that in an hour and ten minutes.

Astrology and Therapy

Two further comments on the relationship between astrology and therapy, from Mike Harding (an astrologer who works as a therapist and teacher of therapy) and Christeen Skinner:

Mike Harding: What does come back, again and again—it's very challenging for therapists, and particularly for people who work in both these areas [astrology and therapy]—is that you see something going on in somebody's chart, people come to you wanting change when Pluto is aspecting something, they come feeling 'all at sea' when Neptune is over their ascendant (or whatever), and changes seem to take place in their lives at very astrologically appropriate moments.

When I've worked with people who have been in therapy for many years, they often say that familiar thing: "I've been doing this for years, I now know what my problems are, but I'm no nearer solving them." Then they get their Pluto transit, and the therapy suddenly becomes effective. That's a challenging one, because many therapists would suggest that somehow the therapist and the client can make changes—but not quite when they decide to. The idea that there may be some other deep factor in play is something that therapists and clients themselves, too, maybe are reluctant to take on board. Changes do seem to come at astrologically appropriate moments. But it may well be that the change would not have its efficacy if people hadn't been struggling with their personal issues for many years beforehand, getting into the frame of mind where they could acknowledge the importance of change.

Christeen Skinner: I find astrology joyful. Yes it's technical, yes I do a lot of study—but I find it brilliant, there is a great sense of fun. That's where it's at. If it lost its fun, I couldn't deal with it. Hence, my particular hassle with counselling; I've yet to see counselling being experienced as fun. Incidentally, the lady who was here the other day said that she'd been in therapy for eight months, and she'd found the hour she spent here more healing. Now, I don't think she would have found the hour so healing if she hadn't been through the eight months of therapy. But I do think that one is privileged to be able to explore somebody's potential with them, and that should be met with enthusiasm. ·

From the Case-books of Astrologers

It may be useful to touch on some actual cases at this juncture, to anchor this discussion in real examples of astrologer–client interactions. Such work often involves many different strands—imagine talking about everything in your life for an hour and a half—so the cases that follow are much simplified, covering only a single, striking, theme in a reading.

> **Robert Zoller:** A lady friend of mine had a daughter who some time ago was looking to get into a permanent relationship, with a view to getting married; and I predicted for her the day on which some fellow would present her with the idea that he was the guy, and said that he would actually fit most of her criteria. It did turn out exactly as I said it would happen, and she decided that she didn't want to go ahead with the liaison because she was afraid she was going to lose her independence. She had the young woman's conundrum— you know, "How do I get the wealth that I am looking for, the love that I'm looking for, and the freedom that I'm looking for—all at the same time?" That really made a big splash in certain quarters and I got a lot of work on the partnership end of things on the basis of that one prediction.
>
> When I first got into astrology, I was at the Institute for Medieval and Renaissance Studies. There was a young lady there who was also an artist. She had all kinds of hang-ups, and she wanted to know what the outcome of her life was going to be. In the process of reading her chart I could see that there were thirteen degrees between two planets in the fourth house, and the fourth house cusp; one of those planets was Saturn, which was the ruler of (or had honour in) the eighth house, and the other planet had honour in the fifth house. So I asked, as cautiously and compassionately as I could, "Were you raped by your father at thirteen years of age?" She hadn't even told her mother about that. She was duly impressed, and I was impressed with the art.

Both of the cases to which Robert Zoller refers show a 'forecasting' approach—in the second instance, his 'forecast' was of an event which had already happened, but since he knew nothing of it the principle applies. To illustrate the 'character interpretation' level of a reading:

> **Mike Harding:** I remember a consultation with someone … it was as if he had ten planets in Capricorn in the tenth house*. His whole life had been devoted to the family business, and he was a man in his forties. But he also had Moon

---

* Mike Harding's astrological shorthand for, "He was very serious, controlled and work-orientated."

in Gemini. Occasionally this popped out, but he felt somehow that he shouldn't have a light-hearted side, he should only have his nose to the grindstone. In the consultation, really, I spoke just about Gemini—in a very simple way that one could probably have got from any book. I touched on some experiences that he half-admitted having.

After the session, I suppose a few weeks later, he rang me and said that he had thought a lot about our meeting. He realised that this [Gemini] was a side of himself, it wasn't something he should try and educate himself out of. There was a playful, enjoyable, light-hearted aspect to him; he had made enormous changes in his life. He said that he felt really happy for the first time, and couldn't praise astrology highly enough.

It was a sobering thing, because I'd got all my charts, all my midpoints and harmonics, yet what had changed his life was a very simple discussion about Gemini. [The discussion had been a] typically Gemini thing in itself: light, fun, and at one level seeming not to have much substance. It was good basic astrology, and also a reminder that things happen in a session regardless of what astrologers, with all their techniques, plan. Sometimes it is a very simple observation that's important.

The following example also shows how a relatively simple observation can lead to a more fulfilling lifestyle:

Robert Hand: The other day, a woman wanted me to do the chart of her seventeen-year-old son. I found a Moon-Venus-Jupiter T-square on the angles. Well, there are two possible manifestations of this. One of them is a guy whose self-indulgence gets him into a lot of trouble; the other one is a really powerful, artistic kind of thing. Well it turned out to be the latter. He had Mars in the 12th square Uranus, and his mother was afraid he was too undisciplined, and that his interest in music was simply some sort of teenage fantasy, even though she acknowledged that he was awfully good.

She wanted to send him to a military school. And I thought, "Mars in the 12th house square Uranus—this kid would be a disaster in a military school!" Absolute disaster! Boy, was he grateful! He'd been trying to talk his mother out of this. The chart just said, overwhelmingly, disaster! But if he's encouraged in his art, his music, there are real possibilities.

While I thought it might have indicated a kind of self-indulgent slothfulness, I didn't form that conclusion until I began a dialogue with his mother. A lot of astrologers like to amaze and astound the client by calling all sorts of shots without getting any input whatsoever. That's very good entertainment, and it's certainly useful to get people over the hump of "Does this stuff really work?" But fundamentally, I think the chart must be done in the context of a dialogue between the client and the astrologer, so that the polymorphous symbolism of astrology can be pinned down.

Quite frankly, given the proper dose of *agnoia* [ignorance], that chart could simply be the chart of a kid who is totally self-indulgent, pleasure-loving, with no drive or motivation, and probably everything going wrong because of the T-square. But it could equally well have been, as I said, highly artistic. There were other things which elevated it, including Neptune; it wasn't just Venus. Venus by itself does not create an artist; but Venus and Neptune do. He plays rock music. His mother's comment was, "His music is beautiful." Now that's not a comment you can make about a lot of rock!

Diagnosis and Remedy

There is an important distinction between diagnosis and remedy. Adrian Duncan describes the problem of dealing with clients whose behaviour generates problems for them:

Adrian Duncan: They often think of it as being somebody else's problem, so they haven't owned it. You have got to get their total, embarrassed acceptance that, yes, they do this. Reaching that point is a wonderful experience, because when people accept that they have a behavioural pattern that is embarrassing, when they own it, you reach this point in the consultation where they say, "Oh God—is that what I do?" Then they ask, "What can I do about it?" Until you reach that point, you can't do anything.

As soon as they say that, they can do something. I must say, finding out how to help people change behaviour like that—I never thought I'd reach that point. For years, I diagnosed problems—and there it was. People recognised the problem and said, "Oh no!" And I just said, "Hmm, well, you mustn't do that."

Astrology is such a fantastic diagnostic tool, but so far as I know it hasn't had much development as a healing tool. In Indian astrology they have remedies. There is always a yoga exercise, or a mantra exercise, that is a remedy. In western astrology there is this diagnostic influence, and the remedies are few and far between.

The discussion with Komilla Sutton naturally turned to the range of 'remedial measures' which exist in Vedic astrology. She began by explaining her reservations about the most simple remedy—dealing with problems by wearing an appropriate gem:

Komilla Sutton: I have seen many cases of people spending lots of money on very expensive gems. I am someone who has worn them all—and now I have taken them all off! Basically, if you want to enhance your chart, you need to understand the hub of the matter, and you need to do something about it physically or mentally. That means that you have to change your attitude to things. So if you are storing anger, for instance, and start wearing pearl to calm yourself down, you are not going to get rid of the anger problems! But it can calm you, so maybe in some subtle way it can encourage you to look at the anger.

It's very important, if you have an issue, to talk about it, to think about it, to see what you can do. One of the greatest remedial measures is to give something of yourself that really hurts—not money. So, working for the poor, or giving your time, your own energy. And accepting is very important—so if you have a problem with Saturn, you fast for it, you try to do things so that it starts working its energy for you. So I'm not very much in favour of the gems!

Q: It sounds as though, gems aside, there is a science in jyotish of how to *use* the chart.

Komilla Sutton: Yes.

Q: It's struck me that some astrologers can be quite brilliant at dissecting a chart and laying bare its problems without being able to string three words together about how the chart's owner might resolve, or at least cope with, those problems.

Komilla Sutton: There are lots of ways in which you can deal with things. Perhaps the most basic one is to wear the gems—or wear colour. Today's Tuesday, so it has the colour of Mars. If you want to activate Mars energy, wear red. I used to be an actress, and when I was starting to get interested in jyotish, when I went for an audition I would wear the colour for the day! So I was using that. And whether it was helpful or not, my mind used to say, "Today's Thursday—Jupiter, so put on a yellow outfit" (we use yellow for Jupiter)—and I would feel psychologically boosted. But this isn't really solving any issue, it's just giving you a feel-good factor. Colour, herbs, oils— you can work on all these levels, but finally you have to work on your mind. Everything is really based on inner balance.

Q: Could you give an illustration of a problematic chart, where you introduced some 'remedial measures' into someone's approach to life in order to turn a difficult aspect into a source of strength?

Komilla Sutton: I can give you an example. When Manju* consulted me in July 1997, she was going through a particularly difficult period of her life. She was living in the United States, and her career was not going anywhere; her company had been taken over and she was not sure whether she would be

---

* Born: 8 July 1958, 17:35 IST (–5.30), New Delhi, India. The client's name has been changed to preserve confidentiality.

kept on in her present position. She wanted to move house. And her father was not well in India. The general stress factor in her life was very strong.

From her chart, I could see that Manju was going to go through a difficult period over the next year. Firstly, I try to explain to my clients that since they are going through a difficult time, it may not be a good idea to change careers, homes, etc., as it will only add extra stress and tension to their life. Knowing that there was a reason for her difficulties gave Manju the strength to get through a difficult time. She was able to see her career in a different light. She was not so willing to make changes at a time when she felt that the astrological energies were working against her.

Being Indian, she was very much open to remedial measures that I could prescribe for her. Firstly I asked her to fast for Saturn—Saturn will always create problems and by fasting for Saturn you are giving yourself a difficult task. The day for fasting is Saturday—Saturn's day. It is the most difficult day to fast. The concept of fasting is that it gives you mental strength as you learn to cope with voluntarily giving up food. I only give remedial measures for those who ask for them, as I feel it is a personal choice. The fast helped her focus her mind.

She was wearing a very large emerald on her left finger. I pointed out to her that emerald is the stone for Mercury and Mercury is the most difficult planet for Scorpio ascendants—so it would be better for her not to wear an emerald as it was enhancing the negative energies. I suggested yellow sapphire, the stone for Jupiter. Jupiter is a good planet for Scorpio ascendants. Also, it is the planet which can withstand the negative energies of Saturn. To wear these gems, it is important to have them specially set so that the stones touch the skin and then solar rays are absorbed into the body through the gems.

Through fasting, as well as wearing the yellow sapphire, Manju found that she was getting more strength in facing her problems. When a natal chart presents problems, it is not possible for the problems to go away entirely. But you can make your situation such that the problems do not have such an impact on you. Manju was able to deal with her problems. She firstly recognised that it was a difficult period, so she would need to be cautious with her choices; secondly, by using gems and fasting, she felt strengthened.

As Adrian Duncan suggested, astrology is incomplete if it is limited to a diagnosis of problems. In fact, an astrological reading can itself turn into a problem:

Pat Harris: I was with a client a couple of days ago who had a very dynamic chart (no obvious easy contacts). She had been told by an 'astrologer' when she was 17 that she would always have bad relationships, always be unlucky in love. She is now in her late thirties. She had had a difficult marriage and felt that this interpretation, so early in her life, had influenced her thinking (i.e. was a self-fulfilling prophecy), so eventually came to me for a professional consultation. She asked, during the two hour session, if she could change what her chart said about her or if she was simply doomed to live it out.

I was reminded of the philosophy I learned from Cordelia Mansell, my FAS tutor, when I had only been studying astrology properly for a year. She told me that we are never given challenges without the resources to deal with them because the same configurations which describe the problems also represent the resources to solve them. I have utilised this philosophy in my astrology and health psychology research. It has been very, very helpful to patients who wish to develop better coping strategies for the challenges in their lives, but it is true for all of us whatever our problems are.

Free Will and Other Short Stories

There are several factors in play here. One is the astrologer's sense of how to relate appropriately to any given client. Another is whether the client believes that their life is fated, or that they can exercise free will and change their destiny—which, in turn, is linked to cultural conditioning. Komilla Sutton commented on the different approaches between western astrologers and their Indian counterparts:

Komilla Sutton: I suppose in some ways, Vedic astrologers (and I'm not talking about those who practise here [in Europe], but those in India) would benefit by learning a softly-softly approach, rather than just telling everything to everyone!

You see in India, people are concerned with different things to what they are here—people go to the astrologer to ask, "When am I going to get married?" Or, very often, "When is my son or daughter going to get married?" Or, "When am I going to have a child?", "When am I going to get that money?" The astrologer's job is to tell them the answers to all these things. And if the astrologer can see that, quite obviously, something's not going to happen, to say that as well. I suppose if you are not prepared for it, it's quite difficult to take—"You know, your chart doesn't suggest that you are going to get married, so it's better for you to focus your energy somewhere else." And with that approach, you are energising your chart to its best potential, rather than focussing your energy on marriage and being disappointed and having a nasty experience. You focus your energy on something else, which can be just as fulfilling. But it can be difficult, if you are in your twenties, to accept that. Easier if you are in your forties!

We must understand the pattern to get the best out of life. This is part of what Vedic astrology—all astrology—is trying to get at; if you understand this pattern, you can have an extremely good quality of life. It doesn't mean that a pattern is negative, just because it doesn't fit with a traditionally accepted view of life, where you get married at 18, have 2.2 children and then become

Astrology in the Year Zero

very rich. That doesn't mean you will be satisfied.

But deviations from this norm mean that you have a special focus—and you have to change your mind, and move towards that. Unhappiness comes from not accepting your own focus.

A western astrologer who sees his role as being primarily to provide information is John Frawley, who (uniquely amongst the astrologers I interviewed) focusses only on forecasting and horary work.

Q: Why don't you do natal charts [i..e. character analysis]?

John Frawley: I just prefer to concentrate on horary. I'm very careful to make it clear that what I offer is just astrology. I'm not a counsellor, not a validation service. Also, all the classics say that the first thing you do when you tell someone about their chart is to tell them when they're going to die, and you're not allowed [in modern astrological circles] to do that!

Q: Are there any things that you might see in a horary that you wouldn't tell the person?

John Frawley: Yes, there are. One has to get involved in issues of privacy, in particular. Once you have accepted the question, you have to give the answer. But there are some questions that I wouldn't accept. Third party questions: "When is my daughter going to get rid of this dreadful boyfriend?"; "When's Granny going to kick it?"

Q: But if someone asked, "When am I going to kick it?" would you have a problem with that, or regard it as their choice to ask?

John Frawley: My attitude is very much that you ask at your own risk. If you don't want to hear the answer, you shouldn't ask the question. But I do temper that with a consideration of the way society sees such things, so I would only answer a question like that for a regular client. Also, since all of my work is done over the telephone, I have a very limited knowledge of a person's current state, whether they are sitting there with a gun to their head, waiting to end it all, for instance.

Q: So all of your work is over the phone?

John Frawley: Yes. The only time I would see somebody here is if they were interested in the astrology and want to work through the chart as a tutorial.

Q: I guess since it's not natal work, it isn't really a problem.

John Frawley: I'm not doing hour-long consultations. Sometimes a judgement can involve a long conversation, up to, say, half an hour. More usually, though, it's quite short. And I don't think there's much point in someone spending an hour getting here, just to hear me say, "The answer is no!" and then going away again.

Q: What does it mean to you, to help a client?

John Frawley: You're probably helping people a lot of the time in some way or another—but more likely in ways that you don't know about. What you might regard as helping them is not necessarily helping them at all. The real help is probably just the exposure to the process, the opening of an awareness of what astrology implies.

Q: Could you give some examples of specific judgements you have made for clients?

John Frawley: A mother asked about her daughter who had been suffering severe headaches for some months. Medical specialists had been unable to find the cause. The astrological chart clearly showed that they were the consequence of a liver disorder, a conclusion at which the specialists themselves arrived some weeks later. This was done purely from astrology, without seeing either mother or daughter, or having knowledge of any medical history.

Recently, an elderly woman had gone out wearing a valuable shawl; she had hung it up somewhere but forgotten where. The chart showed that it was in a French restaurant a couple of doors away from her house. This was without any indication that such a place existed or that she had even been to a restaurant.

Another client had a pair of pistols missing. He was convinced that workmen who had been in the house must have taken them. The astrological chart showed that they were still in the strong-room, just where they ought to be. He denied this—but went back, looked again and found them in there.

A client was planning to hold a garden party on a particular day in a couple of months' time. The astrology showed that it would rain all day, which it did. Knowledge of this enabled her to make alternative arrangements.

As an aside, reeling off a list of successes in such fashion may create the impression of boastfulness on the part of an astrologer, but such an assessment would be unfair. Getting this kind of detail from John Frawley and other astrologers was a bit like drawing teeth.

Returning to the issue of fate and free will; the issue could be discussed forever, and forever won't fit in a book, so, briefly, here is an analysis that many western astrologers would probably more or less agree with:

Bernadette Brady: One of the things I put a lot of time into was developing an opinion about fate. That enables me to know what I can predict and what I can't predict. For example, with my model of fate, I am confident that I can't predict what colour socks you are going to wear on a particular day. But I'm extremely confident that I can predict the timing, the nature, and the potential outcomes of events in your life.

The list of outcomes is presented to you, in my model, like a multiple-choice list. And there are two components in you that are not represented in the chart. These components are: (1) your previous history—your tendency to make decisions a particular way in past experiences; (2) this rather elusive little thing called free will—which is a touch of chaos theory!

So the cosmos may give you a list—let's say it's a Saturn transit. Then you've got a list which reads, "Go to jail, do not pass go; your father dies; get caught for tax evasion; get a promotion in your job..." You've got a list ranging from the really negative expression of a Saturn transit right through to a very positive expression. When the astrologer sees that, if they are working blind, they can get the timing—and through using technique, that is all they can get (with my model of fate, anyway).

Once they start talking to the client, and start to ascertain the client's history, then they can reduce that list considerably. So if you present yourself as someone who has always handled Saturn well (or at least is in there trying), and you are definitely going for this new job... you can reduce the list! But you've still got free will in there. So what I'll do with a client is apply a lot of effort to technique—the actual 'doing astrology', applying my model of fate. Then it gets down to a short list; and then, with the client, I'll take an intuitive leap. With them fully aware that that's what I'm doing. I'll say, "Given this, and given what we've been talking about, my best bet is that you will do this..."

How Astrologers Prepare

A major difference between astrologers is the complexity, and duration, of their preparations for a reading. One of the quickest must be Warren Kenton:

Q: How much time do you take to prepare before a reading?

Warren Kenton: I draw up a chart but don't look at it in detail before I sit down with the client. I then look at them, to ascertain their level, and then consider the chart. First I give an outline, and ask, "What do you want to know?" That's when the reading becomes interesting, as the reason for the consultation emerges. Sometimes the real question is avoided, so prompting may be needed—or the subject is avoided as it's not the right time to discuss it.

Q: When you talk about looking at someone and finding out what level they are at, is that something that is basically applied common sense, or is there some kind of psychic faculty involved?

Warren Kenton: It's experience. An old doctor can look at a patient and say, "Measles." How does he know? It's because he has seen measles hundreds of times. It's a mixture of experience, observation and intuition. If you've done hundreds of charts, then one comes to a point when a glance at a chart and face will conjure up an insight or comment... by the time one is 40 (and I'm now 66) one should know something about life, and be able to recognise things about people who come along. By the age of 50, one should no longer rely on books.

As previously noted, Warren Kenton's approach is a synthesis of astrology and kabbalah. Space prohibits a more detailed investigation of this approach here and the interested reader is referred to Mr. Kenton's books on the subject. Another astrologer whose work cannot be adequately summarised is Pamela Crane, whose 'Interdimensional Astrology' approach involves the use of many different charts, the connections between them, plus the role of asteroids. Here she describes the charts that she prepares if someone is coming for a consultation:

Pamela Crane: The basic tropical pattern; the basic helio[centric] pattern; the draconic; the sidereal.

I don't always print them out separately, but [either way] the four get put into the quadriwheel. Normally I just put the usual tropical at the centre, because that's what the person will recognise if they've had any contact with astrology anyway, and it is also the framework in which you can see where the draconic fits—that is an important side to it. So those are the 'mastercharts'.

Then... the current crop of solar returns, including the draconic; the secondary progressed; secondary converse (because we make a splash in time); then any relocation charts that are important—either because [the client] was born somewhere else, or is going to live somewhere else, or work a long way away and commute long distances.

And then I do a quadriwheel with the normal tropical at the centre, the secondary next, the converse next, and then the related return. So you can see how everything is interacting, and what themes are coming up there.

And where possible I put in the dwads, certainly in the main tropical chart. If it feels important, I put them into the tropical and sidereal too.

Then—eventually—we get onto the asteroids...

There are more than 6,000 of these. The difficulty of summarising Pamela Crane's approach is probably apparent, so we must regretfully limit ourselves to a brief glimpse of the rationale behind her use of multiple charts, and refer the interested reader to her works.

Pamela Crane: There are different levels of yourself. There is your deeply true self—the heliocentric—and that is no illusion. This [i.e. the everyday world and the everyday self] *is* illusory. Everything looks as if it's going round us, but it isn't. That's geocentric. Everything geocentric is to some extent illusory. Heliocentric ain't! Heliocentric is the true perspective from your God-self, from your spiritual centre. That's where you really see the viability of the organism, you see the viability of the self, you see very often patterns of entrenched disability—it's very important in medical work. You also find entrenched patterns of pathology at the psychological level as well if you're looking at criminal charts.

Moving from complexity to greater simplicity: Adrian Duncan is one of several astrologers who advocate the use of a 'consultation chart'—that is, a chart drawn up for the moment astrologer encounters client—and even suggests that the most important themes can often be seen in this one chart:

Adrian Duncan: I use the consultation chart, which cannot be recommended strongly enough. It transforms the consultation from a woolly explanation to laser-sharpness. You can ask any question of that chart. The chart speaks. What does it want to tell you? This guy had a daughter who couldn't have children. In the consultation chart the Moon was in Cancer in the 5th—and he said his daughter couldn't have children! It was going to trine the Sun in Pisces. I said, "She will have children." He said, "No, physically, she can't have children." I said, "She's going to have a child in a year"—because the aspect wasn't far away.

He was a big business guy in Denmark. It came true, and he was astonished—it was very good for business. It's absolutely sure if you see it in the consultation chart, no matter what you have got in progressions or anything else. The one that is really sure is the consultation chart.

Q: Taken for the moment the client walks through your door?

Adrian Duncan: Yes, the moment of meeting the client. It's not so surprising. The whole point about astrology is that it is working all the time. You don't have to have a consultation for a consultation chart; you just have to have an event, a meeting.

At any point, everything in the environment is screaming at you, telling you what is happening now; and what is going to happen. That's the great thing about horary (if you want to call it that)—it's the astrology of now.

What is Astrology Capable of?

A few specific cases have been mentioned where astrology has been of benefit. At a more general level, what do astrologers think they are achieving through their work?

Dennis Elwell: Anyone interested in self-realisation (and a perusal of the advertising pages shows this is by no means a universal preoccupation!) must work to tune the various instruments of the cosmic orchestra, so that each is making its proper contribution to the whole. You might say the unfolding planetary patterns are a sort of curriculum or agenda. At this time you may have an opportunity to develop your relationship with Mars, next month or next year it may be Jupiter, and so on. Each cosmic principle has to be developed to its proper height, so to speak, and ideally none exaggerated at the expense of another.

One of our tasks is to establish ourselves as a creative centre. We are not automatically at the centre of our life activity, and it is something to be worked at, to be achieved by stages. This function relates to the Sun. But not everybody is living creatively. I don't mean we should all be painting watercolours or doing embroidery. It is a matter of being creative in the life-situations that come our way, through the conscious exercise of spiritual intelligence. We can leave the stamp of our own personality on the opportunities and trials that come our way, or we can react robot-like according to our immediate feelings of pleasure or hurt. Such feelings are lunar: they arise as a sort of conditioned reflex, and come laden with the experiences of the past. The Sun on the other hand declares: behold, I make all things new!

I believe that at this stage of human evolution the creativity of the Sun has to struggle for expression, while the Moon function is too active for our own good. That is to say, our lives tend to be little more than a bundle of reactions.

It is so important to get this Sun-Moon polarity right, and a large book could be written on the subject. If we want to see a sign of the zodiac at its creative best, we should study people born with the Sun there. On the other hand the Moon tends to highlight the 'faults' of the sign, simply because she is so robotic, so swayed by feeling. The Moon placement can almost be regarded as the Achilles heel.

I am reminded of the contrast between the Sun and Moon every morning when I fetch the papers. There are the tabloids, urging us to emote over the latest ephemeral sensation, and there are the broadsheets, trying to address central issues, geared more to intellect and responsible intention. Every day the tabloids win the circulation war, which tells us something about human nature as it currently stands.

The mirror we hold up should perhaps be a magnifying mirror. We are after all relating the individual to a larger scheme of things. I like the ringing dictum: "Magnify to each his own soul!" Equally important, we should be revealing the significance of the biographical dimension. By that I mean we can help to reconcile people with their individual destiny by explaining it in terms of what nowadays might be called a 'mission statement'. Left to themselves, people tend not to magnify but to minify their worth, and their contribution to the whole. From astrology's unique vantage point we can restore their self-esteem, give them back the dignity that may have been undermined by the false values of today's society.

I asked Robert Hand whether he felt that astrology had a role to play in assisting people to realise their potential:

Robert Hand: Yes! I think this may be the twentieth century's outstanding contribution to the history of astrology: the use of astrology as a developmental tool. I think any decent counselling astrologer has two issues to deal with. One is nuts-and-bolts questions—"What's so, and how does it work?" That's always been the case. But the other is to get people to accept themselves. Because the lack of self-acceptance is the primary cause of ignorance. As it used to be put in the old EST training, "There is always the conflict between who you are afraid you are, who you think you ought to be, and who you really are." Insofar as you are labouring in that conflict between who you are afraid you are and who you think you ought to be, you're ignorant about who you are; and you pervert your life.

Charts, astrology and the readings we give, by taking a little bit of the load off the person, and putting a little bit of it onto the cosmos, allows them to look at themselves and say, "This is what I am; it's OK." That is a first step—it's not the last step, but it is the first step. The reason why it's not the last step is that your perception of what you are is not necessarily accurate; but it's a start! The point is, you *stop resisting*. This, I think, is something that astrology helps us do already. But there's a next step, which is described by Plotinus—in irritatingly vague detail—where he says (I'm paraphrasing): "When the object of contemplation, and the contemplator, are one, and there is no longer any boundary between them, then the contemplation is perfect." That's a very free paraphrase, I hasten to add. Now what he says around this passage is, "Action derived from a perfect contemplation is perfect."

Now, what does that mean in terms of the chart? Well, even with a humanistic approach to astrology we tend to think of Saturn as being an external attribute that either signifies or does something. But it's external. The contemplated Saturn would be you and it being one totally; and everything you do follows out of a perfect sense of the continuity of you and it. The astrologer, instead of prescribing courses of action that people follow—to take evasive manoeuvres during a rotten transit, for example—would actually help that person become the 'rotten transit' and it wouldn't be rotten any more. It would simply be 'one doing what one is'.

Now, this sounds very exalted, and how can you ever experience this sort of thing? It's actually very simple. People experience the perfect contemplation all the time. My favourite example is walking—it's that trivial. You don't *think* about walking. You *are* walking, when you walk. There is no sense that the walking is an external activity—unless you're tired, of course. When you learn any new skill, there's a period where there's a gap between you and the skill—like if you ride a bicycle, when you first of all learn it, it's very foreign and alien. Then all of a sudden you become the riding of the bicycle. That's contemplation; that's it.

Now, if astrologers can develop the art to the point where we can assist people in achieving that with the symbolic map of the psyche we call the chart, then astrology will make an enormous leap forward. That's when it will really become a tool to make people move on the spiritual path. Quite frankly, we don't know how to do this. So we have to go with a slightly inferior form, of getting people to a state of self-acceptance and maybe mapping out some practical strategies for dealing with gooey situations. And maybe, eventually, we'll learn how to do this other thing.

Unfortunately, Plotinus gives you no hints whatsoever as to how to bring this about. Iamblichus, who is the more magically-oriented, indirect disciple of Plotinus, said that one way you can do this is through magical ritual. Had his school of philosophy survived intact, we would have a school of Tantric Platonism. That's what he was—a Tantric Platonist. So we would have a Platonism that is like Tibetan Buddhism. Since we don't have it, we might as well use Tibetan Buddhism—or ceremonial magic, or whatever. I think astrology *does* have a role to play in that, but we have a learning curve here. Bit like a cliff, actually.

Chapter VI
Astrology and Health

Amongst the objections raised against astrology are (1) if it was a serious subject then people would study it at university; (2) if it was effective then it would be used to help people at a practical level. So it was with some interest that I talked to Pat Harris about her post-graduate work on the use of astrology in hospitals.

Q: I suppose you must be one of the few people in the country with an MSc in… well, I guess it doesn't say 'MSc in Astrology' on your certificate, does it?

Pat Harris: It says 'MSc in Health Psychology'. But in order to get it I had to do six different pieces of research, and a dissertation. One of the pieces of research was the application of astrological counselling to the understanding of coping strategies of chronic pain patients. It meant looking at the psychology of these patients in terms of their birth charts.

I worked with a clinical psychologist who created the pain-management programme in a hospital in Wiltshire, and gave him astrological reports based on interviews with each patient (which were about 90 minutes long). He then used those reports to further interview his patients, to see if he could get a better understanding of any problems they had with the programme. He found it was much more helpful than conventional psychological techniques, and has been extremely supportive of my work.

Now I am registered at Southampton University to do a PhD in 'The Applications of Astrology to Health Psychology'. My thesis is about how astrology can work in a social science setting, related specifically to health psychology.

I'll be doing that for about three to four years, but I'll be publishing various studies along the way. The first study will look at various forms of infertility treatment, including in vitro fertilisation (IVF). With IVF treatment, the relevant factors include contacts from Jupiter and Saturn to the potential mother's chart during times of treatment. There has been some research done on this already: Dr. Margaret Millard has carried out some interesting work on the correlation of Saturn with failure of IVF (Millard, 1993). In her exploratory study, there were indications to suggest that if Saturn was in a certain configuration with the natal chart of the woman undergoing IVF, she would not conceive. That study will be subject to both quantitative than qualitative methods of analysis.

Q: How do they differ?

Pat Harris: Qualitative is favoured in research in counselling because with this approach you are exploring individual case histories, whereas with quantitative analysis you are using models and specific tests to analyse the data and understand what the resulting probability levels are telling you.

I had done some research, with my own clients on Jupiter transits and Jupiter contacts, which was briefly quoted in Eve Jackson's book on Jupiter (Jackson, 1986). Jupiter appears to correlate with conception and success—not in IVF itself, but in the process of becoming pregnant, or through a pregnancy. So I'm using that research, plus some social science research about anxiety levels and tension (stress... Saturn!) which can block successful conception. The study may take quite some time, perhaps much of the time I am researching my PhD, and will form a substantial part of it.

As noted, it is unusual to encounter someone doing post-grad research into the use of astrology in health care, so I asked Pat how she began:

Pat Harris: During 1993, on a weekend course at Southampton University on death and dying in different cultures, I met the director of the then soon-to-be-launched health psychology course, which had first been developed in the States. She invited me to apply for the course, an MSc. in Health Psychology, but I was hesitant because of my non-academic background—I had no A levels and no first degree. She said, "Yes, but you have a different background—apply for it. We have an assessment process with interviews, and you have to write a piece—so you don't necessarily need a conventional academic background, as long as you can display the ability to cope with the course's demands." So I went through the interview process, which took several months. I had to sit with the head of psychology, the resident psychology tutor, and the course director herself, and explain the value of my diploma in astrology. They were very interested, and asked some very good questions about the discipline of astrology. After a three month process I was finally informed that I had been accepted on to the course.

Once I got into health psychology, I began to realise just how important belief and attitude and self-perception are to health, well-being and quality of life. It's not about recovering from illness, it's about enjoying your life while you have it. And whether you die at this point or that point becomes irrelevant; because if you are enjoying the process of living, you forget about dying. And in a lot of cases, people then actually have a better survival rate. There is a considerable amount of research to show that depression appears to suppress the functioning of the immune system, so techniques that help people cope and enjoy life in spite of health problems are likely to encourage the development of a better level of health—this is a very good positive upward spiral.

Good understanding between health care practitioners and their patients is a key component in the upward spiral and astrology is so vital in this process, because it can open gateways to understanding that conventional psychology is simply at a loss to find. Discovering this through my personal research, I became more committed as I went on, and now I'm driven by this conviction that astrology is absolutely necessary in health psychology—it helps to reduce stress through developing a better sense of health and well-being in the patient.

Q: Could you give an example of the kind of interactions you have with people?

Pat Harris: Yes. Let's go back to difficulties in conceiving children. A client of mine had one child, but although she wanted more, she had been waiting for three or four years. She couldn't understand why they could have one, then no more. She was getting more and more anxious about this. I explained that traditional astrology indicated that there are certain times in your life when you are more likely to be able to have children. Perhaps it was just a question of timing, waiting and accepting. So we had a look at the next few years. I said, "Well, you are going through three years when you could have a child in each year if you wanted. So the best thing is just to forget about everything now, because I'm sure it will happen."

She did forget about it, and of course she had two more children. But one wonders. OK, the astrology indicated it; but I think that she was also causing a lot of problems for herself by becoming very anxious and tense about the prospects of never having any more children. If you have Saturn directions it seems likely that you are going to experience tension, resistance and blocking—which has been demonstrated to correlate with failure to conceive.

The beauty of astrology is that it is so multi-layered in its expression, you can explain one thing and the other with the same factor. You can say, "You are likely to experience tension and stress and inhibition under Saturn; and Saturn does correlate with failure to conceive. Relieve the stress and the possibility of conception increases." It describes the mind and the body as being one, through the energies of the planets, which can manifest in more than one way in a person's life. And it may be that one must wait out the Saturn stress until it gives way to a more stress-free Jupiter-like phase in order to achieve successful conception and birth. But this is a somewhat simplified way of presenting it and individual cases may need more consideration, especially when Jupiter and Saturn play out patterns in the would-be mother's chart which need careful understanding and navigation.

To give you another example of astrological cycles in health: a male client got in touch with me after he had been suffering from a type of cancer which had gone into remission. He was seeking an understanding of why he had suffered from the tumour over several years and why it suddenly seemed to disappear, inexplicably. We explored his case history and the astrological patterns of it which suggested that the pattern of his cancer was linked with finding a vocation that really fulfilled his needs. The cancer would respond to treatment for a while and then suddenly become a threat, again—and it was coinciding with a particular factor in the horoscope that appeared to be linked to his need for a sense of fulfilment in a vocational capacity.

Understanding Migraine

Sometimes astrologers are put in the position of having to call on their knowledge of astrology to help themselves with a health problem:

Pamela Crane: One thing that I, along with another umpteen percent of the population, suffer from is migraine. And that was okay when I was intact, because it came at a particular time of the month. I knew roughly when to expect it and therefore to say no to any potential commitments, so that I didn't let anybody down. But in 1989 I was whisked into hospital and given a total hysterectomy. So, bang went my calendar. I could expect this appalling, debilitating illness—which it is, because it prostrates you for up to five days at a time when it's really bad. People who've never had it don't realise. Once you have had it, you do—with a vengeance; it's a whole system thing, your whole system crashes. We now know that it's a chemical thing, at least in part.

Anyway, there was no way for me to know when I was going to be ill. And the current medicine wasn't sufficient to deal with it. And so my life was in ruins for years. I carried on with astrology, but I wasn't able to commit myself to very much and kept letting people down—which is a horrible experience. You want so much to go and do the talk, do the tutorial, see the client, and then you are ill and you can't. And it's sudden; it's short notice, and you're suddenly have to cancel things. And all I could do was apologise to all the people I had to cancel. Because there was just nothing else I could do. I was very, very sick. But this got beyond a joke and so I thought, "OK, is this astrology worth anything? Let's see if astrology can help." To at least get a handle in the timing. It looked as if it ought to be a Mars issue, because all the phenomena centre around Mars. It's in the head, Aries, all to do with inflammation, temperature, noise sensitivity, blood vessel expansion, stress levels, dietary triggers that excite the system—it's all Mars stuff. So I started to study the transiting positions of Mars—tropical and draconic—at that time against my natal chart (tropical, draconic and helio) and the progressed patterns. I also looked at the daily progressed angles, because I knew how important they were... literally our clockwork.

And, you know, when I had Mars at an angle, I knew I was going to have a very hectic day, because all the adrenaline would be running. So I looked at this and have actually come up with a three year study that tells the whole story. Whenever I had a really bad ongoing migraine that crashed me out, it was when there was a whole constellation of patterns from different directions all homing in on the same few days. And when there was only a light set of symptoms there would be perhaps just one. And this was consistent. But the tropical and the draconic were very noticeably active. And the daily progressed angles were just as important as the natal angles. That was of huge value—it meant I could predict the periods when I was likely to be ill, and, when people asked me to do things for them, avoid those periods. I mean, when you're a little Virgo rising and a draconic Virgo, you are a helpful little soul, you don't like to let people down. So that was nice. I was able to get some control back. I was still ill, but I could do stuff in between.

And then some wonderful people in the laboratories found a substance to help migraine, which has just transformed everything. Not only can I control the timing now, but I have help, which normally works. Please God may it continue.

I would like anybody out there who is a migraine sufferer, has an accurate birth time and is willing to keep a migraine diary (either for themselves if they have the software, or let me have their details at some point), to let me check it out and see if this is a consistent phenomenon, or if it was just my pattern. They surely will have a pattern of some sort. Must do. It's very simple because it's just one planet, and one set of very strong criteria, just the natal angles, the progressed angles and usually the lights—perhaps Mercury, but usually just the lights [the Sun and Moon]. These are the main foci. It should be able to be subjected to statistical work. And it's been so helpful!

Another intriguing astrologer who is involved in medicine, at the cutting edge of the discipline, is Dr. Igor Podolsky, whom Maurice McCann mentioned:

Maurice McCann: I met Podolsky in Moscow a year or so ago. He is a surgeon who controls nine theatres in a hospital in southern Russia and he uses astrology to time the moment the other surgeons begin the operations by making the first incision. There is a computer with astrological software in each theatre. He is very highly respected by the medical profession in Russia and also by his fellow astrologers.

A Practice in Medical Astrology

Graeme Tobyn uses astrology extensively in a healing context (he is also a qualified herbalist). We discussed why people typically come to him:

Graeme Tobyn: You have people who have an illness and aren't getting anywhere with their GP, so want to try something else. There's a lot of bridge-building to give them confidence in you as a fully-qualified practitioner, issues of confidentiality and so forth. That's already a big step for people. When it comes to astrology people think of Sun-sign stuff, and some believe it. A lot think 'these people are stupid' and disbelieve it. So to introduce astrology... that can be a bridge too far for my colleagues (the other alternative practitioners I work with), let alone clients!

Working, as I do, in the Shires, there are going to be patients who have strong religious views, and think 'this is of the devil' or whatever. I can think of one patient who came along. I know that her doctor had a very dim view of alternative medicine, but she'd come along to see me anyway. At the end I asked her if I could cast her horoscope. She threw up her hands and said, "I knew this would happen if I came to an alternative practitioner!" Needless to say I didn't see her again, but that was well-indicated in the decumbiture chart. I think the ruler of the ascendant was applying to Uranus in the ninth house, which was very pertinent.

Q: So how do you work out whether to break it to people that you use astrology?

Graeme Tobyn: I've struggled with this for quite a time. Historically, the decumbiture chart is the chart for the patient first taking to their bed in recognition of their illness; that's what the root of the word means. But it has also been taken in the tradition to be that time when the question is first put to the astrologer—so nearly all my decumbiture charts, 99%, are the time of either the first consultation or the phone-call to book the consultation in the first place. And you can cast that without the patient knowing.

So you've already got the decumbiture chart. But then trying to get the natal chart (and Culpeper says, 'if you have the natal chart as well you shall not fail') gets difficult. You can ask where they were born on some pretext, but ask the time—and it starts to ring.

I believe that I have to have a mandate to cast horoscopes for a patient. They have to express a positive desire in that direction. Of course, that embodies other work as well—drawing up the horoscope and so on—so really, that introduces a different scale of fees. But it's very difficult, in the same practice, to charge one person this amount and another person that amount— that's not very comfortable. So what I have done in the past has been to look on this as an area of my own study. There have been two types of situation in which I would put it to the patient that I would like to use astrology to help me in treating their condition. The first is with patients who I think might be open to it. The second is with those whose condition doesn't have a clear orthodox medical diagnosis and nor is it clear from my point of view as an alternative practitioner. That gives a clinical reason why I might want to use astrology.

Most times, there has been a positive response. But I'm doing that for free, as it were. Now I get patients from other sources—through the world of astrology—where astrology is part of what they are coming for; it's absolutely clear, and so there is no hesitation, no ambivalence. That's what they have come for, I need that data, they give me it, and are charged appropriately.

But it is the case that I'm not using astrology for every patient. That brings up another issue—it's an awful lot of work! I think it was Paracelsus who talked about how you can't have too many patients, because then you aren't doing any of them any good. You don't want to have too many patients where you aren't treating any of them with the attention that their case deserves. So the astrology inevitably will be limited to a certain extent in that way as well.

Q: It's the case, I believe, that someone can develop an illness because there's something wrong at a deep level—in which case, it might be possible to deal with the immediate symptoms but not really address the cause of the illness. To what extent do you see it as being your task to dig and find out why the person is getting ill in the first place?

Graeme Tobyn: I would have said that symptomatic treatment is often the stamp of orthodox medicine, and if patients come to an alternative practitioner that's not what they want. Furthermore, especially with modern drugs—I'm thinking of drugs which have been designed in the last thirty years—they have been designed to interfere with the body's physiological mechanisms. Those specially-designed drugs, of course, can suppress the symptom. Herbs don't really do that, because they're not chemically specific enough to do so.

Now, judiciously used to spare the tissue under stress, these designed drugs can do the job. But the idea of 'keep on taking the tablets' is the start of a very slippery slope.

People are looking for something different. My training in herbal medicine is trying to deal with causes rather than symptoms. These, however, will be couched in a nineteenth century naturopathic mode—so there is the idea of cleansing the body, working on the liver, supporting the kidneys, supporting the ways in which the body rectifies itself by using its channels of elimination. If those channels of elimination are blocked, they need opening. By doing that, you are looking to remove the symptoms—because they will go when you treat the cause.

Graeme Tobyn provided some case studies:

Graeme Tobyn: A patient came to see me last year. She opened the consultation by saying, "A friend of mine went to see a herbalist, and she's cured. That's what I want." She complained of feeling bloated all the time; she had aches and pains all over her body; she had excruciatingly painful headaches and periods. She had been put on oral steroids for headaches.

Now, I don't know another patient who has been put on oral steroids for headaches. Clearly the doctors recognised that the head pain was due to some inflammatory process. She had been to see a rheumatologist about these pains all over her body and in her joints, and she was overdosing on brufen for the period pains. Her doctor had rightly told her off about this.

Having taken my case history, I diagnosed that she had an allergy to gluten—normally that means wheat, modern strains of wheat. So I put her on a gluten-free diet, looking to introduce oats and rye in the second month (because, as I say, it's normally wheat) and I got her off cow's milk and related products (she could take goat's and sheep's milk)—so she wasn't on a dairy-free diet, but she was avoiding cow's milk.

After four days, the headaches went, the aching all over went, the bloating went. The period pains lessened, but they were still there. So that's an example of treating the cause. Food intolerance is a classic thing that doctors are not interested in. If they suspect an allergic reaction, then you get an antihistamine. But they didn't even suspect that here.

Q: How did you identify the specific allergy?

Graeme Tobyn: There are certain symptoms that, when they have no other medical explanation, are seen to be connected to allergy. So I recognise things like fluctuating weight, and swelling of the hands and feet coming and going. Those are two signs of allergy where there are no other apparent reasons. About gluten in itself—she absolutely loved bread. This is called a masked allergy.

You have to know Seley's adaptation syndrome; but most people who have a food intolerance are actually intolerant of foods they eat every day. So we're talking really about wheat, cow's milk, and the potato family. You can imagine that when I ask a patient, "What foods do you eat every day or nearly every day?", those things will come up. That means that they are going to be in stage two of the adaptation syndrome. On first exposure to this thing that they have (let's say suddenly) become intolerant of, they have an acute reaction but they don't put two and two together; they don't know it is the bread. So the body goes from the stage one acute reaction, which people do recognise ("Oh, I'm allergic to shellfish—every time I eat it I vomit and have a headache") to stage two. In stage two, they have to keep ingesting the thing that they are intolerant of, in order to remain in stage two. Otherwise—if more than three days elapse of not being exposed to it—when they are next exposed to it, they go back to a stage one reaction.

So they stay in stage two, and the body is madly secreting endogenous cortisone to damp down the inflammatory reaction.

Q: Is that experienced as a craving for the thing to which one is allergic?

Graeme Tobyn: Often. This woman ate loads of bread, she loved bread. So that was my clue, and I hit the nail on the head.

So that is an example of treating the cause, rather than the symptom. Giving steroids for the head pain and brufen for the period pain is looking at the symptoms; same with going to a rheumatologist—the thing they say about rheumatologists is that they are good at diagnosis but their medicine is terrible. It's all looking at body parts—"You look at that part, I'll look at this part"—whereas I try to look at the whole picture.

That's another reason I try to treat causes and not symptoms—because I claim to be a holistic practitioner, so I'm looking at the whole picture. Not only physical symptoms, but any emotional difficulties that might impinge—a spiritual orientation, because often, people are spiritually sick.

Astrology helps to bridge these worlds, because it is a tool with a holistic paradigm, a cosmic view of things.

Let me give you another example of a holistic orientation, one without herbs or astrology! A woman was referred to me by her GP. She was a district nurse with perennial rhinitis. I took a case history and examined the membranes of her nose and decided there was too much heat in the body. Towards the end of the hour I asked her about feelings of anger (which could produce excess heat in the body, being under Mars). She told me that she used to work for a GP practice as a nurse but had been overlooked for some kind of promotion in the surgery. She subsequently left that practice, but, she told me, every time she passed its doors, anger would rise in her. At this point she burst into tears, her face flushed red, her blood pressure went right up (I took it before she left the consulting room). I prescribed a cooling mixture of herbs for her and she was better in days, not having any rhinitis at all, but personally I believe it was the releasing of the anger through confessing it that made her better. So, a holistic practitioner will want to understand every facet of the patient in order to discover what really is wrong.

Q: If someone comes to you with an illness, how do you decide if it's psychosomatic in origin?

Graeme Tobyn: A psychosomatic problem would be functional, like the rhinitis case I have just mentioned. So the first step would be to eliminate the possibility of any organic disease. One of the worries of the medical profession about alternative practitioners is that, if they miss serious disease and fail to help the patient, not only are they not helping the patient (that would be OK in light of the Hippocratic maxim of 'at least do no harm'), but by not referring them on to their GP having not recognised a more serious illness that is beyond their capabilities to deal with, they are actually delaying the treatment that the patient needs. This is a concern.

So my first step would be to rule out organic disease. How much of that you can do through a clinical examination—without recourse to blood-tests, x-rays, scans and so forth—is an issue. The practice of GPs today is that they will wait for the results of a blood-test, scan or whatever—and feel that they cannot treat a condition if they don't have that 'objective' evidence. Even examination with the hands is seen to be subjective in some sense. (In the tradition, the hands are seen as the organs that have everything in complete balance—the best tools for judging whether there is an imbalance of heat or cold, dryness or moisture). But [now] there has to be this 'objective' evidence from technology.

So physicians of the past—and you don't have to go that far back to get to a much less technological clinical context—spent a lot more time focussing on the clinical presentation and the examination.

A patient is consulting me at the moment, and he has pains and swelling of the upper abdomen—the stomach, really—most of the time. He's had this for about twelve years. So I carried out an abdominal examination, and that was a bit tricky because the muscles of the abdomen were a bit taut, and they have to be nice and relaxed so you can palpate through and see if there are any lumps, or any areas of tenderness. In that way, I'd be looking to rule out organic disease, such as a tumour. And I feel that I have to carry that out, in order to say to myself, "Well, I haven't found any objective signs of organic disease."

Given the symptoms, and the case history, I thought that it was psychosomatic. I cast his natal chart, and a decumbiture chart. It can be the case that one works better than the other; or one is highly meaningful in the context and the other doesn't seem to be. Or sometimes they both work, and there may be some synastry between them. In this case, the natal chart was speaking volumes to me.

I felt that this problem of his was psychosomatic, and was well indicated in the natal chart by a square of Mercury in Aries to Jupiter in Cancer. Those planets were rulers of the meridian—fourth and tenth—and he sees the origin of this problem in the separating of his parents when he was about two. So that fits; the rulers of the fourth and tenth in difficult aspect signifying the parents not getting on; secondly, Mercury rules the mind, Jupiter in the tradition rules the natural virtue (which is to do with digestion and reproduction; so here, it's very much about digestion—Jupiter of course rules the liver, which is a key organ in that process).

For other reasons as well, it all played into that Mercury square Jupiter, which could easily suggest psychosomatic problems, as you can imagine.

So then I started to treat him with Jupiter and Mercury herbs. That's how I would look to decide psychosomatic from organic. 'Psychosomatic' has a particular medical meaning—that it comes from the mind—but of course that really implies the emotional or the spiritual life. So that is where those levels slot in. In this patient's case, it was the separation of his parents when he was very young, and what happened after that.

Can Astrology be Tested?

Q: You're giving examples in which astrology is coming up with the goods. Has anyone ever run a study on the work of medical astrologers from the point of view of evaluating whether astrology works?

Graeme Tobyn: Well, there's Cornell's 'Encyclopaedia of Medical Astrology', which I think was published in the '20s. That had some input or sanctioning from a physician. But I just don't believe it! You know, where has all this stuff come from?

You see, I don't believe that I am separate from any of this astrology that I view. So I need a mandate from the patient in order to actually do astrology in the first place. I cannot take all those patients that I did not do astrology for, but for whom I have a case-history, follow-up visits, a whole course of treatment and what happened in the end. I don't believe that I can cast horoscopes for the decumbiture, maybe a noon chart for their date of birth, and look back in retrospect—because there wasn't the mandate for the astrology.

So I don't believe in objective astrology, actually*. First of all, there has to be the desire of the client that astrology be invoked. And then, when it is invoked, it is invoked by me—I am in there as much as the patient. Interestingly, it's very strongly in the tradition of medical astrology that you do self-reference.

What I mean by self-referencing is that the ruler of the 7th is the astrologer/herbalist, the physician. You're in there; and you have to consider whether you are the best person to take this case on, or whether you are liable to do them some harm. Should you just refer them on? There is that element in the practice of medical astrology, which places the practitioner in there as well as the patient.

It's hard to objectify it, because it's all about that particular astrologer drawing up the chart, seeing themselves reflected, and acting in recognition of that. Astrology is not so much a tool for accessing information, like calling up a patient's records from the computer months later, it is about initiative in the moment. Let the moment pass and the chance to take the initiative in the matter at hand in that moment has passed. You cannot treat retrospectively.

About research—I have a load of patients I've treated astrologically, and my knowledge of astrology is built upon that experience. That's the experience side, then the theoretical side is my continuing studies of the subject—because,

---

* This is an important statement—and perhaps a surprising one in the context of medical astrology, which seems as if it ought to offer ideal conditions to practise, and either validate or falsify astrology in objective, scientific terms. The whole issue of whether astrology should be thought of as an objective science (or as a subjective art, or as something in between) will be a recurrent theme in Chapters VIII – XII.

of course, astrology is a bit like medicine, it just goes on and on.

You see, I don't think there is any point in trying to establish objective evidence for it. For instance, there are doctors (I think there's a group in Glasgow) who do proper research (by which I mean controlled clinical trials, because that's the 'gold standard' of it) on homeopathy. I can't remember all the details, but I think they produced cases where homeopathy seemed to work; they submitted it to 'Nature' magazine for peer review, and it was included but it was argued in the journal that it didn't stand up to scientific scrutiny. The doctors who carried out the research had to say, "Either you are working according to these objective, scientific principles, which we have fulfilled—and homeopathy seems to work in this controlled trial—or else you are not doing that, in which case why are we bothering with controlled clinical trials?" You see, beyond that realm of 'objective, scientific ideals' is the human realm, where it is not in the interests of medicine to have this kind of material validated. Astrology is so far removed from the orthodox medical model that to imagine that it is going to be included is very naïve, I think.

Q: Bernadette Brady recounted how, when she first discovered astrology, she was a microbiologist. She says that she got angry with astrology when she started to find that it seemed to work—she wished that more astrologers could have this experience, so that they might understand the anger that the scientific community have against astrology. If it's true, of course, then their worldview, even their life's work, is undermined.

Graeme Tobyn: That's right. Richard Dawkins heads that group for communicating science to the general public. He did his thing against the 'X-Files' and all this mysticism stuff, suggesting that people's rational understanding is being undermined by these things. Yes, it is a great threat. But he writes books which smack strongly of genetic determinism; and you might well be worried about the new class of drugs that will come along where you're told, "You're not ill yet —but if you take this drug it will interfere with your DNA and save you from the development of this genetically inherited problem in your forties." That's mega-bucks for the pharmaceutical industry; selling medicine to people who are well!

The Designer Health Industry

Graeme Tobyn: The thing with high cholesterol is a case in point. High cholesterol is a risk factor in heart disease, but it's not the only risk factor. By itself, it doesn't necessarily warrant too much consideration unless it's extremely high (this is my understanding). But what happened was that a drug was brought out, some level was set that is 'normalistic' for the human body (treating the body like a machine). Then, lo and behold, every place had its little testing machine, taking your cholesterol level and telling you whether you needed to take medication. And you're not ill!

There is an inherited condition—hyper-lipidaemia or hyper-choles-terolaemia—and there will be a history of heart disease in some families. But that's a small number of people. Now we have the whole population concerned about their cholesterol levels. There's an alternative view, a naturopathic view, which relates to diet. I think diet is extremely important in this regard, because you have the issue of trans-fatty acids—which don't occur in nature, and are caused by the process of hydrogenating vegetable fats. So if those conditions are more prevalent, it's probably a problem of modern food technology and lifestyle.

Q: When astrology interfaces with medicine, does it only do so with the alternative approaches? Can astrology make sense of things like Viagra or chemotherapy?

Graeme Tobyn: I've seen Pluto symbolise antibiotics, a heart pace-maker and the contraceptive pill. But that's still from the 'alternative' point of view, where you are seeing a patient whom the doctor has told, "You need a four-month course of antibiotics for this acne," and the Moon is quincunx Pluto applying.

But no, I can't see it, because the modern medical model is of the body as a machine, so the parts are interchangeable. Your machine is the same as my machine; this part of your machine is broken, we can take it out and put another part in. That's so reductionist. Astrology isn't reductionist in that way. I reject any understanding of astrology as reductionist*.

So the answer would be no. But having said that, a doctor has quite a degree of clinical freedom to do this or that in the interests of his or her patient. So it's not inconceivable that a doctor will practise orthodox medicine but do natal astrology as a separate issue, in the same way they might use a faith healer.

I want to make a firm distinction between the astrology of disease and the astrology of health. The astrology of health is there for straight astrologers to dip into. I'll explain what I mean by 'the astrology of health' (I outlined it in my book, 'Culpeper's Medicine').

The astrology of health is based on the natal chart—from which you derive the temperament of the individual. Culpeper says that you need the natal chart, because maybe the patient has lived in a different climate, or maybe they have had illnesses in their life, or maybe they have just got older, and that changes their baseline temperament. The natal chart should show that; that is your starting point.

---

* Reductionism—the approach of reducing a whole to a collection of parts and dealing with the parts—appears again in Chapters X and XII.

The Six Non-Natural Things

Graeme Tobyn: Once you have identified the temperament of the person (and usually that's a combination of two, not just one simple one), that feeds you straight into what was called (in the western medical tradition) 'the six non-natural things'. They are things that are not innate in the body, but are required by the body. In fact they are unavoidable, and they have to be in good order for the body to be maintained in health.

The first one is air that you breathe; in our day that tends to mean pollution, which is very important. But it could mean the difference between living half-way up a mountain or living in a valley; living by the sea or living on a plain in a land-locked area.

The second one is diet—food and drink.

The third one is the balance between exercise (activity) and rest. I was listening to the radio this morning; some woman was running a half-marathon, extremely fit, and she dropped dead. They are saying, "We need more defibrillators." You imagine people running these marathons, really being healthy, yet there's this demand for defibrillators all down the course. You think, "What's going off there?" It's this 'no pain no gain' mentality; if you're getting pain from exercise, you are doing yourself harm. That would be the old view. In terms of rest—you speak to some people and they go to work, they get home and cook, potter around, do knitting, they don't really watch TV because they can't sit still for long enough. Their inactivity thing isn't very good, so they should be doing something like yoga.

The fourth is sleep and wakefulness. Insomnia: big problem.

The fifth one is bodily evacuations. Herbalists are good on this, they always ask patients about their bowel habits. The English are supposed to be very bad at talking about it, and that's why so many cases of colon cancer go untreated. Herbalists do ask about bodily functions, because that is a part of their orientation.

The sixth one is the emotions. Passions in the mind transmit things to the heart (this is in the old understanding) and when the heart is disregulated by these emotions, the whole body is put out of sorts. So the emotions that a person is experiencing—prolonged grief, anxiety, depression, anger—these things can upset the body.

So those are the six non-natural things. You could have a straight astrologer—not a medical practitioner—but with a knowledge of the energetics of food. We know that garlic, and onions, are extremely heating. We know that lettuce and cucumber are extremely cooling; that is why, as a group, we eat them in summer. We know that strong tea is very astringent, it puckers the mouth (think what that is doing to the kidneys...)

You see, you don't have to go very far to be able to understand what someone of a certain temperament needs. Because the temperament means that there is not perfect balance between the humours, or the elements. No-one is in perfect balance—that would probably confer immortality! So everyone is slightly out of balance, but still within the bounds of health. That is what the Greeks called the *eukrasia*, the 'good mix'. The idea of the six non-naturals is to get better health than you already have. An astrologer can do that by looking at the six non-natural things; and that would put the astrology of health within the remit of natal astrology. That's where medical astrology should make its first big step in recovering its status; but illness frightens people off, and you do have to have a certain medical discipline to deal with that.

Q: Do you get into evaluating the temperamental balance of someone and telling them that they should, say, sleep more (or less)?

Graeme Tobyn: Yes. I had a case a week ago. I was phoned up by a journalist, who was writing an article for a new health and fitness magazine that's coming out. She wanted to compare what a GP, a reflexologist, and (of all things) a medical astrologer could tell her. I was at a disadvantage, in comparison with the others, because I didn't see her; we had to do it over the phone. I asked her to make it clear that this isn't my normal practice at all.

The GP had said that [the journalist] was tired. I don't know what the reflexologist said. I got my caller's natal details, and also cast a horoscope for the moment of her enquiry—which, initially, didn't look promising, but in the end I decided that it would be beneficial for me to be involved in that way. That change of view really depended on me identifying myself in the 7th—not as Saturn, the ruler, but as Uranus, the co-ruler, which is very pertinent for astrology.

I drew up the natal chart, evaluated the temperament, then considered my six non-natural factors. I also wanted to suggest herbs that she could take. I decided that she had problems sleeping because she was choleric/melancholic. Both those are dry, so I decided that one problem lay in the dryness. The dietary advice, then, would be to eat moistening foods. I didn't want her to exercise too excessively. I thought that sleep would be a problem, so I noted down: Chamomile. Chamomile tea is the first step in self-help for people who are having difficulty sleeping; a cup of Chamomile tea before bed.

The natal ascendant was Leo, ruled by the Sun. You always want to strengthen the ascendant ruler—especially as the ascendant is the cusp of the house of life and health. So Chamomile was my constitutional remedy for her. And because, as Culpeper says, it purges heat (and she was, first and foremost, choleric) that would be ideal in that way.

The other two were really medicinal herbs that you would use to treat insomnia: hops (which, although a herb of Mars, purges heat from the system, like curing like) and the third was a herb of the Moon, Californian Poppy, which is cooling and moistening; it removes the dryness, and is a known hypnotic herb. So I jotted these down. She rang for the consultation, and I went straight into saying, "Well, you are this balance; do you have dry skin?" Yes, she does, there is a history of eczema in the family and she has had eczema from time to time.

The chart was great for her career as a journalist: Moon in Aquarius, sextile Mercury and Venus in the 10th house. So she's good at writing, there is a charm to her writing. Sun in Aries on the cusp of the 10th—she is ambitious, as you would expect from a choleric melancholic; both those temperaments will be ambitious. And liking to work on her own—the Aries thing, of course.

And yes, she does have trouble sleeping. She works frenetically (she has Moon square Mars) and then has a period where the work is not going so well, or there isn't so much of it. She has Saturn in the tenth, square the ascendant— the main signifier of melancholy in her horoscope.

So that worked out. I told her of the herbs for her insomnia, and she found the whole thing "uncannily accurate" (her words). I described her physique, as well: with that temperament you would expect her not to be fleshy, but slim. I thought she would be middling height or lower—not tall. She was middling height, actually. Nothing to do with temperament, but with so many planets in the tenth house and no strong ruler of the 5th, I didn't think she had children; she didn't. Very much the career woman at this stage.

That went well, and that's the astrology of health. I think astrologers can take that on without [necessarily] getting into disease issues.

Chapter VII
The Varieties of Astrological Experience

Astrology has been brought into play in many people's efforts to understand themselves and the world in which they live. This chapter is a further examination of some of astrology's developments, and its interactions with other disciplines.

Psychology and Psychotherapy

The psychologist C.G. Jung (1875-1961) once wrote: "I am particularly interested in the particular light the horoscope sheds on certain complications in the character. In cases of difficult psychological diagnosis, I usually get a horoscope... I have very often found that the astrological data elucidated certain points which I otherwise would have been unable to understand." (Jung, 2000.) Whilst Jung's knowledge of, and interest in, astrology was more limited than this quotation might suggest, the psychological model that he developed as he emerged from the influence of his mentor Freud was largely informed by alchemy, which shares its ancestry with astrology. It was, therefore, natural for astrologers to incorporate Jung's ideas into their work—witness Dane Rudhyar, writing in 1936: "We are... stressing values and using a terminology which are found in C.G. Jung's works, because we are deeply convinced of their inherent validity, and also because they dovetail so remarkably with the general set-up of astrological symbolism." (Rudhyar, 1970, p.92.) For astrologers in the mid-twentieth century Jung provided a modern philosophical framework for their work, whilst also lending it an air of scientific respectability.

    The attempt to marry astrology and psychology has been a major theme in western astrology over the last seventy years, with Jung generally being brought in to sanctify the union. In addition to Rudhyar, Liz Greene and Howard Sasportas—founders of the Centre for Psychological Astrology (CPA)—and Stephen Arroyo have been prominent exponents of this approach.

    Psychology comprises many different, often conflicting, ideas and theories, and it would be inaccurate to leave the impression that astrologers with an interest in psychology are unanimous in their praise of Jung. The existential therapist and astrologer Mike Harding, for instance, has reservations: "If we accept the Jungian ideas as described, then the infinite complexity from which social and racial identities would seem to emerge can be conveniently ignored in favour of—at best—rather smug generalities, which are of dubious accuracy, and refer to virtually every corner of our lives. Astrologers already come perilously close to this attitude without any outside help." (Harding, 1992, p.59.)

    Psychology provides models to help analyse and understand the mind; the related discipline of psychotherapy involves a trained therapist using psychological insights in order to help an individual client—usually in a series of one-to-one sessions. The value of psychotherapy has been increasingly emphasised in the astrological community over the last twenty years—for instance, students of the CPA's 'In-Depth Professional Training' course are expected to receive regular therapy for at least one year, and the Faculty of Astrological Studies (FAS) has initiated a 'Counselling Within Astrology' course, with a similar requirement for ongoing therapy.

In addition to his commitments as a teacher and practitioner of psychotherapy, Mike Harding has worked on the FAS's counselling course. I was keen to hear how, in his experience, psychotherapeutic skills can contribute to astrology.

Mike Harding: At a basic level, counselling is about listening to somebody. It's about being able to identify issues. It's about being able to make appropriate interventions, hopefully in a relatively sensitive way, and recognising some of the issues that can come up when two people talk about intimate or personal things. So at that level, I think it's probably useful for all astrologers to have some experience of it—even if they work in a very traditional way, like giving horary readings. I've seen some examples where people have been given readings from horary charts at public meetings—very insensitively: "Well, your dad *is* going to die next month…"

If a person asks a question like that of an astrologer and wants an answer, then they can't complain if they get it. But there are better and worse ways of addressing powerful emotional issues and I think that counselling can help the astrologer here.

At a deeper level, for people who want to see clients a number of times, counselling obviously—by its nature, by its structure—gives one a way of thinking about, and working with, multiple sessions or how clients may want to use time in each session.

So there are quite a few practical skills, ideas and experiences that can filter through. For me it's about the issue of practical qualities that help the astrologer to work more effectively—rather than the feeling (which I don't follow) that somehow the astrologer should take on some of the therapeutic or counselling models of the human being and see people in those terms. It's more about skills and sensitivity.

Q: How did your involvement with psychotherapy begin, and how did it develop?

Mike Harding: Like many people, I first saw a therapist for my own personal reasons: I was going through a very difficult time. I decided that I wanted to take this seriously, and in fact went into analysis, not with a psychoanalyst (although I have had some experience of Freudian group work). I saw an existential therapist for many years.

Then there was a period when I did quite a lot of training at North London polytechnic (as it was then) in group therapy and group dynamics. That all went by the wayside when I discovered astrology. My interests then went mainly in that area, and it wasn't until about ten years ago that I started to get back into the area of psychotherapy more formally. Obviously, I'd used astrology in a counselling way—probably that was the main way in which I worked. But I decided to go back and complete my rather fragmented training and get properly registered, etc. So that's what I did.

There was quite a gap when I wasn't particularly interested in the practice of psychotherapy—some of the ideas in it, but not the practice of it.

Q: What does your practice of psychotherapy consist of these days?

Mike Harding: In practical terms, I spend most of my time working as a psychotherapist or teaching at Regent's College*—teaching both in the area of psychotherapy and philosophy. I certainly haven't given up astrology, but I don't see many clients at the moment. I do a certain amount of supervision, I do a small amount of teaching, but I don't see many clients. There just isn't the space for them at the moment, because what time I have free I want to spend writing. I can see this changing in a few years' time, but at the moment, at a professional level, astrology plays [only] a small part. It is there in my life all the time, I always look to see what's going on [in the ephemeris], and still do charts for myself.

Q: You mentioned in your book 'Hymns to the Ancient Gods' that you were in analysis for twelve years. On the basis of that experience, as well as your own work counselling people, what do you feel that psychotherapy can offer?

Mike Harding: It's a very, very difficult question, because it has a lot to do with how someone is in their life at a particular moment. I think there are times when psychotherapy can offer very little, and other times when certain approaches, at certain important moments in someone's life, can offer a lot. I don't think I could write a description of what I think psychotherapy can offer per se. I think one would have to think about particular examples.

At a very simple level, an ability to talk about what is going on for you is extremely important. The empathy (or lack of it) that you get is also important. Research clearly indicates that it isn't a particular approach that clients or patients see as significant, it's the actual person. Interestingly—and also rather challengingly, for someone whose life is spent teaching—research shows that it doesn't make a lot of difference whether the person is trained or not, in terms of whether the person experiencing therapy or counselling finds it beneficial.

That's quite a challenge. It doesn't mean that I think training or teaching is of no value. It *is* of value, and the more we can learn and the more we know, the better. But the idea that, if you are taught well, you automatically become a good therapist doesn't work. You can't make the jump—if you are taught to do plumbing or woodwork or something you can achieve a certain level with it, you can be competent, but that doesn't carry across to psychotherapy. I think there are imponderables that can't be taught.

* In the School of Psychotherapy & Counselling—details in Appendix 1 .

Q: How has astrology affected your approach to counselling?

Mike Harding: First of all, the issue of *time* is often ignored in therapy—except things like missed sessions; do you work for forty five minutes, fifty minutes or an hour; and how do you get the client to stop when the time is up? But the philosophical concepts of time are left out of most therapies, and obviously it's a central aspect of astrology.

Working with astrology makes one sensitive to time in a slightly different way than perhaps one normally might be. One recognises that something very profound is going on in time. That thought is not often there within the psychotherapist.

So far as the actual practice of astrology and the overlap [with therapy] is concerned, with the clients I work with therapeutically I deliberately do not ask their birth date. I do not even know the years in which they were born. There are some people who I do work with astrologically and therapeutically, but that's slightly different.

Obviously one gets a sense of somebody, and one feels, "This might be Libra here" or "This sounds like a Saturn-Neptune issue." So the language of astrology comes in at a subliminal level for me. It's there all the time.

I suppose it's really the issue of not drawing a tight boundary (which can often happen) between the person and the world. You really do see that we and our world are one, and that is something that comes across very strongly from astrology. Some therapies would certainly look at the ebb and flow of the world through the individual, but often that is done in a pathological way—one is talking about repressed unconscious desires which come back to you as a car accident, or something like that. Astrology doesn't take that stance, it just recognises that skin is not necessarily a boundary—that our world and what happens to us are one and the same.

Putting Astrology on the Map – Astrolocality

There are many ways of seeing the web of interconnection that astrology implies. Mike Harding mentions the awareness of *time* that astrology provides; in the next section, we consider how astrology can be applied to *space*. It is possible to view planetary influences as spreading out in space—across your living room, around the planet—so that specific astrological influences will come into focus in particular locations and directions. I spoke to Martin Davis shortly after he had completed his book 'Astrolocality Astrology', and I was particularly interested to hear about the use of astrolocality* to harmonise one's living area—an area that brings astrology face to face with the oriental discipline of Feng Shui.

---

* Astrolocality—a generic term introduced by Martin Davis, which embraces all techniques for applying astrological information to physical territory, particularly Astro*carto*graphy and Local Space.

Martin Davis: When you work with Local Space in the home, where you place an object can make it either positive (harmonious) or not positive (inharmonious) depending on your lines*. For instance, the dreaded Saturn line might not resonate too well with the fireplace (unless you wanted the fire to go out all the time!). In the book I talk about the work of Ralph and Lahni DeAmicis, Angel Thompson and Steve Cozzi. Their remedial measures modify energies based on (1) general ergonomic principles; and (2) personal Local Space directions. So you try to soften things or strengthen things with colours, shapes, forms, certain kinds of objects.

Ralph and Lahni have a wealth of experience in getting clients to modify their homes on these principles. For instance, if there is a Uranus line running through the bed, the energies in the bed will be very exciting—so one client had a great sex life, but she couldn't sleep!

Q: On a practical level, how might it work in an individual's living space?

Martin Davis: I can advise at a what-to-do-until-the-doctor-arrives level. I'll create a Local Space map for use in your house (I go into this in greater detail in my book; it's called a 'Geomantic Compass'), which will reveal, for example, that a bed might be in a Uranus direction, exciting but not the best place for sleep. That bed can be moved or the energy 'played out' by the use of specific objects or colours.

And there are things that one can do that go beyond astrology. For instance, a Feng Shui expert visited me in my office and told me that my rickety office furniture meant that I'd have a rickety business, and my stuffed and overflowing wastepaper bin would also impact negatively, etc. I made adjustments because of that and my business actually did improve.

As another example: after you do your Local Space lines, you might find that a Mars line intersects your telephone—you are getting a lot of angry calls. You move the telephone somewhere else to counter or improve this. You know, it's amazing how *even astrologers* will look at me in disbelief and say, "Come on! You're going to tell me that moving my telephone to a Venus line in my house will mean that I get more romantic phone calls?!" I say, "Yes!" Yet these same astrologers would very much accept that if Venus is moved to the fifth house in a relocation chart they are going to have a better romantic life.

I think the main lesson is that it really matters how we lay out our houses, and in fact how we lay out our very lives. In essence, everything matters. And we are being called now, in modern life—as an archaic revival, really—to open our awareness to the space around us.

Q: Could you say more about how astrolocality can help people? And, for

* Local Space lines map an individual's natal chart as lines of planetary influence, spreading out horizontally from their current location.

that matter, do you think it can ever be a negative influence?

Martin Davis: Normally it's used to suggest a move to a new location or movement in a specific direction, to draw upon the specific energies represented by the lines. Or, it may be used to assess a current location—especially if we have an option to move or remain there. This type of information can be very helpful in modern life where we not only have the opportunity to travel but where job or relationship requirements may even demand that we relocate.

Negative influence? I think there are two types. The first is when a line frightens us from going to a location. Saturn and especially Mars and Pluto lines are notable for the fear they can strike in the hearts of astrologers. Jim Lewis* himself magnified this by writing of the dire events that can happen under their influence. But locations under these lines may be necessary for our growth. For example, twice in my life events drew me to Saturn locations and this was before I knew anything about astrolocality. I did feel inhibited at them, seemingly blocked from the action I wanted to take. However, I was able to do other things such as reflection and study. It turned out this was just what I needed to prepare and lead me to the next major events in my life. So we shouldn't automatically run from Saturn or even Mars and Pluto locations, as we might be avoiding some important learning situations.

The second type of problem we may encounter is when we are too passive in the face of our astrolocality information, comfortably sitting back and remaining as we are, waiting for the new goodies to arrive. No way! It is important that we actively and courageously participate in the events that we meet at a new location.

You can step off the boat, or the plane, or the London underground, and it's still you that is there. New influences may be coming at you, but are you ready to participate in the situation or not? That's a very big issue.

The subject arose of how Local Space lines can even be used to understand the type of experiences that can occur when travelling in a certain direction:

Martin Davis: A good example of that, which I use in the book, is a very attractive, dynamic lady who lives in London. She met a Brazilian man in London, and became infatuated with him. She decided to go to Brazil to see him. I noticed that she would be travelling on her Mars Local Space line to Brazil. That will often happen—women travel on their Mars lines to meet men. Not only was she travelling on her Mars line, but the Moon was exactly in the east for her Local Space chart in Rio de Janeiro. Moon in the east is like Moon on the ascendant in its interpretation.

Bear in mind that the Moon has to do with motherhood issues. When she

---

* The pioneer of Astro*Carto*Graphy—see bibliography.

flew to Brazil from London, the seat they gave her happened to be next to several children, who were Brazilian. The stewardesses immediately assumed that she was their mother, asking her for parental decisions about them. So motherhood issues arose for her as she stepped onto the aeroplane! She wasn't in Brazil yet, but she was already experiencing the Moon in the east, as found in her Local Space chart for Rio.

Q: What would you put forward as being cases that emphatically show that astrolocality techniques work, for the benefit of skeptics who need further persuasion?

Martin Davis: I think the problem with astrolocality skeptics is the same one astrologers have with skeptics in general. The good news is that in many ways astrolocality astrology is verifiable. I show this in my book with very practical examples. Lindbergh flies on his pioneering journey along his Mars Local Space line. A perfect correlation. Amelia Earhart is lost and runs out of fuel on Neptune and Saturn crossings. Another perfect correlation.

Q: In the Afterword of your book you speak of astrolocality as a 'stepping stone' for astrologers en route to the rediscovery of the 'magical possibility' in astrology. Could you explain a little more about this?

Martin Davis: Astrolocality astrology takes our noses and points them to the ground. We have to look upon Mother Earth and ask: "Why am I located here? What kind of experience can I expect in this place? What is the earth saying to me? Where am I going next?" This change in emphasis from sky to earth is a revolutionary shift in the thinking of astrologers. It moves us closer to a fuller view of space/time, and also to a shamanic attention to the earth. This is a very important point to stress. If you are familiar with Tarot cards, 'The Magician' has one hand raised to the sky, and one hand pointing to the earth. As astrologers we've been great at pointing to the sky but I believe, with astrolocality, we have the opportunity to make the magical connection between earth and sky.

The Astrology of Megaliths

Thousands of years ago, our ancestors made their own connections between earth and sky with astronomically-oriented megaliths such as Stonehenge. Robin Heath has a particular interest in discovering the secrets of these ancient monuments.

Q: What is the astronomical and astrological significance of the megaliths?

Robin Heath: The astronomy of the solar system and the nightly risings and settings of the stars were understood better by these ancestors of modern Europeans than by anyone else up to the time of Kepler. Our present culture is deeply in denial of this indigenous culture and there are thousands of years of overlain repressions, persecutions and religious confusion behind the reasons why very few people to date have awoken to the outstanding observational and measurement skills of these guys. They left a big message for us, a message I convey in my books, tours and lectures... either we believe 'as above, so below' or we don't. I do, and so did early Man. My two published books show that we are dealing with an extremely sophisticated culture that is quite unlike our present one. This scares many people.

Q: What can people gain, do you believe, through an awareness of this message?

Robin Heath: We talk so much about heritage and roots these days, yet virtually ignore our own. 5000 years ago in Britain (and Ireland, Brittany and a few other places), someone knew the length of the solar year and the lunar month to a high degree of accuracy and was manipulating these numbers of days to forecast eclipses and calendars. They could also, with this information, predict tides to within minutes. I have personally taken groups of ten and eleven year olds through this process and they have been able to predict eclipses two years in advance to within a few hours, using just marked ropes and a little rule or two taken from Stonehenge.

We never really know what people gain from anything. If you think it's important to be more conscious of what the sky is doing, where the Moon is, what phase she is, what stage the tide is in, then this work is vitally important. These were also the main requisites of a Druid or a learned man, as the ancient 'Song of Amergin' or the tenth century epigram 'Saltair Na Rann' informs us. These are the remnants of an oral tradition in astronomy which almost certainly dates back to the late Stone Age. It has no truck with Babylon, the 360 degree circle, our 'western' astrology nor the farcical Roman Calendar. It was closer to the 28 lunar mansions of Vedic astrology, and there would have been thirteen months in the year.

Q: What do the people on your megalithic tours make of it all?

Robin Heath: My tours are, in addition to letting people try hands-on work at ancient sacred sites, an informed rant about the importance of being conscious of the cosmos. They're about Sun/Moon integration. Some participants have reported enormous changes in their worldview as a result, just as some of my astrological clients have! Both processes are about expanding consciousness and learning to listen better to cosmic messages.

Q: Are we heading towards a future golden age, or receding from a past one?

Robin Heath: I think this kind of question can be usefully changed to "Am *I* heading towards a (golden) future, etc." Then the landscape shifts and the onus is on the individual to access any golden age. Culturally, much of what is going on in the outer world appears to be a sell-out to the lowest common denominators in human culture. Mass hypnosis via the media is probably how the denizens of the 22nd century will see this period. But within the rather sad and depressing tableau some individuals are really moving things along. We have access to so much information from the past now and it is very easy to take a more elevated path. People have always written about golden ages, but I've never seen a postcard sent from one saying, "Having a great time, wish you were here."

Astrology in Politics

There are many ways of working towards a 'golden age'. In the interview with Pat Harris, the subject of her work on the peace process in Northern Ireland arose after we had finished a (relatively trivial) discussion on the astrology of horseraces:

Pat Harris: Astrological analysis of political trends and processes is a much more serious business. It involves very careful and painstaking observations over, in the Northern Ireland case, a number of years, in order to establish identification of patterns within charts for events in a process. This can then provide a model for forecasting how the process is likely to unfold and even resolve. I've recently had several conversations with political executives about the timing of decisions and talks...

Q: (Interrupting) Really!

Pat Harris: In my conversations, with representatives from all political sides, I was aware that the astrological input was appreciated. The fact that this input was encouraging was welcomed by every political representative with whom I discussed my analysis and prognosis for the talks. Whether or not my input and information were actually used, other than as a source of inspiration, I am afraid I cannot say. But I would judge from my exchanges that everyone to whom I talked, no matter from which side of the political divide, found it comforting and encouraging during some very depressing episodes.

That, unfortunately, is all that I was able to get on tape regarding this subject. There is, however, nothing new about astrologers being involved in politics. From Mesopotamia to the English Civil War, astrologers have guided politicians—and the practice continues, sporadically, to this day. The contention of 'The Sunday Times' that Boris Yeltsin had a team of twelve astrologers advising him* remains unproven, but the Reagans' use of astrologer Joan Quigley is undisputed and well-documented†.

Here are two more instances of astrologers acting with contemporary politicians—in the first case as a paid consultant, in the second on an informal footing.

John Frawley: The President was on trial for corruption, and was certain to be found guilty and dismissed. [John prefers not to disclose the country involved—it was not, however, the USA.] The chart showed that he would cut a deal with the judiciary—who were determined to unseat him—and charges would be dropped. The client, who was close to the seat of power and in a good position to know, assured me that this was quite impossible—yet it is exactly what happened.

Warren Kenton: In one case an astrologer who happened to be living opposite a cabinet minister advised the minister's wife to put off a crucial meeting on a foreign issue until an eclipse was over. She said, "He won't take any notice, but I'll mention it anyway." Later on, it was announced on the news that, "The minister has decided to postpone a decision pending further talks…" After the transit had passed, the difficult negotiations took a turn for the better and were satisfactorily completed.

It is rare nowadays for an astrologer to be retained by a politician. But there are several other reasons for astrologers to take an interest in mundane astrology (the study of political characteristics and trends). One is that this type of work allows the astrologer to test and hone techniques by predicting clearly defined and publicly-reported events. Another reason is that—as Nicholas Campion found—this type of work can increase an astrologer's earning power:

Q: What would you regard as being your greatest predictive success?

Nicholas Campion: It was writing in 'The Daily Mail' in December 1988 that 1989 would be the year that the Cold War ended. For this, I was spontaneously awarded a £60 per week pay rise by 'The Daily Mail'— something unheard of. What I particularly liked about that one was the headline I chose: '1989: The Year the World will be Turned Upside Down.' That was the title of a book by Christopher Hill about the English Revolution, which occurred around the time of the 1648 Uranus/Neptune conjunction. So

---

* The Sunday Times, 28 March 1999 p.29—referred to in 'Media Watch' in the Astrological Association's newsletter 'Transit' May 1999 (Vol. 4 No.3).
† In her book about her work for the Reagans (Quigley, 1990), Joan Quigley claims that she deserves credit for putting the 'Teflon' into the 'Teflon presidency'. Her account of her work is full of jaw-dropping asides: "I only allowed Ronald Reagan to go any place, including outside of the White House, at safe times" (p.83); "My control over the departure times of Air Force One when the President was aboard was absolute." (p.82)

what I was anticipating was a repeat of that. There was a newspaper called 'The Sunday Correspondent', and at the end of 1989 they looked back and chose the headline '1989: The Year the World was Turned Upside Down', a headline obviously written by somebody also familiar with Christopher Hill's book. What I think I predicted there, fundamentally, was the headline in 'The Sunday Correspondent'!

Of course, the end of communism was predicted independently by Michael Baigent—who forecast very exactly the collapse of communism in the Soviet Union in the AA Journal in 1980 (Baigent, 1980). The same forecast is found in Liz Greene's 'The Outer Planets and Their Cycles'. Dane Rudhyar also predicted the crisis in communism, based on the Uranus/Neptune conjunction, as did Andre Barbault, not to mention Katina Thedossiou, who was a popular Sun-sign astrologer back in the '50s and '60s: she predicted it in a lecture at the Astrological Lodge in the '50s.

So that's a notable astrological success for astrologers, and more than makes up for the fact that astrologers failed to predict the Second World War, something they have never been allowed to forget. After all, they did predict the fall of communism when Mikhail Gorbachev, the CIA and everybody else failed.

Two other successes that I find interesting—they were the most precise—were two by-election forecasts, both published in 'Old Moore's Almanac'. One was the forecast of Roy Jenkins' by-election victory in Glasgow Hillhead in 1982; the other was the forecast of a Liberal Democrat victory in the Eastbourne by-election which I think was in 1989 or '90. The first one was, "There will be an SDP by-election victory"; the second one, "The Liberal Democrats will be in a strong position to win a by-election." One was written about six months in advance, the other about eighteen months in advance. So both were very exact—to the day—and were published well in advance of the trains of events which led up to the elections. The Eastbourne by-election happened because the incumbent MP was assassinated by the IRA; so a lot had to happen for there to be an election on that date. It was the first major Liberal Democrat victory after the party was formed.

The Liberal Democrat forecast was easy, because the Liberal Democrat chart's 11th house Moon is conjunct [the fixed star] Spica—which basically means good luck with popular opinion in legislative matters. And there was a new Moon on that, on the day of the Eastbourne by-election. So eighteen months in advance I saw it, and thought, "Hmm—good day to win a by-election!" Paddy Ashdown was reputedly impressed!

This type of result certainly does have the power to impress people and give pause for thought about astrology. As Noel Tyl remarks:

Noel Tyl: This is a real test, because you can publish these mundane predictions [say] five years ahead of time. I was able to publish, almost two years ahead, the prediction to the month of the fall and dissolution of the Soviet Union. I was able to publish, 18 months ahead of time, that a new government would take over in elections in Israel, and that, in the second week of September in (I think it was) '93 that new government would sign a peace treaty with the PLO*. Those are probably two of the most astounding predictions of the last fifty years.

The Astrology of Disaster

Aside from political events, many of the most high-profile events in the world are disasters—both natural and man-made. Astrologers who look at world events often find themselves reluctantly prophesying disaster. A recent example is Peter L Cook, who wrote on 3 August 1999, "…I think that there is a real danger of a serious natural disaster, most likely an earthquake, occurring in Turkey within, say, the next month." (Cook, 2000) On 17 August a major earthquake occurred in north-western Turkey.

Two more such predictions—this time of man-made disasters—were made by Dennis Elwell in the 1980s. These predictions gained a good deal of attention in the media at the time, and I was interested to hear the story behind them:

Dennis Elwell: The reason I burst into prophetic activity in 1987 was because I had promised my publishers I would try to draw attention to astrology in general, and 'Cosmic Loom' (Elwell, 1987) in particular. So I had to cast around for a promising strategy. Because of heightened Neptune activity it seemed that sea disasters were a good bet. As it turned out there were more sea disasters in 1987 than in any other year since Lloyds began to keep records.

As a veteran journalist I knew it was pretty feeble merely to proclaim that sea disasters were imminent. Such disasters are not uncommon, and with so many sibylline voices in the market place why should mine be given special attention? Not only that, I did not want to create the impression that I believed in absolute predestination; on the contrary I think there is usually room to manoeuvre, because astrology shows us where the hidden levers are. So it was a question not so much of oracular pronouncements as issuing warnings of the possibility of a Titanic-like disaster to specific companies to see how they would react. One was P&O, who had recently acquired the Herald of Free Enterprise, and the other was Cunard, about to re-launch the QE2 amid much media hype. (The charts of these companies indicated they were suitable for such an exercise.)

The 'Herald' capsized ten days after P&O wrote back to say the

---

* "With its new political leadership in place in the Fall of 1992, there is strong indication that Israel will yield on its position, either in February 1993 [when the Oslo talks began] or around the second week of September 1993 [when an Accord was signed]"—Noel Tyl writing in '1993 Moon Sign Book' (Llewellyn, p.283). The book was published in Autumn 1992, with Noel's article having been written in March that year. Cf Tyl, 1996, p.115 n.259.

company's safety procedures were designed to cope with an emergency from any quarter, thank you very much. There followed a good deal of self-publicity on the theme of 'the warning ignored', with newspaper and magazine articles, and interviews on radio and TV. Needless to say, journalistic skepticism had to be overcome by a careful scrutiny of the relevant correspondence and so forth. One journalist wanted to know what else the sage could see, so I said that in the autumn I was worried about disasters on underground transport, and that such companies should be examining their safety and security. I also mentioned the danger in an Astrological Association lecture [see Elwell, 1987a]. The basis for these fears was the upcoming eclipse, which had Mercury conjunction Pluto, with trimmings.

The morning after the terrible Kings Cross [underground station] fire the regional evening paper, 'The Express & Star', rang to ask if I recalled the interview I had given them, in which I had cautioned about such a tragedy. They carried a report [about the interview] alongside their story.

My letter to Cunard brought a courteous reply, reminding me that it was their company that had rescued the Titanic passengers! I was assured my fears would be passed upwards. That April the QE2 duly began her maiden voyage after her refit, but things soon began to go wrong. Half way across the Atlantic she received notification of ice in the area where the Titanic lay. What to do? It was decided, to the annoyance of the already inconvenienced passengers, to make a 250 mile detour through fog. The ship arrived in New York late.

It has to be remembered that there had been considerable publicity regarding the 'Herald', and Cunard knew they had received the same letter from me. One of the stewards on board for that journey later told me the ship was abuzz with the tale of the astrologer's warning. Cunard were put in the amusing position of having to explain to one newspaper that the ship would have changed course without the astrologer's advice! But who is to say that my letter might not have helped to avert a disaster—after all Titanic had ploughed on into the ice regardless.

On the BBC's 'Kilroy' show I was asked if I had expected P&O to listen to me. Of course not! But you have to start somewhere, and perhaps eventually a sound astrology will be given a respectful hearing. People also wanted to know if P&O had come back to me afterwards, to seek advice. They had not, and I had not expected them to do so either.

I got my revenge when the company came to launch their new flagship, the much publicised Oriana. A very negative Neptune sky! I wrote to say that if they had come back to me after the Herald I would have counselled against launching Oriana at that time, and I urged them to check certain onboard systems. Well, Oriana's troubles began when she scraped her bottom leaving the German shipyard. She did not sink, but P&O's reputation did! Later that year, after a passenger mutiny, the chief engineer complained that there were 700 things wrong with the ship—including the systems I had cautioned about.

To watch astrology working can give you a certain grisly satisfaction. I was not particularly tuned-in to world events in 1987. I don't rely on tuning in, just the application of simple rules, which anyone can follow. I do have Neptune in the tenth house, so perhaps it is appropriate that my five minutes of fame should be connected with events on the high seas.

Making really businesslike predictions is a chore. It is alarming the way some astrologers risk their reputations—not to mention astrology's reputation—by venturing predictions off the top of their head. You need to check and cross-check from different quarters, using a mix of data and proven techniques. But at the end of the day, who is going to pay you for the trouble, and who is going to listen? There are ways astrology can be turned to good account, but not by ramming it down reluctant throats.

From my point of view, I would not wish to be remembered for predictions, but for trying to point astrology in a new direction. It has much to offer those troubled souls who are desperate to find some meaning in the apparent chaos of events. It also contains the seeds of a radically different worldview, which embraces the mysteries of time, evolution, cognition, personality, and the greatest puzzle of all: the nature of consciousness. But broadly speaking, at the moment, even astrologers do not see the relevance of developing this larger context, because what they are doing is largely client-driven.

To preserve a semblance of balance, I should report that every astrologer who mentioned successful predictions also pointed out that they had also predicted things that did not happen. This, of course, prompts a question about the significance of astrologers' results—how, ultimately, do you evaluate whether they are significant, or merely represent the workings of chance? This issue will receive attention in the last four chapters of this book, but whilst on the subject of world events, it is worth including two incidents that illustrate the problems facing the predictive astrologer.

The Problems of Prediction (1)

Whilst talking with Adrian Duncan about Sun-sign astrology, he wanted to illustrate how a quite simplistic level of interpretation can still yield results in astrology:

Adrian Duncan: If you say that Nato is like Mars. You watch Mars going into Libra, and they're pussyfooting around in Kosovo; then it goes into Scorpio and they say, "We're really going to do you in." Then it starts grinding retrograde, and they don't do it anyway.

This was recorded on 13 March 1999, when rumours of Nato intervention over Kosovo were rife. Airstrikes began on 24 March, so on a simple reading Adrian's comment about Nato backing away from conflict is completely wrong. And yet... Mars went retrograde on 20 March, four days before airstrikes began, and went direct on 5 June, two days after

Slobodan Milosovic announced that he would accept Nato's terms for surrender. Hence Adrian's main point—that there would be a connection between Mars's apparent motion in the sky and military action by Nato—fits the facts well. This illustrates the problems an astrologer faces in making predictions—unless they are right in every detail, a substantially correct interpretation can be totally derailed by one factor.

The Problems of Prediction (2)

In a 21 May 1999 recording, which was played on ITV's 'Predictions 2000' programme on 8 January 2000, Komilla Sutton mentioned that the impending solar eclipse on 11 August 1999 made some strong aspects to Tony Blair's chart, adding, "What is interesting is that Cherie Blair, his wife, has got a similar eclipse indication, so she is also very strongly affected. So one of the things that we will see is some kind of issue concerning some close personal relationship with his wife..." On 18 November, three months after the eclipse, it was announced that Cherie Blair was three months pregnant. This was duly hailed as a successful prediction on the programme. But it also illustrates another problem faced by a predictive astrologer. Given that Mrs Blair was already 45 years old, a pregnancy was not something that an astrologer would likely have considered in evaluating what form the Blairs' 'relationship issue' might take. It is much easier for the astrologer to see that 'something significant' will happen to a person (or country, or whatever) at a particular time, than to define exactly what form this will take.

This brings us back to a point that Robert Hand made in respect of natal chart readings: "Fundamentally, I think the chart must be done in the context of a dialogue between the client and the astrologer, so that the polymorphous symbolism of astrology can be *pinned down*." [My italics] It is in the nature of symbols that they connote and connect different qualities and things in the world. For instance, sky-blue, copper, kidneys, apricots, music and daffodils are all ruled by Venus.

Most of the astrologers I spoke with see the information they get from astrology as adding significantly to the potential understanding of a situation or thing, but emphasise that it is best used in combination with whatever other sources of information are available. This explains Christeen Skinner's comment in Chapter IV, concerning her business work:

> **Christeen Skinner:** I am absolutely certain that no matter what I deliver, nobody will be able to say, "The astrologer chose these people." That's not how it is set up; I am one part of their toolbox. As it happens they find it a valuable tool, but I am not the only thing.

In discussing astrology one often encounters the implicit assumption that, if it works at all, it should virtually confer omniscience. In contradistinction to this expectation, most astrologers emphasise the limitations of astrology (or, amounting to much the same thing, of astrologers themselves) and the responsibility of both astrologer and client to make the best sense of the information that's available. In short, a measure of intelligent questioning is generally encouraged.

Chapter VIII

Doubt in Astrology

One factor that distinguishes astrology from most other subjects is that many people do not believe that it relates to reality in any way. This gives the astrologer problems that are unlikely to face, say, an accountant. Doubt troubles most astrologers some of the time, and some astrologers most of the time: sometimes doubt in a particular technique or application of astrology; sometimes doubt in astrology itself; sometimes it is self-doubt; sometimes the doubts of others. This chapter begins an investigation into doubt in astrology, which will continue within different frames of reference through to the end of the book.

Maurice McCann mentioned two crises of confidence where he was no longer satisfied by the results he was getting from astrology.

Maurice McCann: I had been going through a crisis around this time, because I wasn't satisfied with birth charts. I didn't feel that confident or strong about them; it seemed very unreliable. It was all conjecture and guess-work, nobody seemed to be very positive about it. I thought, "OK—what if, each day, some unusual event was to happen to me? Would that show up in my horoscope?" So I used to be on the lookout for anything that would happen—any sort of an incident: if there was a power cut, for instance, I'd try to get the time, and see if that locked in with my chart.

At times it *seemed* to work; other times it left me still dissatisfied. I began to think, "Well, this stuff doesn't work"—you know? A lot of it was highly implausible, I thought. You read various things, or listen to people delineating charts… I remember, in the [Astrological] Lodge one night, seeing somebody talking about some form of mental problem having to do with Pluto. I thought, "My God, you've got to be able to do more than that, surely?"

Anyhow, I was very dissatisfied. I began to think, "Well, this isn't working—but I'm hooked on it—so where do I go from here?" But Bernard Eccles came along [to a meeting Maurice was at] and started doing horary. I was amazed—it was like looking at a black and white television all your life, and then suddenly seeing it in colour. When he was doing it, I knew… "I know this; I can do this; this is it—this is *really* it!" I knew exactly what he was on about.

The discovery of horary astrology did not, however, mark the end of Maurice's doubts—or of his search:

Maurice McCann: Some years later I was getting very dissatisfied with horary. I was doing quite a lot of teaching, and I was seeing clients at that time—*and the vast majority of the answers were wrong*. It's very embarrassing. When you do horary, it's black and white: you either get it right or you get it wrong. And people were telling me, "You got it wrong." It was OK doing the nativities, because you sort of lumbered your way through the chart; I did predictions on the chart, and would get one or two right—and that was enough to keep them happy; nobody would condemn you.

But when you do horary, you will get condemned! And you've got to be pretty tough to take it. So I was back at that stage of looking at it and thinking, "Oh my God, this whole astrology is rubbish! It's not working!" This was four years ago.

With Derek Appleby's influence, I thought, "It must be OK if he's doing it; and [William] Lilly was getting them right..." But I couldn't figure it out. I was doing all the right things. I was a stickler for all the rules. If it was too early to say, I would tell the client, "It's too early to say." Then half an hour later, the phone would ring and they'd say, "Well—it wasn't too early." And there was nothing too early about it.

I got away with stuff. I met somebody recently who told everyone, "Oh, Maurice! He did my chart years and years ago, and made an accurate prediction that I would meet somebody from a far-off country, who would do business with me and it would be great..." I don't even remember saying that! God knows where I got it from. But every astrologer will tell you stories like this. Because, for some reason, you can hit it, or it might be that you say something that the client misinterprets, to your advantage. But there's no way in the world that you could repeat that again.

I was getting very discouraged. I was teaching and I stopped the class. I stopped seeing clients. I have spent the four years since then on horary—four, five hours a day, often more. I started testing it. I started testing the rules. Because I thought, "How do we know that these work? Who has tested this?"

I bought everything on horary—whether it was any good or not—just to see what people were saying. I used to go to the British Museum and photocopy [the work of] old English astrologers (since they're the most available in this country). I even did a degree on the Civil War period—on propaganda in astrology.

I used to sit here, spending one to two hours every day calculating all the rules—everything. That got very tiring. I thought, "Oh God, I can't stand this." So I wondered if I could get someone to program it all—and that is how the program Tara* came about. Now I can roll off a horary (by computer), and be pretty sure about getting it right, in about four to five minutes.

There's no interpretation involved in a 'yes/no' horary; you just go through the rules. Now what that means is that the program could be updated to answer those questions itself.

Maurice declined the opportunity to boast about his results, however:

---

* Program designed by Maurice McCann. This software calculates the chart for a moment, *and* the horary rules therein. See Appendix 1 for more details.

Maurice McCann: One reason I don't publicise wonderful predictions is that most of my questions are very personal, innocuous and not really that important—"Will so-and-so phone me today?" or "Will I get an email when I log on?" or "Will I get a letter in the post tomorrow morning?" People are going to look at [the results] and say, "So what!" But it's working… it is really working.

Religion and Astrology

Doubt about whether astrology works is not the only thing which might turn someone away from the subject, as I discovered in conversation with John Frawley:

Q: How would you label your beliefs about life?

John Frawley: Capricorn rising sums up most of my beliefs—miserable bastard! I'm a practising Catholic.

Q: How do you reconcile astrology with Catholicism?

John Frawley: 98% of me sees no contradiction at all. I wasn't born Catholic, I came to it through astrology. I found it was the only system that was intellectually rigorous enough to satisfy me. The catechism says that all astrologers are servants of the Devil, and the other 2% of me thinks that that could be quite accurate. I suspect there will come a time when I shall cease to practise astrology because of it. But at the moment I find that the faith expands my astrology, and astrology expands my faith.

Q: Do you feel that astrology can help you find an answer to this dilemma? Or is there a paradox in asking astrology about astrology, which rules that option out for you?

John Frawley: I think it would be impious. There are some things that are more important than astrology. Astrology works with the spectrum, but it is the source of the white light that is ultimately important.

One problem which Catholicism sees with astrology (and it is not unique in this; similar criticisms have been made at one time or another by many critics of astrology, including astrologers themselves) is that the motivation of anyone wanting to know hidden things is inevitably suspect. Thus, Paragraph 2116 of the 1993 Catechism of the Catholic Church states: "All forms of divination are to be rejected: recourse to Satan or demons, conjuring up the dead or other practices falsely supposed to 'unveil' the future. Consulting horoscopes, astrology, palm reading, interpretation of omens and lots, the phenomena of clairvoyance, and recourse to mediums all conceal a desire for power over time, history, and, in the last analysis, other human beings, as well as a wish to conciliate hidden powers. They contradict the honour, respect, and loving fear that we owe to God alone."

The relationship between religion and astrology is complex—within Catholicism itself, for instance, there is room to interpret the Church's doctrine as only condemning the misuse of astrology—as has been done by a Catholic priest, the Rev Laurence Cassidy (Cassidy, 1994). Another angle on Catholicism's attitude toward astrology came from Warren Kenton when I mentioned the Catholic Church's condemnation of astrology to him:

Warren Kenton: That is interesting, as the medieval Popes used to have their coronations set according to astrology.

Q: I take it there are no such problems with the Jewish approach?

Warren Kenton: According to orthodox Jews, it's forbidden; but it's interesting to note that in the Middle Ages most of the astrologers in the courts were Jews. Most of the rabbis were well-acquainted with astrology. It was only Maimonides, the great Aristotelian rationalist, who said it was superstition, but then he was not an astrologer. It is also important to note that many rabbis considered that Maimonides was too rationalistic in his outlook. While the Babylonians and other ancient peoples might worship the planets, the Jews did not. They saw the heavenly bodies as God's servants, the planets as angelic beings. Moreover, Abraham came from Ur of the Chaldeans, which was the city of astrologers. He was considered to be a master astrologer according to Jewish tradition, which led him to question which of the stars was the supreme one. Clearly, none of them are. So he concluded that there must be an absolute beyond the stars.

The distinction between sacred and secular—and a certain amount of jostling for position between religion and astrology—was touched on by Bernadette Brady, who began by praising the work of medieval Arabic astrologers:

Bernadette Brady: I've been *really* taken with the work of Abu Ma'shar, Masha'Allah, Bonatti and Omar—that whole stream; and the Lieber Hermatus. I've found in there as well (and Zoller does lectures on this, this isn't my original work) that those astrologers captured the *soul* far better than I think modern psychological astrology does. They were banned from writing about the soul. The church said, "We own the soul, you own the body—you are not allowed to say anything about the soul." So they actually wrote it between the lines. But if you really look at it, you see that they have ways of looking at a chart and *defining the person's version of God*; defining how (and whether) that individual will be able to gain satisfaction from the spiritual life, and whether they will be able to fulfil their spiritual values, and what their spiritual values are.

When you apply these techniques, it's far more *breathtaking* than anything Jungian or psychological astrologers do in terms of the person's spirituality.

Murder, They Said

Bernadette Brady also reached a point where she was radically dissatisfied with the results she was getting and encountered doubt. The circumstances were dramatic:

Bernadette Brady: What really pushed me into examining my own astrology, deconstructing it and then rebuilding it in more of an Arabic/Bonatti mould, was that I had a client I had seen about four times over four years. The police rang me and said this guy was a murderer. I had not spotted it in his chart [banging the table for emphasis], and that drew me up really fast. I thought, "What the hell am I doing here?"

That was about four years ago when Hindsight* was happening. I'd basically given them my credit card and said, "Send me everything!" because I'd always been interested in this stuff. So basically I deconstructed my astrology piece by piece, quite thoroughly, and rebuilt it again. I stopped seeing clients for a while so that I could do that, and started working much more on predictive work. So, yes, my astrology has changed dramatically...

In another interview, the question arose of how far astrology can go. Seeing that Mike Harding had written, "Very little can be said about the possible process of an individual's psychic development from the birth chart..." (Harding, 1992, p.167), I told him a little about Bernadette Brady's experience with the murderer and asked—in the light of that—whether he thought astrology was capable of identifying a murderer.

Mike Harding: Well for one thing, the chart is not the chart of a person, it's the chart for a moment in time. I can give you a chart and you won't know who or what it is for. So the chart is about 'the nature of time', whatever that turns out to mean. Once we know that it's for a person, that it's for a man or a woman, we can focus our minds and perhaps make some conjectures about how their life might go. But I think they would only be conjectures.

Your particular interviewee could test this quite simply—if you do feel you've got a signature for a murderer, Gauquelin has the data of several thousand murders. Can you tell? Can you split them from another group chosen randomly? I'm not saying this can't be done. I think there is a program that can detect a propensity for alcoholism within the birthchart. I think this

---

* Project Hindsight, an organisation devoted to translating ancient astrological texts. See Appendix 1 for details.

is a possibility. I think that is slightly different from murder... but suggests a testable hypothesis. I would be very surprised if it could be demonstrated, because I don't think murder is a fact, in the sense that I don't think it's one category of something. I think someone who sits down and plans to kill their auntie to inherit a fortune is a totally different kind of person from someone who, in one moment of madness, lashes out and happens to connect with somebody's head, kills them, and spends the rest of their life in the deepest remorse. So I don't think there is murder as a separate category—that would have to be explored.

Predicting Death

As this example shows, astrologers do not necessarily agree on what it is and is not possible to see and to define through astrology. Another area in which this shows is the attitudes which astrologers have towards the prediction of death. Leaving aside questions of if, how, when and why it might be appropriate to tell someone that they are about to die, there is a big question over whether this is something that astrology is capable of finding in any case. Here are two points of view, beginning with John Frawley's response to the question, "Is it possible to predict death?":

John Frawley: Yes, it is perfectly possible, from both natal and horary (and in practice as well as theory).

Nicholas Campion: There are no reliable, fool-proof techniques for predicting death. The prediction of death, astrologically, is a highly subjective business, and there can be no rules for predicting death, because if they applied in medieval times they would apply now—but now we have a much longer life-expectancy, and the planetary cycles have not stretched.

Here is a third perspective on death, which goes some way toward resolving the apparent conflict between the previous two:

Bernadette Brady: One [set of medieval techniques] that I've studied a lot is the length of life—but not for "You are going to die next week!" Because if you really read what they are saying, they'll give you the formulas and algorithms and methodologies and then they'll say, "However, he may get run over by a chariot"—so what you are really looking at with that work is the *life-force* in a chart. Think about it: the one thing that modern medicine has done is not extended our life-expectancy, but got more of us there. The astrology hasn't changed, the planets haven't changed. So therefore, you could say that's an argument against the techniques for assessing the length of life. But what I would say is that these techniques look at the *life-energy*, and there are quite a few people who can live on once they have run out of time—once the charge in the batteries has gone—because modern medicine gets them there. Which is good.

So that's a precise algorithm… a wonderful technique, because it gives you the ability to look at a chart and say, "This child's got problems with their health, and it's serious." It's not the standard stuff you think of in modern astrology; you can look at an apparently normal-looking chart, but as soon as you apply these algorithms it shows that there's a huge crisis of health.

The modern use is that, if the parent knows about that, then when little Mary starts to develop symptoms they can act straight away—don't go to the GP, go straight to the casualty department, you know? And the child can be saved. So that's a really valid thing. Also, when you start studying that, you start to see something: everybody in their life has a health crisis every now and again. I'm not a medical astrologer, but this gives you another insight as a predictive astrologer in terms of what to look for in health crises.

I have said to clients, "I think it's time you got life-insurance." The client is appreciative of this, and they can avoid crises. I say, "Why don't you get income protection insurance just for this period of time?" There are very real and tangible things you can work with. When the time runs out, that can be a time of crisis. They can get through it—but if they know that it's a serious time, then they can take that headache (or whatever) seriously.

Natural and Judicial Astrology

A problem which arises for contemporary astrologers in considering doubts and disputes within the subject is the lack of a common worldview, the lack of a common philosophy, in which discussion could be grounded. Individual astrologers may have quite different views of what astrology is and how it works—hence the diversity of views about what it is and is not possible to do with it. At the heart of this diversity, there is a fundamental split between two ways of seeing astrology—natural and judicial astrology:

Nicholas Campion: The doctrine of 'the baby and the bathwater' is, I think, crucial to understanding astrology's nature. This notion is due to Kepler, the idea being that astrology contains a core of demonstrable truth, which is the 'baby', surrounded by an ocean of false superstition, which is the 'bathwater'. To Kepler, the superstitious bathwater included almost the entire weight of astrological tradition. The same point of view was also put forward in this century by the people who wanted to research astrology scientifically, as they saw it, and still underpins most efforts to 'research' astrology, in which the goal is to find out which techniques 'work' and which 'don't', or to establish statistical correlations between celestial and terrestrial events. John Addey and Michel Gauquelin are the twentieth century's two most famous exponents of this approach. I tend to agree that the 'baby-bathwater' polarity is a useful one, and that it is possible to view astrology in two completely different ways, I also have considerably more respect for the 'bathwater' because without it there is no astrology!

In fact this distinction is first found in Cicero's 1st century A.D work, 'On Divination'. In this he argued that there is a reliable, verifiable, useful form of divination that he called 'natural divination', based on reasoned evidence and measurement—what today we would call science. Then there was 'judicial divination', in which everything depends on the diviner's ability to reach a judgement through irrational or supernatural means. Cicero disapproved of this and [classed] such practices as entrail divination and horoscopic astrology as 'judicial'. From this we get the division of astrology into two types, natural and judicial*, a distinction which was very common in the middle ages but which we seem to have forgotten.

Natural astrology survives today in astro-physics. We know there's a common mathematical order linking the Earth to the rest of the universe; these are the laws of physics and nobody disputes them. What arouses disagreement is how far they affect human society. There is very little evidence to suggest that they do, but at the same time it seems perfectly logical to suggest that there should be links. If human rhythms and cycles are linked to annual cycles, they are linked to the Sun and the Moon, and solar and lunar motions are part of the rest of the mathematical order in the solar system. So I see no theoretical reason why one day we shouldn't be able to substantiate the existence of planetary connections with human affairs to the satisfaction of society as a whole, not just astrologers. That would seem to me to be the basis of a perfectly workable natural astrology—especially mundane astrology.

But most of what astrologers do, it seems to me, must be classed as judicial astrology. It is quite clearly not demonstrable under the sort of repeatable, controlled conditions required by contemporary science. Much of what astrologers do is actually not demonstrable according to the standards acceptable in astrology, either. Witness the number of wrong predictions astrologers make about their own lives, let alone other people's. There may be various philosophical justifications for everyday astrology, but there certainly is no justification for the idea that what most astrologers do can be measured and proved.

The distinction that Nicholas Campion draws between two types of astrology will be significant in the remainder of this book. In brief, the distinction is between 'natural astrology' (the study of links between planetary movements and nature as general trends) and 'judicial astrology' (the art of reaching a judgement on a specific issue).

---

* For more on this important distinction, see Curry, 1989 p.8 ff; Cornelius, 1994 p.72ff.

The Astrologer as Magician

Patrick Curry (Curry, 1989, p.9) points out that natural astrology tended to be based on rational, Aristotelian philosophy, whilst judicial astrology was based on neo-Platonic philosophy—which shades imperceptibly into magic. A consequence of this is that, as Nicholas Campion observes, natural astrology is much more amenable to scientific analysis than judicial astrology. And it leaves a question waiting to be asked—is the astrologer a magician?

Robert Hand: Do you mean in the technical sense of the word? No. Do I believe that ceremonial magic is a valid set of techniques? The answer is yes. But I do not practise. Partly it's a lack of time—it hasn't grabbed me enough to pull me in that direction. I also realised—I've read Dion Fortune many times, but this was the first time I'd read the book called 'Psychic Self-Defence'—that unless I find a really good teacher, I'd better not do it. I could join one of the magical orders, of course. But I've thought of that a couple of times, and the spirit just is not going in that direction. I'm intrinsically more of a mystic than a magician. But I believe that the mystical and occult worldviews have considerable validity. In fact, there are certain kinds of things that I think can only be explained by the Neo-Platonic, kabbalistic views of a multi-layered world. Astrology, for example!

The way I like to describe the physical planets is this. In kabbalah you have the four realms. Atziluth is the highest realm of creation. (There's the uncreated of course; but of creation, Atziluth is the highest realm. It is the so-called emanational realm.) Then you have Briah, which is usually translated as 'the archetypal realm', but actually means 'the realm of carving' (or 'scraping away'). Atziluth means 'next to', by the way. Then you have 'Yetzirah', which is translated as 'formation'—which is a formation done by moulding, and shaping a somewhat fluid entity. And then there is 'Assiah', which is action (in Sanskrit, 'Assiah' and karma mean the same thing).

As you descend through the worlds, you become increasingly determined, less free, and more multiplied. This is directly descended from Platonism, of course. I think there are probably some kabbalists who would be offended by that, but kabbalah is essentially a Judaic Neo-Platonism, with lots of Hermetic stuff too. Or it's coming from the same roots, which is also possible.

Now, human beings—according to kabbalah—are the only entities that can travel up and down in the four worlds. For the most part we stay in the bottom two. Yetzirah is basically what you are when you look inside; and Assiah is what you are when you look outside. Well the physical planets are Assiatic (to coin a word); the astrological planets are Yetziratic. *They don't exist out there.* But they are the *cause* of 'out there'. So the physical planets don't cause anything. The Yetziratic planets cause the physical planets; and they also are the source of the same movements of the soul, which is Yetziratic. So what astrology is really doing is not examining a physical phenomenon at all, but rather a phenomenon on the soul level—Yetzirah, formation. Which prefigures, and underlays, the physical universe.

I would say that, in the proper sense of the word *cause*, the planets are the effect. But the reason we use them is because they are so reliable. And why are they so reliable? Because they are *utterly* Assiatic; they are totally determined. The physical planets are totally determined by the movements in these inner worlds, or underlying worlds, or whatever you want to call them. And we can use them to describe the less-determined movements in the upper, or inner (or whatever!) worlds. This is what we are doing. We are essentially using the planets to tell us what 'soul-time' it is. They really are a clock. But the soul sets the clock; the clock does not determine the soul. So the physical planets are the final result; they have no freedom... actually that's not totally true, they have a tiny bit. There's a certain amount of chaotic factor in the solar system—but very low, otherwise we wouldn't be here.

So I think this multiple-world approach—kabbalah, Neo-Platonism and so forth—really goes a long way to explaining, at least in a qualitative way, a lot of the phenomena. I think astrology may in fact be *proof* of these realms, because I don't see any way you can explain the 'Mars Effect' of Gauquelin due to mechanical interaction; I don't see any way that can be done.

What Robert Hand outlines here might be called a magical approach to the cosmos—that is, a model in which humanity plays a creative part in shaping and defining the way things are. Some of the implications of this can be difficult to take for astrologers (not to mention the scientific world), seeming to threaten a fall from a world of rational symbolic order into total anarchy.

An issue which can be particularly threatening for astrologers is the 'wrong chart' issue. This was raised by many of my interviewees, from quite different perspectives. Here are two takes on the subject:

Adam Fronteras: You do a really brilliant reading for someone and they're really impressed, then right at the end of the reading you hand them the chart and they tell you that you've got the year wrong. I'm sure I'm not the only one—this has in fact happened to a lot of astrologers. Some of the best readings have been with wrong charts. You try working that out! So I think that there *is* a pattern, but I think a lot of what you get from astrology is actually psychic ability.

Geoffrey Cornelius: [Astrologers] get *correct* readings from wrong maps on sufficient occasions for it to be, clearly, an astrological phenomenon. One has to be very sparing with that, because it is *so* ruthlessly undermining of the status of astrology. It's as if we could just pick a moment in an ephemeris, and that would be as true as a genuine horary moment that has come to us. No, it is not. But the genuine horary moment's truth isn't *caused by* physical planets at a certain time and space, *either*. It's subtle!

A very different perception of the 'wrong chart' phenomenon was that of David Hamblin, former Chairman of the Astrological Association, author of 'Harmonic Charts', and once a figure of considerable stature in the British astrological world. He was so troubled by an experience of getting a 'right reading' from the wrong chart, together with other discrepancies and problems in his practice of astrology, that he eventually felt compelled to stop practising altogether.

Q: Why, and how, did your feeling toward [astrology] change? Was it gradual, or sudden? Was there an external event that set things off, or was it primarily internal?

David Hamblin: It was gradual, and primarily internal. I always had some doubts about whether astrology was true, and I wrote an article called 'The Need for Doubt and the Need for Wonder' (Astrological Journal, Summer 1982) in which I expressed the nature of these doubts. But for a long time I felt that my doubts were healthy and, indeed, helped me to be a good astrologer, since I did not accept astrology unquestioningly. In the end, however, the doubts increased to a point at which I felt I could no longer continue to practise astrology, since I was too unsure about whether what I was saying was true.

I was always unimpressed by the predictive side of astrology and especially by the more arcane techniques such as day-for-a-year progressions—I never really found any evidence that these techniques had any validity. But my main interest was in natal astrology, i.e. in using the birth chart as a tool for interpretation of personality and for psychological guidance, and at this level it seemed to me for many years that astrology was quite extraordinarily valid and accurate.

Eventually, however, I began to wonder whether this apparent accuracy was mainly the result of the incredible ingenuity of the human mind, which, if it finds a fact that does not fit in with its theory, can easily find ways of explaining the fact away while still retaining the theory. In my article I wrote, "There are so many different factors in a birth chart that, if one finds a lack of fit between some factors of the chart and the personality of its owner, one can always explain it away by referring to other factors. If I find a very meek and unassertive person with five planets in Aries, this does not cause me to doubt that Aries means assertiveness. I may be able to point to his Pisces Ascendant, or to his Sun conjunct Saturn, or to his ruler in the twelfth house; and, if none of these alibis are available, I can simply say that he has not yet fulfilled his Aries potential. Or I can argue (as I have heard argued) that, if a person has

an *excess* of planets in a particular sign, he will tend to suppress the characteristics of that sign because he is scared that, if he reveals them, he will carry
them to excess. But if on the next day I meet a very assertive person who also
has five planets in Aries, I will change my tune: I will say that he had to be like
that because of his planets in Aries."

A number of events contributed to these doubts. One was when I
interpreted a birth chart for a client, who told me that my interpretation was
very accurate and useful; but then he realized that he'd given me the wrong
data, and that in fact he'd been born in a different year. In other words, I had
given him the right information on the basis of the wrong chart! Another was
when my wife, who is a non-identical twin and has virtually the same birth
chart as her sister but a very different personality, sent her birth details to a
well-known astrologer and received in return an excellent interpretation, not
of herself, but of her sister. Of course these things do not show that astrology
is untrue, but they do show that it is not *reliably* true. And I feel that, if you are
talking to a client about their innermost nature, their hopes and fears, their
pain and anguish, you cannot afford to have unreliable techniques.

Astrology is based on the theory of 'as above, so below'—the belief that
the movements of the planets are mirrored by events on earth. But in fact the
'above' world is very different from the 'below' world. Up there, all is
exactness and mathematical precision; down here, all is chaos and
unpredictability, due to the interaction of innumerable factors that cannot
possibly be measured. When I watched the solar eclipse in August 1999
(though the Sun was obscured by clouds), I was struck by the fact that
scientists can predict, hundreds of years in advance, exactly when the eclipse
will occur and where it will be visible, but down here they cannot predict the
weather from one hour to the next! What applies to the weather applies even
more to the complexities of human behaviour. It may well be that the planets
affect human behaviour in some of the ways that astrologers believe in, but,
because of the innumerable earthly factors that intervene, this relationship can
never be simple and straightforward.

There's another reason I moved away from astrology. As an astrological
counsellor I came to feel that the birth chart was a barrier between the client
and myself. Rather than focussing on each other, we were both focussing on
this piece of paper that lay on the table between us, and I was talking to the
client about what the marks on the piece of paper meant. In this way we were
inhibited from really coming into relationship with each other, and from
seeing each other as we really were; also the client was inhibited from forming
his or her own insights about his or her own nature. This is not always true:
if two people come together who are both equally conversant with the
language of astrology, they can use that language to gain great insight. But if
the astrologer is the 'teacher' and the client is the ignorant 'pupil', then the
relationship is too unequal. Astrology gives the astrologer too much power.

Q: What is your attitude to astrology now? Do you ever use it at all?

David Hamblin: No, I never use it, apart from occasionally glancing at the ephemeris to see where the planets are now. But this is mostly because, since my computer broke down, I haven't been able to calculate birth charts by computer, and I've forgotten how to do it manually. I think that if my computer were still working I would still be calculating the birth charts of famous people, out of curiosity.

Q: In retrospect, how do you feel about the role that astrology had in your life? Was it a Good Thing or a Bad Thing? Do you miss it? If you had your time over again, would you do anything differently?

David Hamblin: It was a Good Thing, and sometimes I miss it quite badly. I see astrology as a necessary stage in my life-long journey from the head to the heart. At the University I was entirely head-centred, and feelings were nothing but awkward encumbrances. I took up astrology because, although it is essentially an intellectual system, I felt it was also imbued with heart values. Then I switched to psychotherapy in an attempt to cast off the intellectual baggage of astrology. Now I'm feeling that even psychotherapy is too head-centred, and I'm drawn towards the approach which is typified by Jack Kornfield's book 'A Path with Heart'.

If I had my time again, the only thing I'd do differently is that I would not become involved in the running of the Astrological Association, which caused me a great deal of heartache. I never was a committed enough astrologer to be able to do this effectively, and I think that, if I had remained on the sidelines, it might have been easier for me to retain my links with astrology even when my doubts became stronger.

Q: How do you feel now about the work that you contributed to the interpretation of harmonic charts?

David Hamblin: I'm still very proud of it, and I still think that if astrology is true at all (and I want to stress that I still think it may be true) then harmonics must be an essential part of how it works. Astrology says that the universe is governed by laws about the relationship between heavenly bodies, and this relationship can only be expressed in terms of numbers. Harmonics is based on the Pythagorean view that numbers are the building blocks of the universe and that each number has an intrinsic meaning. Even if the theory of harmonics is not true in a scientific sense, it is still to my mind very beautiful, and Keats said that beauty was truth.

Q: What is your attitude to science in astrology? Do you think that statistical analysis is capable of establishing whether astrology is true?

David Hamblin: Yes, I do think so. If any of the claims made by astrologers are true, it should be possible—with properly controlled experiments and with a large enough sample—to prove them to be true. There really isn't any escape from this. I say this in spite of the fact that I don't much like scientists and statisticians, and I often feel annoyed by the excessive skepticism that scientists display towards all kinds of phenomena which don't fit in with their worldview. But astrology lends itself so beautifully to statistical analysis. It says, for instance, that if you're Aries you're more likely to be extrovert (or 'fiery') than if you are Taurus. If there is any truth in these statements, they must be capable of being proved statistically. Of course it may be difficult to agree on a measure of 'fieriness', and also of 'Aries-ness' (are we talking about Sun sign, Moon sign, or Ascendant sign?), but it's not impossible.

Q: If someone were thinking about learning astrology would you recommend them to go ahead, or to avoid it?

David Hamblin: If they were genuinely enthusiastic about astrology I would recommend that they go ahead. As I said, I don't regret my own involvement in astrology. It was the right thing for me to be doing at the time.

Q: What do you think of as being the best things about astrology and astrologers?

David Hamblin: Even if it isn't really 'true', astrology is still a wonderful thing, a fantastically complex and beautiful construct, which draws your eyes up to the heavens and makes you aware that you are a tiny and yet still significant part of the workings of the universe. Most astrologers, I believe, are affected by this, and have a quality of beauty in themselves. The annual astrological conferences that I attended were wonderful experiences because of the quality of the energy and the sheer excitement generated by the exchange of astrological ideas.

Q: What do you think of as being the worst things about astrology and astrologers? Do you see any way in which these things could be changed?

David Hamblin: The worst thing about astrology, I feel, is astrological gossip: "Oh dear, he's a Gemini, I don't get on with Geminis, you can't trust them. With Sun in Gemini and Scorpio rising, no wonder he ratted on his girlfriend." This is turning astrology into a force for destruction and division, rather than love and understanding. But I have to admit that it's not much worse than the habit of many psychotherapists of sticking labels onto people (narcissistic, anal-retentive) and then judging them according to the negative characteristics of those labels.

The second worst thing about astrology is when it leads people to regulate their lives according to the movement of the planets (delaying action until the stars are in the right position), so destroying their spontaneity and their freedom to act in the present moment.

No, I have no idea how these things could be changed. Every human activity has a dark side; astrology is no exception.

Chapter IX
Research into Astrology (Part 1)

Introduction

In contemporary western society science is commonly seen as the final arbiter between reality and illusion, and this book would be incomplete if it did not represent the scientific view of astrology. I chose to approach Geoffrey Dean—an experienced researcher who is well-versed in scientific methodology, astrology, and what happens when the two collide. Dean suggested that he recruit others to help out, and the upshot was that I interviewed by email a team of five prominent researchers scattered across the globe. Their collective answers led to further questions, and also to changes and clarifications, which (to meet size constraints) we then collectively edited down to what follows in this and the next chapter*.

We have endeavoured, in this interview, to cover the main issues that arise between astrology and science. Trying to accomplish this in a finite number of words made compromise inevitable—in the questions asked and not asked, the amount of discussion and illustration possible for any given topic. The Researchers asked me to point out that, although they are similar in their scientific approach, they are capable of disagreement amongst themselves. They report that some of my questions led to differences of opinion (for example on the relevance of religion to astrology), but that once these differences were explored they tended to disappear. These explorations do not appear in the interview, whose hard-won unanimity may therefore be deceptive. My sincere thanks and gratitude go to each researcher, and particularly to Geoffrey Dean for collating their input.

Why the Interest in Astrology?

Q: It seems rare for scientists like yourselves to be involved with astrology. How did it happen?

Researchers: We were intrigued by astrological claims, and by the depth and complexity of the subject. Was astrology true? Could the stars really correlate with human affairs? How could it work? Scientists love challenges like that. The problem was the lack of evidence—a situation no longer true. So we set out to explore the claims in depth. That was how our research started. Along the way some of us became practising astrologers, so we were able to approach the subject from both the inside and outside.

Q: How did the astrologers become astrologers, and what effect did your researches have on your astrological practices?

*An expanded version is presented on my website:
http://www.astrozero.btinternet.co.uk
and on the website: http://www.smitpotze.demon.nl/Astrology-and-Science

Researchers: One of us (Mather) was a self-taught student of astrology and was sufficiently impressed by results to become Research Co-ordinator for the Astrological Association 1971-1978. Two of us (Dean, Smit) were full-time practising astrologers and teachers of astrology. Dean was the founding president of the Federation of Australian Astrologers WA branch. Smit was the founder of NGPA, the only Dutch society for professional astrologers, and while in Australia was the distributor of Matrix Astrological Software. Both of us have lectured at international astrology conferences, and in 1988 we both received an AMR Commemorative Bi-Centennial Award for contributions to astrology, specifically for our work in research. (AMR is the Sydney-based Astrological Monthly Review. The Award was an international one and recipients included Doris Chase Doane, Liz Greene, Robert Hand, Alan Oken, and Lois Rodden.)

We started in much the same way as any astrologer starts—we calculated charts, saw that they seemed to work, and were hooked. Astrology became our passion. Every spare moment became devoted to it. We read more and more books, we did more and more charts for more and more people, we went to meetings and talked to more and more astrologers (whose experience was much the same as ours), and we became more and more convinced that astrology worked. Nothing we saw or experienced told us otherwise. Astrologers were generally nice people, they seemed intelligent and well-educated, they spoke from the heart, and they based everything on practical experience. Other than Sun-sign columns, which most of them rejected, there seemed to be nothing for anyone to complain about. We did not understand why some people should be so hostile to astrology. Nevertheless problems remained: for example, chart readings still seemed to fit when the wrong chart was used by accident.

Q: So what happened next?

Researchers: Those were the days when scientific tests of astrology were hard to come by. So we began to make our own tests. That is, we controlled for artifacts and other sources of error, something astrologers rarely did. (An artifact is something spurious that mimics a genuine effect, for example the varying number of days per month will mimic a dependence on month unless we adjust the arithmetic.) We were dismayed to find that artifacts and errors seemed to explain everything. Our beautiful world of astrology began to collapse. For example, when Mather used the data for 900 major earthquakes to test the claim that they tended to occur when Uranus was on the MC or IC, the claim could not be confirmed (95 earthquakes fitted but so did 91 out of 900 non-earthquakes). When Dean used volunteer clients to test charts that, unknown to the clients, had been altered to reverse their meaning, the reversed charts were accepted as readily as authentic charts. When Smit tested the main predictive techniques on people who had died an accidental death (nothing ambiguous here), the claims in astrology books could not be confirmed.

Ultimately we took heed of the mounting evidence and ceased actual practice, as did a few rare astrologers like David Hamblin (a former chairman of the Astrological Association), Terry Dwyer (a former tutor for the Mayo School of Astrology), and Jan Kampherbeek (a former editor of the Dutch magazine 'Spica'). As Aristotle might have said, astrology is dear to us, but dearer still is truth. But we did not lose our interest in astrology. Of course such U-turns can be personally traumatic. For example, Smit was originally an amateur astronomer highly skeptical of astrology, so his conversion to astrology was of momentous personal significance, making his unconversion even more so. When he realised that astrology seemed to have no basis in scientific fact, and probably never would, his rich and rewarding astrological life suddenly lost its meaning. He fell into a mental depression that lasted several years, and which was perhaps the main reason for the breakup of his marriage at the time. Even today he finds it painful to realise his initial skepticism of astrology had been justified, albeit for reasons more valid than those given in astronomy books, and that for over a decade he had been neglecting his original interests in favour of astrological ones. If nothing else, his experience illustrates the passion that astrologers can have for astrology. To dismiss them as frauds (as some skeptics do) is to miss the point.

Q: How did the non-astrologers become involved?

Researchers: We had long been interested in related matters, namely solar effects on people (Ertel) and lunar effects on people (Kelly), so in due course we also became interested in how astrologers conceive of relationships between heavenly bodies and people.

Q: How did this new interest affect you?

Researchers: As with the others, we experienced a kind of conversion, not from science to astrology or vice versa, but from bad closed-minded science to good open-minded science. By forcing us to be neither believers nor disbelievers, astrology has helped us to be genuinely open-minded, so it is easier to be open-minded in other areas. In short, astrology has made us better able to observe the spirit of science, which ironically seems quite the opposite to its effect on astrologers.

Basic Issues in Research

Q: How would you define scientific research as applied to astrology?

Researchers: In astrology there are millions of opinions and we can have them for nothing. But for knowledge we must work: we must do research. Scientific research in astrology has the same aim as scientific research in general—to improve what we know and to improve what we do. To us it reduces to four simple guidelines: (1) be careful because pitfalls are everywhere; (2) consider other explanations for claimed astrological correspondences; (3) investigate all promising ideas; (4) follow wherever the results of sound investigation lead even if they conflict with existing beliefs.

Q: These four guidelines really look like applied common sense. Are they really any different from what a competent astrologer would do?

Researchers: The four guidelines may look like applied common sense but to our knowledge few astrologers actually follow them. Even the most competent astrologers seem unaware of pitfalls: they do not consider other explanations, and they do not follow where the results of sound investigation lead. In fact these are the main objections that scientists hold against astrologers. Nevertheless, your point is true in one sense—researchers investigate the same testable claims as do astrologers. The crucial difference is that researchers are more careful and more rigorous. Researchers and astrologers differ not so much in their ideas as in the approaches used to test those ideas.

Q: Are there different schools of thought advocating different methodologies for scientific research into astrology, or are researchers unanimous in their approach?

Researchers: Yes and no. Methodologies in science generally may differ in detail but all involve the critical examination of ideas. The same applies to scientific methodologies in astrology—nothing is accepted just because astrologers say it works. What matters is whether it stands up to critical examination, of which tests are an important part.

Q: What sort of questions do researchers investigate?

Researchers: Is it true that positive signs are extraverted, that an elevated Neptune is musical, that adverse Mars transits indicate accidents, and that bucket patterns become agitators? What is the best zodiac, house system, aspect system, dynamic technique? Does Saturn mean the mother, the father, or neither? Are Sun-sign columns plausible? Should the signs be reversed in the southern hemisphere? What about distance, latitude, the 99th harmonic? How important is experience, intuition, a friendly client, an accurate birth time? Do astrologers perform better than computers, graphologists, palmists, psychics, tossing a coin? Is X easy to see in charts? How strong are astrological effects? How important is the search for new techniques? What makes a good astrologer? And so on. But perhaps the most important question is one that astrologers rarely ask, namely, "Could we be fooling ourselves?" Could astrology seem to work for reasons that have nothing to do with astrology? This, too, has been carefully investigated.

Q: Are there some astrological claims to which scientific research might be irrelevant?

Researchers: Some astrologers claim that scientific research is impersonal or unspiritual or insensitive to deeper truths. For example, they claim that the personal direction and purpose revealed by astrology cannot be tested. Or they claim that astrology involves subtle factors not yet known to science. In each case they conclude that science is unsuited to astrology, period. But apart from its emphasis on critical evaluation, science requires only that events be observable in some way. Astrology is the same, or so the textbooks imply, even though astrological observations can be little more than mere impressions. Nevertheless, if astrologers can observe it, so can scientific researchers, and vice versa. Does this mean that science must apply to all areas of astrology? Not at all. If no possible observation could rule out a particular claim, then the claim is untestable, and scientific research is irrelevant. It is as simple as that. We can test the idea that Leos are more generous than other signs, say by analysing the tips given in restaurants, but as yet we cannot test the idea that Leos were Cancerians in their previous life. Even so, we can still compare astrology to other systems that claim to give direction and purpose to our lives (astrology has no monopoly here), in the same way that we can compare the origin and maintenance of religious beliefs. Perhaps more importantly, we can explore the distinction between subjective and objective astrology.

Subjective and Objective Astrology

Q: Are you putting 'subjective' and 'objective' forward as distinct categories of astrology? I'm sure that many astrologers view astrology as existing half-way between subjectivity and objectivity.

Researchers: For such astrologers the distinction is a philosophical one, as for example in whether or not we create the world we live in. But this is not the distinction we mean. For our purpose, we can put subjective and objective at right angles to each other, as shown in Figure 1.   Figure 1 shows that subjective/objective is not a matter of black/white but of shades of grey. Nevertheless we can still describe what each dimension represents, as follows:

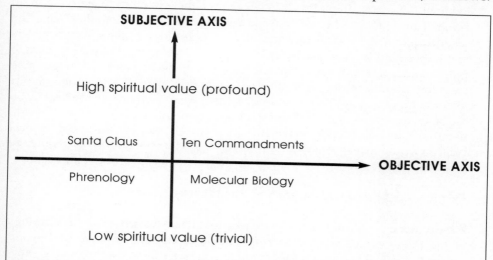

Figure 1: Subjective (vertical axis) vs objective (horizontal axis)
To illustrate the subjective/objective distinction we have aligned them with spiritual/material values.   Alternatively we could have aligned them with, say, benefit/truth or religion/science. Of course the terms are not strictly equivalent, but our aim is to illustrate the distinction without being dogmatic about what the terms should mean.

In subjective astrology only subjective values matter. The correctness of a particular statement, or of a chart reading, or even of the chart itself, is of no direct concern. What matters are issues like: Does astrology give a direction and purpose to our life? Does it provide benefit, self-understanding, insight, empowerment? Do astrologers feel that it always works? Are clients always satisfied by astrology? Does it enrich our lives in ways that the rational cannot as religion, myth, poetry and fiction do? *To be accepted, subjective astrology does not need to be true.*

   In objective astrology our subjective values do not matter. That millions of people may feel empowered or dismayed by astrology is of no direct concern. What matters are issues like: Are the statements of astrology true? Are Leos more Leonian than non-Leos? Which techniques are the most accurate? Do rectified times agree with actual times? Can astrologers pick the real chart from a control? Can clients pick their own interpretation from a control? Does astrology provide information not available from elsewhere? *To be accepted, objective astrology needs to be true.*

Figure 1 also shows how we cannot conclude that a false or problematic belief is due to nothing more than simple-minded gullibility. The belief might be due to its spiritual value, its social value, or its cultural value. A material feast cannot appease a spiritual hunger, a point underlined by the sheer longevity of major religions. In other words, there is more to astrology than being true or false. Let us look at this crucial point in another way: the distinction between subjective and objective astrology reflects how believers and critics tend to view astrology differently. The typical believer is looking for a spiritual experience that transforms the self (does astrology give meaning, understanding, direction?), but the typical critic is looking only for material proof (is astrology true, what is the evidence, where are the tests?). So the believer sees the critic as having missed the point, and vice versa. If we do not make the distinction between subjective astrology (sought by typical believers) and objective astrology (sought by typical critics) we could be creating conflict where none may exist. Which is not helpful to either side.

Q: How does this affect the aims of scientific researchers?

Researchers: It is not for researchers to dictate which kind of astrology (subjective or objective) is important. Their aim should be a more modest and respectful one—to point out for astrologers the need to be careful, and to show what happens when this need is neglected.

Research Methods

Q: So what is your own approach to scientific research? From start to finish, what do you actually do?

Researchers: Our own approach is quite ordinary. First, we survey the literature to determine what research already exists. Very little research into astrology by scientists existed before the 1950s. Today there is a great deal, although few astrologers seem to know about it. Second, we perform tests of promising ideas according to our interests and resources. Thus we might test astrologers to see if they get the right answers, or we might test the charts of, say, extraverts to see if they differ from those of introverts, or we might re-examine old studies to see if they might provide new information. Third, we submit the results to informed critics and act on their comments. If flaws are uncovered, or if we fail to follow up a promising line of enquiry, then we must try again. Science is a tough business. Finally, at the end of years of painstaking work (nobody said research had to be easy) we survey the totality of results to get an overall indication. No individual study stands alone.

Q: What types of test are there?

Researchers: Tests can be qualitative (what kind?) or quantitative (what amount?). A qualitative test involves categories (yes/no, male/female, Jupiter/Saturn), so shades of grey are not allowed. A quantitative test involves numbers that express position on a scale (20 kg, 50% certain, orb 5 degrees), so shades of grey are allowed. Which is best? Some astrologers say qualitative, but to us this applies only if people were never shades of grey. So we prefer quantitative. Indeed, much of astrology is already quantitative, as when astrologers use orbs or when they weigh factors prior to chart synthesis, which they presumably would not do if qualitative really was better. But qualitative tests may be preferred by astrologers because they are easier to apply non-rigorously and are therefore more easily persuaded to give the desired outcome. Or because they are more open to creative interpretation, which amounts to the same thing.

Q: I'm not sure I can agree. Quantitative tests require using statistics, but many astrologers feel very strongly that the statistical approach is quite unsuited to astrology.

Researchers: There are two kinds of statistics. If astrologers mean *descriptive* statistics, as in births and deaths, their argument is that statistics deal with groups, whereas astrology deals with individuals. That is, each chart is unique, so the success or failure of judgements for other charts is irrelevant. But this is like saying each day is unique, so whether the Sun rose on previous days is irrelevant. Those who depend on the Sun might disagree. Alternatively if astrologers mean *inferential* statistics, as in p = 0.05, their argument is invalid. Astrology is said to incline rather than compel, so we have no way of knowing whether a particular chart judgement is a hit or miss until after the event. Astrology works only sometimes. In other words it is essentially probabilistic, which means that probabilistic (i.e. statistical) approaches could hardly be more suitable.

Q: What do you think astrologers could learn from the discipline of the researcher?

Researchers: What we do is no different to what astrologers do in that we both make observations. But we are more careful. In fact, hugely more careful.

Q: What does this mean in practice?

Researchers: Consider first how astrologers do things. Each time they erect a chart they see how remarkably it corresponds with the person or event. They see with their own eyes that astrology works even though science (apparently) cannot explain it. This is their everyday experience, and on this experience they rest their claims. What could be more fair, more reasonable, and more disarming of criticism? Who could argue against 'it works'? But consider what 'it works' actually means. It means that *all non-astrological influences leading to the same result have been ruled out*. Astrologers seem to take this proviso for granted, but researchers have to be more careful. Ruling out non-astrological influences is harder than it might seem. We are too easily misled.

Q: And you see this as being where your approach differs from that of most astrologers?

Researchers: Yes. We want to avoid being misled, and avoiding being misled is part of what being scientific is about. Unless we are careful, unless we are aware of where we can go wrong, we can look at the Earth and conclude it is flat. Things are not always what they seem, a point most astrologers seem unaware of.

Reasoning Errors

Q: Can you illustrate what you mean by 'things not always being what they seem'?

Researchers: Here's an example anyone can try. With a ruler draw a vertical line a few centimetres long, then close underneath draw a horizontal line of the same length. The vertical line looks distinctly longer. The illusion prevails even though many credible authorities might claim the lengths are equal. Worse, it prevails even though you re-measure the lines to check their accuracy. This example shows how, without measurement, without tests, the error would never become apparent. The thing is not what it seems. The dangers of error become immensely greater at the higher levels of reasoning, i.e. at the levels where astrological ideas are formed, taught and applied, which is why we are so easily misled. Indeed, errors at these levels are as diverse as human experience itself.

Q: Can you give examples?

Researchers: Ordinary people have embraced countless things now known to be untrue, such as the belief that the Earth is the centre of the universe, or that the number 13 is unlucky, or that sleeping in moonlight sends you insane, or that rubbing frostbite with snow is helpful, or that the Moon is covered in ice 140 miles thick, or that bloodletting cures illness, or that the Fox sisters were genuinely psychic, or that the 23,28,33-day cycles of biorhythms work. Books such as Charles MacKay's 'Extraordinary Popular Delusions and the Madness of Crowds' (Noonday reprint 1977) and Martin Gardner's 'Fads and Fallacies in the Name of Science' (Dover 1957) attest to the pervasiveness and often amazing longevity of delusions (false beliefs). N-rays, polywater, and canals on Mars are examples where even scientists saw things that subsequent investigation showed not to exist. Cold fusion may be another. Such delusions (other than optical ones) are almost always due to our poor reasoning skills, and here the example closest to astrology is phrenology. A look at phrenology is enormously revealing about astrology.

Q: How so?

Researchers: Phrenology is a system of philosophy based on reading character from brain development as shown by head shape, or in popular terms by the bumps on the skull. Phrenology is now effectively dead but in the 1830s its popularity exceeded that of astrology today. Thus in the UK one quarter of the then 25 million population was illiterate, and a phrenology book cost one quarter of the average weekly wage. Yet roughly 1 person in 3,000 was practising or studying phrenology, roughly three times the proportion practising or studying astrology today. It was just as popular in Europe, the USA, and Australia. So in terms of popularity it compares more than favourably with astrology. No obscure restricted system here.

Like astrology, phrenology predicts the general tone of life (albeit not specific events), and it encourages you to assess yourself and act on its findings to achieve harmony with the world. Like astrology, its ideas were expressed with complete authority, it lent itself to cookbook interpretations (feel your bumps and look up the meanings), and it attracted people of intelligence and a vast literature wherein every criticism was furiously attacked. Most important of all, like astrology, phrenology flourished *because practitioners and clients saw that it worked.* So believers in phrenology were unmoved by what the critics said, and for what seemed the best of reasons. As in astrology, their views exuded overwhelming confidence. For example, according to the '1896 Year Book of the British Phrenological Association', phrenology was "so plainly demonstrated that the non-acceptance of phrenology is next to impossible." No ifs or buts here. Nevertheless, scientific research upset everything.

The experience-based claims of phrenologists were shown to be completely wrong. Character was not indicated by brain size and shape because the brain did not work like that. Nor did character break down in the ways required by phrenological theory. So a certain head shape did not mean what it was supposed to mean, nor was there any way it could possibly do so. The system that millions of people passionately believed in, and passionately acted upon, was totally without foundation. Note the problem: experience led phrenologists and their clients to believe in phrenology, just as experience leads astrologers and their clients to believe in astrology. In each case the reasoning is the same—the interpretation seems to fit the client, therefore the system works. But the reasoning was wrong for phrenology, so why should it be any different for astrology? Might astrology be just a figment of our poor reasoning skills?

Q: But if the claims of phrenology were wrong, how could experience lead to the opposite belief? How could the experience of practitioners and clients support non-existent effects?

Researchers: What matters here is that systems like phrenology and astrology rest on correspondences, otherwise known as reasoning by analogy; the assumption that things similar in some respects are also similar in other respects. Thus a high forehead or a strong Mercury indicates a strong intellect. The number four and the fourth planet have the same qualities. Big handwriting indicates power and dominance. Mars the red planet indicates blood, anger and war, and by extension anything vaguely red, hot, or aggressive.

Reasoning by analogy seems at first sight to be similar to ordinary reasoning. Size indicates strength, so a big man is stronger than a small man. Loudness indicates activity, so a loud noise suggests more danger than a faint noise. The difference is that these statements involve clear causal links, so we have reason to believe them. They do not claim to tell us anything new. By contrast, reasoning by analogy involves no causal links. It requires only that X correspond with Y in some way, from which correspondence we supposedly discover something new. The problems should be obvious.

Q: Such as?

Researchers: First, it is impossible to specify any two things, no matter how dissimilar, that do not show some kind of correspondence. A raven is like a writing desk because both cast shadows. But knowing something about ravens does not necessarily tell us anything about writing desks. Second, we have no way of deciding between conflicting correspondences. Are black cats lucky as in ancient Egypt or unlucky as in medieval Europe? Is the keen edge of our intellect blunted by over-use or sharpened? Is Mars unfortunate because red equals blood and war or fortunate because red equals blood and life? Who can believe any correspondence when it is so easily contradicted by another? Third, our chances of being correct are not good. No longer do we believe, as Aristotle did, that death can occur only at low tide. No longer do midwives open the door to ease a painful labour. No longer do doctors use the lungs of foxes, noted for strong respiration, to cure asthma. No longer do alchemical ideas appear in chemistry courses. In fact, reasoning by analogy is generally so spectacularly wrong that it survives in scientific textbooks only as an example of fallacious reasoning.

Q: But what if the correspondence actually exists?

Researchers: We still have problems because we are so bad at judging correspondences. Even if the correspondence is strong, as between human height and weight, we are still bad at judging it accurately. We can also see correspondences where none actually exist, so a system such as phrenology can seem to work even though it does not. This is why researchers have to be so careful. They cannot afford to be misled.

Q: Please explain how we can see correspondences where none actually exist.

Researchers: Consider the Draw-A-Person test. You draw a person on a sheet of blank paper, and the person's size, detail, clothing, and so on, supposedly reveal your inner conflicts. This is reasoning by analogy. Close-set eyes mean you have a suspicious nature. Big eyes indicate paranoia. A big head means you worry about being clever. This is an example of the correspondences that have been widely accepted. Nearly everyone believes these particular ones. It is also an example of the correspondences that have been critically examined, and in this case dozens of studies have found them to be wrong—people with such features do not draw such pictures. But it does not end there.

In one famous set of studies, groups of 56 college students were given 45 drawings of a person from a Draw-A-Person test. Each drawing was accompanied by six personality statements about the drawer from which each student had to work out the meaning of features such as head size. So they were rather like astrologers trying to work out the meaning of a new chart factor, say a new asteroid, using the traditional method of comparing charts with their owners. But unknown to the students the personality statements were deliberately unrelated to the drawings. For example, the statement 'worried about being clever' appeared just as often for small heads as for big heads. So did the students see what was actually in the data, namely nothing? Not at all. Nearly every student saw the correspondences even though they did not exist in the data. Worse, they continued to see them despite corrective strategies such as repeating the exercise, sorting the drawings into piles for closer study, and even when offered money for accuracy. Worst of all, when the statements totally opposed the correspondences, so that 'worried about being clever' appeared only for small heads, never for big heads, the students still saw them, albeit to a lesser extent.

In other words the students saw only what they expected to see. They reasoned by analogy. The actual data (the only thing that mattered) had almost no effect. Or as the late Professor Eysenck would say, "My mind is made up, don't confuse me with facts." The important point is that these studies could not have made it easier to avoid seeing non-existent correspondences, yet the students still failed miserably. So there is no reason to suppose that astrologers do any better once their minds are focussed on astro-symbolism—and this process is only one of the many ways we make errors in our reasoning.

Q: Can you say something about other errors?

Researchers: Reasoning errors are the focus of dozens of books and thousands of published studies, where they are given intriguing names like anchoring, Barnum effect, cognitive dissonance, confirmation bias, Dr Fox effect, halo effect, hindsight bias, illusory correlation (this is the one we just described), misattribution, placebo effect, Pollyanna principle, Rumpelstiltskin effect, regression effect, stacking the deck, and vividness heuristic. And a fascinating lot they are. For example, the Dr Fox effect involves blinding you with style and jargon rather than content (we just did exactly that). Cognitive dissonance is the painful consequence of holding incompatible views—if we are committed to astrology then it is painful to find evidence against it, so we search for confirmation, almost anything will do, and ignore the painful bits. The Barnum effect is where we read specifics into generalities, and is often thought to be the most important error in astrology. But other errors can be just as important, such as the placebo effect (it does us good if we think it does), the Pollyanna principle (the power of positive thinking), hindsight bias (afterwards we knew it all along), stacking the deck (asking only confirming questions), safety in complexity (so even the wrong chart fits), and vividness heuristic (judging by vividness not content). There are many more, all of them leading us to believe in seemingly spot-on correspondences where none actually exist. They prevent us learning from experience, a result that says it all. Perhaps the cruellest blow is the absence of errors leading in the opposite direction, which means we are stuck in a one-way street—a point to keep in mind when reading what astrologers say in your other interviews.

Q: But wouldn't prejudice, the rejection of astrology for emotional reasons, be an error leading in the opposite direction?

Researchers: No, because we are talking about the reasoning errors made by astrologers, who presumably are not prejudiced against astrology. The only thing that might persuade astrologers to disbelieve in astrology is the informed critical mind, which of course is not a reasoning error but rather a defence against reasoning errors. Fortunately, anyone can have an informed critical mind.

Intuition and ESP

Q: You have focussed on reasoning errors. But many astrologers would claim that successful chart reading isn't possible without some degree of intuition. Might this avoid reasoning errors?

Researchers: Intuition has been a rich source of inspiration in all fields of human endeavour, including science. Yet it can be totally unreliable simply because it is not self-verifying. We have no way of resolving opposing intuitions except by reasoning. So intuition does not avoid reasoning errors. Furthermore, the golden rule of considering the whole chart is immediately broken if we select a focus, yet this is what intuition encourages us to do. Astrologers generally seem unaware of this conflict.

Q: But is intuition really so unreliable? I know quite a few astrologers who would disagree with you.

Researchers: Their disagreement with us might be more persuasive if they did not disagree so spectacularly among themselves. If their intuitions were in fact reliable, the disagreement between astrologers, between astrological schools, and between traditions (Arabian, Aztec, Burmese, Chinese, Hindu, Jewish, Mayan, Tibetan, Western and so on, excluding purely cultural differences) should not exist. But astrologers are here in the same boat as palmists, phrenologists, physiognomists, numerologists, and the readers of cards, colours, tea leaves, and so on. Such people frequently claim to rely on intuition, as if this somehow allowed them to home in on the truth despite the disagreement between astrologers on how to read charts, between palmists on how to read hands, between numerologists on how to read numbers, and so on. They are like mechanics who claim that intuition allows successful repairs to cars despite having no workshop manuals.

To be sure, our intuitions, for all their unreliability, serve us well in everyday life. To adopt alternatives would be unrealistic. Nobody seeks formal arguments to decide between strawberry and vanilla ice cream, and most errors are of little consequence. It would also be incapacitating—life is simply too short. But this does not alter the fact that intuitions are unreliable. Just take a look at selection interviews, which rely for their success on the interviewer's intuition. Here many hundreds of studies are virtually unanimous in their findings—interviewers frequently disagree completely with each other, with the same candidate rated top by one and bottom by another. So much for the supposed benefits of intuition.

Q: The word 'intuition' is often used quite loosely, so maybe we should define exactly what we are talking about.

Researchers: In psychology the word 'intuition', also called insight or hunch or gut-feeling, refers to the method of arriving at a conclusion, not to any property of the conclusion itself. The key features of intuition are: (1) everything happens in our head; (2) answers pop up out of nowhere, especially after a rest period, so we end up knowing but without knowing how; (3) we are usually confident of being right; (4) we may be right but we can also be spectacularly wrong. However, there is no reason to believe that an answer that pops up has actually come from nowhere, or that ESP is involved (at least not during a chart reading). Instead the evidence suggests that such answers are largely based on previous experience. The relevant experience may not be quickly remembered or even remembered at all, so the rest period in (2) can be essential to allow for unconscious retrieval and unconscious processing of possibilities. Thus the supposedly effortless and unanalysable nature of intuition means nothing—driving a car requires endless decisions of exactly this nature, but judged by our first fumbling steps at learning to drive they clearly owe little if anything to intuition as traditionally conceived.

Conscious problem solving (i.e. high cortical arousal) narrows the pool of possible ideas and suppresses our unconscious workings, which is another reason why the rest period (i.e. low cortical arousal) can be essential. If having gone to sleep on a problem we wake up to find the answer mysteriously before us without effort, this is intuition at work. Sleeping, or doing nothing, has worked better than thinking furiously. Most scientists, including ourselves, have had many such experiences.

Q: What if there is no rest period, as in a chart reading?

Researchers: If there is no rest period, intuition can still apply, the main feature here being a quick confident conclusion based on a small (and therefore seemingly inadequate) number of clues. Studies using problems with known clues and known answers have revealed two underlying dimensions, namely clues (few-many) and answers (correct-incorrect). The dimensions are independent, so correctness is generally unrelated to number of clues, which is not what we might expect. Correctness also increases with IQ but only slightly. Interestingly, a person's position on these two dimensions seems to be inherent. Thus a person can be few-correct or many-correct, or few-incorrect or many-incorrect, just like any personality trait, where correct = intuitive and incorrect = non-intuitive. These are not rigid categories, so most people are a shade of grey. Intuition is not a yes/no quantity but something we have more of or less of. These two dimensions also align with the personality dimensions of tough-tender mindedness (few-many clues), and emotionally stable-anxious (correct-incorrect answers). Non-intuitives tend to be tender-anxious. Intuitives tend to be tough-stable (also creative and unconventional). On this basis the genuinely intuitive chart reader is tough, unemotional, and uses only a few chart factors. This is so different from the warm caring emotional (and therefore non-intuitive) stereotype using the whole chart that we might doubt whether intuition really does play a part in chart reading. Even if it did, it could only work if the chart factors thereby selected actually had the meanings they are said to have, which (given the research results to date) seems doubtful. In any case, the bottom line is that unconscious processes are as fallible as conscious processes, which is why intuition (despite our confidence) is not necessarily correct. Even self-proclaimed psychics cannot tell when their intuitions are correct, otherwise they would rule the world. No wonder that intuition has been defined as the strange instinct that can tell us we are right even when we are wrong.

Q: You mentioned there are reasons for believing that ESP is unlikely to be involved in a chart reading.

Researchers: At first sight it might seem that ESP (if it exists) could account for all astrological predictions that are difficult to explain yet appear to be correct, whether personal, electional, horary, or whatever. Similarly it might seem that ESP could also explain any successes due to palmistry, tea leaf reading, and so on. But if ESP were really responsible, planets would be interchangeable with tea leaves, and we would have no grounds for claiming that such methods are valid in themselves. In fact the study of astrology would become irrelevant, which presumably is not a view supported by astrologers. This alone is good reason for believing that astrology is not merely ESP in disguise. Furthermore we should recognise that ESP can be defined as *not the result of any means we know of.* So if an outcome can be explained by normal intuitive processes in the brain, no matter how mysterious they may seem, we are not entitled to invoke ESP. We can invoke ESP only if all other explanations can be ruled out, which would require safeguards that are generally never present during a chart reading.

Q: Are you saying that ESP could never be involved in a chart reading?

Researchers: Parapsychologists have explained such ESP effects as may occur in terms of two models. In the *reduction of sensory-noise model*, the key is relaxation and a constant low-level sensory input. If the subject is relaxed, hears white noise, and sees only a featureless warm glow, sensitivity to ESP (should it occur) begins only after 15-20 minutes of habituation to these conditions. That is, under conditions of unvarying sensory input it takes 15-20 minutes for the brain to stop attending to the senses and become attentive to internal mental events instead. But if the astrologer is having sensory inputs, as is necessarily the case when reading charts for clients, habituation cannot occur and ESP is unlikely to manifest. Alternatively, in the *reduction of bias-and-rigidity model*, the key is the absence of preoccupations and constraints. ESP can then be triggered by need, e.g. to avoid a not-consciously recognised hazard, but not too much need, which produces stress and impairs performance. If the subject is preoccupied, e.g. with finishing before the next client arrives, or is constrained, as is necessarily the case when addressing particular issues for clients, ESP is unlikely to manifest. In both cases, contrary to what some astrologers have claimed, the process of reading charts, or focussing on mandalas, seems not conducive to ESP. Nevertheless, if astrologers could consistently score above chance under conditions where ordinary explanations could be ruled out, then ESP would have to be considered. But the prospects do not seem promising, given that a direct test of top psychic readers found them to be no more accurate than matched non-psychics.

Q: Could you describe this test?

Researchers: It was a remarkable five-year study finished in 1988. It monitored a total of more than 200 readings by the top 15 counselling psychics in the Netherlands, and then rated their accuracy against matched groups of non-psychics. Over 10,000 statements were obtained, of which 10% were sufficiently specific to be tested, of which 10% turned out to be correct, i.e. only 1% of all statements were both specific and correct. No difference in hit rate was observed between psychics or between psychics and non-psychics. It was concluded that psychics were no more accurate than non-psychics, but their sensitivity to human ills and their huge experience (their own lives were often traumatic) still made them useful counsellors.

Q: What might this mean for astrology?

Researchers: It would seem to deny that intuition and ESP (or at least claimed ESP) could play a useful role in the reading of *charts*, though intuition might play a useful role in the reading of *clients*. But regardless of whether astrologers use intuition, they are in effect claiming that chart factors have real intrinsic meanings as opposed to ones imagined by the ancient Greeks, and that their permutations can be accurately disentangled by astrologers as opposed to the mere appearance of disentangling. You have interviewed many astrologers. Generally speaking, did they have any doubts, do you think, that chart factors have real intrinsic meanings?

Q: There is a range of opinion. Certainly, all the astrologers I interviewed believe that they can access real information from the chart, but views differ as to how this happens. Some see astrology as an empirical science where each chart factor has an intrinsic meaning, much as H_2O always means water to a chemist. Others consider that meaning does not inhere in chart factors per se, but is created by the coming together of chart factors with the astrologer's mind, so H_2O could mean Antarctica, emotion, making tea, ships, or anything else with watery connections. These are extreme positions, with most astrologers existing at points on the spectrum between them. So do astrologers think that chart factors have real intrinsic meanings? Some do, some don't, and most are somewhere in the middle.

Researchers: The issue boils down to our distinction between objective and subjective astrology, so it is good to see how well it agrees with your astrologers' responses. Some believe that chart factors have real meanings, so theirs is objective astrology. Some do not, so theirs is subjective astrology. Others try for both, quoting scientific evidence if positive but ignoring it if negative. Astrologers can check their position by asking the questions listed in the discussion of Figure 1.

This chapter has focussed on questions that science raises about astrology in principle. The next will cover some of the research which has been carried out to test astrology in practice.

Chapter X

Research into Astrology (Part 2)

The Picture Emerging from Research

Q: What has been going on in the world of astrological research, and what kind of picture is emerging?

Researchers: If only subjective values matter (see Figure 1) the objective results that have been reported to date will be irrelevant whether positive or negative, as will much of this interview. Otherwise we can summarise the emerging picture as follows. If we are to accept the claim that astrology provides reliable knowledge and accurate diagnoses, it has to do this under conditions where errors in our reasoning cannot intrude. Yes, the chart may fit the person, but does it fit better than other charts? Yes, clients may identify with their reading, but can they pick their own reading out of several? Yes, the prediction was a hit, but how many were misses, and is the hit rate better than that achieved by informed guessing? Many such tests have been made, some by scientists, some by astrologers, and some by scientists and astrologers working together. Many have been made by ourselves since the 1970s when we first started our researches. But over the whole range of approaches the answer has been generally negative. The occasional promising result has not been confirmed, which illustrates the importance of not depending on just one study. Half a century of research into astrology, using techniques incomparably more powerful than those available to the Babylonians and Greeks, has failed to reveal effects (or at least effects commensurate with astrological claims) beyond those due to ordinary causes such as errors in reasoning. Which of course is very disappointing to those of us who have been astrologers. On the other hand it does not deny that future tests may be more positive, or that astrology may be fruitful in subjective ways.

Q: Could you give an example of a promising result that was not confirmed?

Researchers: What got newspaper astrology columns off the ground was the apparently amazing accuracy of the British columnist R H Naylor. Unlike columns today, his column included predictions of national and world events as well as birthday predictions, then made by birth date rather than by Sun-sign. In the 5 October 1930 edition of the London 'Sunday Express', he made this prediction among several others: "Earthquakes will occur, mostly near deep-sea levels, and affecting peninsulas, in the autumn quarter of 1930. They may not actually occur in October—though from the 8th to the 15th is a real danger point—but they will be exceedingly likely in November or December. British aircraft will be in danger about the same date." On 5 October 1930 the great British airship R101 crashed in a storm near Paris. There were 46 dead and 8 survivors. Newspapers showed pictures of terrible wreckage. Naylor said this about his success: "My prediction last week was based on a very simple observation. It can be proved that, whenever the new Moon or full Moon falls at a certain angle to the planet Uranus, aircraft accidents, electrical storms, and sometimes earthquakes follow. Now... the configuration referred to [New Moon conjunct Uranus] occurred on October 7; the destruction of the R101, therefore, prematurely fulfilled the indication." At first sight Naylor's hit seems quite amazing, which is why his column took off. But the hit is ambiguous. Naylor's forecast said 8-15 October, during which time no aircraft crashes, electrical storms or earthquakes were reported by British newspapers, so no hits can be counted there. The crash occurred when the Moon was 33 degrees from conjunction, a long way from modern orbs of a degree or so. And later studies of air disasters did not confirm any link with the Moon and Uranus. So was it a hit or a coincidence?

In fact an isolated hit is no more meaningful than an isolated chart factor. It is the totality of research that matters. Interestingly, in the days when few tests existed, most astrologers held that astrology was demonstrable and therefore testable. Just try it, they said, and you will experience for yourself how well it works. In fact those of us who were astrologers said exactly the same—it was how we got hooked in the first place. But the advent of scientific tests and their predominantly negative results has caused a U-turn. Today many astrologers hold that astrology is not testable after all, thus denying the bad news, as if this did not also deny that astrological correspondences could be confirmed by experience or even discovered in the first place.

Q: Astrologers who say astrology is not testable may do so because they see it as a divinatory tool more akin to a ritual that prepares the mind to intuit what needs to be said. In their view the working of this tool is not necessarily testable in a scientific way.

Researchers: Their view is hard to understand. It is like saying that we don't know how gravity works and therefore cannot test the fall of apples. The issue is whether the astrology ritual works better than a control ritual, e.g. by providing new information or by improving self-esteem. Much is testable here.

Q: You are certainly painting a gloomy picture. What would you consider to be the most convincing research in favour of astrology, and what are the weaknesses in it?

Researchers: Astrologers tend to quote the Gauquelin results as the most convincing evidence in support of astrological claims. (These results showed that eminent professionals tended to be born when the planet relevant to their occupation was just past rise or culmination; this tendency was later called the Mars Effect, but depending on the occupation it could equally well have been called the Moon, Venus, Jupiter, or Saturn Effect.) Indeed, two of us have worked for some years following them up. Gauquelin's work was certainly the most rigorous of its time. But his planetary effects, even though independently confirmed by us, are too tiny to be of the slightest practical value. For example, given that Mars tends to be just past rising or culminating in the charts of eminent sports champions, this information is of no practical value unless your client is eminent (say 1 in 20,000 of the population), in which case the information is already superfluous. Furthermore, Gauquelin's other results showed no effect for half the planets, or for signs, or for aspects, and work by one of us (Ertel) has disconfirmed initial hints of a planetary link with character traits, all of which is contrary to astrological claims. So the relevance of the Gauquelin results tends to be overstated. On the other hand some astrologers claim that the Gauquelin results are at best peripheral to astrology. Here again our subjective/objective distinction resolves the conflict.

Q: But doesn't the Gauquelin research deserve more acknowledgement of its implications? Consider the statement made in 'Recent Advances' (Dean, Mather et al 1977) that the Gauquelin results "provide, for the first time, rigorous and objective evidence about the basic fundamentals of astrology, upon which everything else depends...something that astrologers themselves, despite millenia of study, have consistently failed to do." (p. 394.)

Researchers: A lot of research has occurred since that statement was made in 1977, and the results require it to be modified. There are two separate issues at stake here. First is the reality of the Gauquelin findings. Research by one of us (Ertel) has found that, despite some deficiencies, the basic findings withstand rigorous tests. Second is their relevance to astrology. Research by another of us (Dean) has found that they may have an ordinary explanation, hitherto unsuspected, in which case it would be premature to conclude that they are relevant to astrology. Real yes, relevant perhaps not. The reason is a simple one—the Gauquelin data show evidence of manipulation by parents. For example there is a consistent deficit of births on the 13th. But if parents can manipulate dates then why not hours and thus planetary risings and culminations? So the Gauquelin findings might be due to parents, not planets.

Q: Are there no other promising areas of research?

Researchers: Twenty years ago they seemed quite numerous. As well as Gauquelin's research there was John Addey's harmonics ("Promises to revolutionise astrology," said 'Recent Advances'), Donald Bradley's Jupiter

Pluvius (the tendency for heavy rainfall to occur if Jupiter aspected the local meridian when the Moon entered sidereal Capricorn), John Nelson's radio propagation quality (worsened by hard heliocentric aspects), the Mayo-Eysenck Sun-sign zigzag ("Possibly the most important development for astrology in this century," said 'Phenomena'), and Vernon Clark's matching experiments [see later]. Even the mathematics (of aspects, of orbs, of probabilities, and so on) seemed promising. Interest in research grew accordingly, only to fade away as artifacts were discovered. As in the above cases, once artifacts were controlled the supposed astrological effects disappeared. The most recent example is Gunter Sachs's best-selling book 'The Astrology File' (Orion 1998), a supposed proof of Sun-sign effects. One of us re-analysed his results but found only artifacts. The whole massive study (it involved several millions of cases) was not careful enough.

Q: Let me come back to some of the research areas you mentioned right at the start, starting with Sun-sign columns. What work has been done here?

Researchers: Lots. When labels and other cues are removed, people cannot pick the sign that is supposedly theirs. Yes, some columns might be uplifting, but the point is: does the use of Sun-signs add otherwise unattainable truth and uplift to Sun-sign columns? Or do they merely con columnists and readers into believing that their 'twelve thoughts for the day' are more meaningful than if they appeared in, say, Kahlil Gibran or a desk calendar? Research indicates the second.

Q: Moving to the whole chart, has any work been done to test the accuracy of individual astrologers and their procedures?

Researchers: Again, lots. Can astrologers match cases to authentic charts better than to control charts? Can subjects pick their own chart interpretation out of several? In each case the results have been no better than chance.

Q: But I thought some early results, namely those of Vernon Clark, were dramatically better than chance? Or were they all artifacts?

Researchers: Vernon Clark's results and those of most other matching tests have fatal problems due to their small sample sizes, typically 10 birth charts. Imagine a hand of 10 playing cards picked at random. Even though there are equal numbers of red and black in the pack, we seldom end up with equal proportions in our hand. Our hand has been affected by sampling variations. Of course the bigger our hand the closer we get to the proportions that exist in the pack. The same with birth charts. Given that the stars only incline, charts will tend to be of two kinds, those that fit their owners (call these red) and those that don't (call these black). Suppose like Vernon Clark we want to know the proportion of owners with red charts. We collect ten owners and send them to astrologers. If the astrologers know their stuff they will quickly discover which charts are red and which are black. But the reds in such a small sample will be determined much more by sampling variations than by the proportion in the population (which is what we want to know). Worse, for any given study we cannot remove the sampling variations, just as we cannot remove the sampling variations for any given hand of cards. They are there to stay. So our results will not tell us what we want to know. Yes, we may have three or seven reds instead of the five predicted, but so what?

Vernon Clark and nearly everybody else used few charts and many astrologers, which is precisely the combination guaranteed to produce this kind of uninformative outcome. So what can be done? The solution is either to use many charts, or to evaluate the sampling variations by submitting the collective studies (to date we know of 43) to what is known as meta-analysis. But in each case the results are no better than chance. Figure 2 (opposite) shows what we mean.

Visual analysis of 43 Vernon Clark studies in astrology (left) and, for comparison, 107 validation studies in graphology (right), using the plots suggested by Light and Pillemer in 'Summing Up: The Science of Reviewing Research' (Harvard University Press 1984). Here effect size is the correlation between actual personality, ability, occupation, or case history and that predicted by astrologers or graphologists. An effect size of 0 means zero correlation as between coin tosses, 1 is perfect as in 100% hits, and -1 is perfect inverse as in 100% misses. For individuals an effect size below 0.40 is of little practical use.

Left: The 43 studies include studies where only top astrologers were used, or where more information was provided than is normally available in a consultation, or where artifacts might reasonably be suspected, so the indications are optimistic. Nevertheless meta-analysis shows that the sampling error (bottom plot) is so high that it entirely explains the differences between studies. So there is nothing for astrology to explain. The other two plots are just as unremarkable. In short the plots offer no support for the validity of judgements based on birth charts.

Right: The support for the validity of judgements based on handwriting is almost as nonexistent. Content (upper two plots), not graphology, explains what little validity there is, which is the opposite of what graphologists claim. The chances of proving astrology via graphology, or vice versa, are therefore not good.

Reproduced with permission from 'Correlation', Northern Winter 1998, page 75.

Effect size vs. year of study

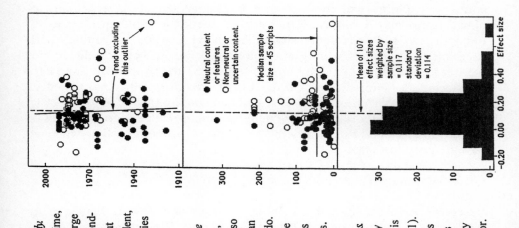

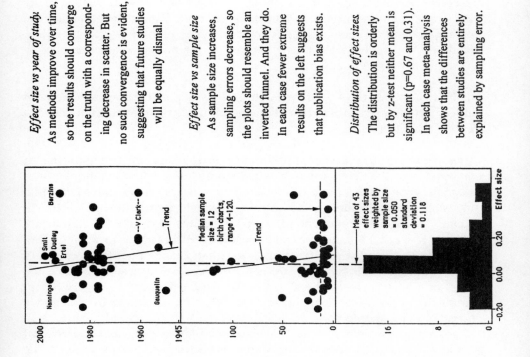

Effect size vs year of study.
As methods improve over time, so the results should converge on the truth with a corresponding decrease in scatter. But no such convergence is evident, suggesting that future studies will be equally dismal.

Effect size vs sample size
As sample size increases, sampling errors decrease, so the plots should resemble an inverted funnel. And they do. In each case fewer extreme results on the left suggests that publication bias exists.

Distribution of effect sizes
The distribution is orderly but by z-test neither mean is significant (p=0.67 and 0.31). In each case meta-analysis shows that the differences between studies are entirely explained by sampling error.

Q: Perhaps a refined and balanced technique is the only one that will work in astrology.

Researchers: The idea that only a refined and balanced technique will work seems incompatible with the high level of disagreement about techniques, all of which are claimed to work. If they actually work, the technique is evidently unimportant, and astrologers should be piling up hits in Vernon Clark experiments instead of scoring at chance level. But if they actually do not work, astrologers are evidently unable to tell. So the supposedly uniquely-true technique referred to in your question would be either redundant or unidentifiable. Nevertheless let us speculate to the contrary. Let us say okay, so elephants don't fly, but given the right conditions maybe tigers might fly, or maybe giraffes might fly. Clearly this won't do. There comes a time when we have to grasp the nettle.

Q: And conclude that nothing in the jungle can fly?

Researchers: The point is that nothing in the jungle is flying. Maybe many things can fly, but this is back to speculating forever. We still have to grasp the nettle, namely that when nothing is actually flying, nothing is actually flying. People do not travel to Heathrow Airport on the off-chance that somebody will suddenly discover aeroplanes.

Q: How complex does your research get? Is it possible to design tests of sufficient complexity to allow for all the permutations of meaning between the various chart factors?

Researchers: Your question implies that astrologers are somehow better equipped to deal with complexity than scientific researchers are. But because researchers are always more careful than astrologers, this is like saying that only sloppiness produces good astrology, which seems ludicrous. It will certainly be news to those who set astrology exams. Actually the complexity issue is a non-issue because we can test astrologers directly as in Vernon Clark tests. If astrologers cannot perform better than chance then the complexity said to be responsible for their success, yet which is supposedly beyond the grasp of scientific researchers, does not exist. Before we worry about complexity or any other detail we need to know if it actually delivers, else we end up chasing phantoms.

Nevertheless, imagine that a level of complexity exists as yet undreamt of, and that it actually does deliver. Can tests be designed to cope with it? The answer is yes. Examples of approaches that take any complexity in their stride are multiple discriminant analysis, which finds the factors that discriminate best between a set of charts and controls, and probabilistic modelling using item response theory, which does everything an astrologer can do short of using ESP but includes what no astrologer can do, namely address astrology's inherent uncertainty directly. Both techniques require a computer. A scan through back issues of 'Correlation' will lead directly or indirectly to examples of tests that address the complexity issue.

Another approach is to bypass complexity issues altogether, notably by a test of time twins (persons born close together in time and place), which avoids all problems of how the various chart factors should be interpreted and combined. A failure to validate Sun-signs might be dismissed as a failure to use the correct interpretation or to properly allow for competing chart factors, but a failure to show that time twins are significantly alike is less easily dismissed. The occurrence of time twins follows what is known as a Poisson distribution (see any statistics textbook). Once we know the mean number of births in a given interval, say ten minutes, for a particular location, say London, the number of births with at least one other birth in that interval can be obtained using a hand calculator. Time twins are surprisingly numerous. Thus in a city of one or ten million people with a typical birthrate of 2% per year, about 4% or 32% of the people will have at least one other person born there within one minute, and 32% or 98% will have at least one born within ten minutes.

Q: Some striking cases of time twins have been reported, such as Samuel Hemmings and King George III. Have you looked into these?

Researchers: One of us has. Legend says that the prosperous London ironmonger Samuel Hemmings and King George III were born at the same hour and died at the same hour after lives showing striking similarities such as being married on the same day. But a careful check of contemporary records showed that the ironmonger's name was not Samuel Hemmings but Richard Speer, and of the events only the simultaneous death could be verified, the rest being most likely fabricated. Several other well-known cases of time twins could not be verified, either through lack of records or evident fabrication. But the number of exact time twins existing even in Western history is so enormous (hundreds of millions) that many striking cases are to be expected by chance alone, so the reported cases are unremarkable. More systematic tests of time twins have recently been made. For example Roberts and Greengrass, in their 'The Astrology of Time Twins' (Pentland, 1994), collected a total of 128 people born on six dates, but they found no clear parallels in personality scores, appearance, handwriting, names, interests, occupation, or life events. The strong similarities predicted by astrology were simply not there.

Now look at ordinary twins. The time interval between births is much the same whether the twins are identical or non-identical. Therefore according to astrology they should be equally alike. But they are not. Identical twins are very alike, but non-identical twins are generally no more alike than ordinary siblings. This is one of the oldest arguments against astrology, but it is generally ignored by astrologers.

Open-mindedness

Q: The subject of open-mindedness came up earlier. What is it, and how is it cultivated?

Researchers: Open-mindedness means a willingness to explore new ideas and arguments. Everyone (especially scientists) thinks they are open-minded, in the same way that everyone thinks they have a sense of humour. But when evidence exists both for and against a belief, most people do not show low levels of conviction, which logically they should, but high levels of conviction either for or against, which logically is indefensible. Logically they should have open minds but in fact they have the opposite. Open minds, like the Scarlet Pimpernel, are damned elusive.

So what is happening? An open mind requires us to embrace uncertainty. But for most of us uncertainty is something we hate. Our need to avoid uncertainty explains the popularity of superstitious beliefs, which can be seen as attempts to reduce anxiety using ineffective techniques when effective ones are unavailable. Or as Bertrand Russell said, "What men want is not knowledge but certainty." No wonder astrologers are amazed when we express no interest in where the astrological chips fall. To them it seems inconceivable that we should not be either for or against.

How to cultivate open-mindedness? Explore new ideas and arguments, and have critical colleagues watch over you and act on their criticisms.

Q: Perhaps it is still necessary to question the underlying worldviews of researchers. How would you describe your own worldviews and how they fit in with astrology?

Researchers: As scientific researchers our worldviews (e.g. that being careful will be productive) are only tentative. Show us a better way of doing things and we will explore it regardless of our worldviews. Success is the arbiter, but so far astrology has failed to deliver. It has not delivered the results promised by astrologers, nor has it provided the evidence required by careful people to adopt an astrological worldview. Astrology may, of course, be more compatible with some world views than with others, but by itself this means little. For eighteen centuries the doctrine of the four elements was compatible with prevailing worldviews, but the doctrine is now known to be wrong. Astrology (like UFOs, channelling, hobgoblins or magic spells) still has to make its own case regardless of its compatibility with a particular world view.

Make a convincing case and we will explore it.

Q: How can you be sure that the results of research aren't just reflecting your worldviews back at you?

Researchers: Presumably an example might be researchers whose worldview requires isolated factors to be meaningful, so they test only isolated factors despite protests from astrologers. The answer to your question is easy—we use as many approaches as possible regardless of what a particular worldview might dictate. Show us a better way and we will explore it. But turn your question around—how can astrologers be sure their claims aren't just reflecting their own worldviews back at them? An example might be astrologers who ignore reasoning errors despite protests from scientists. The question is one that only research can resolve (and in our view has probably already resolved), using as many approaches as possible, yet astrologers show little interest in such research.

The Relevance of Belief; a White Crow

Q: You keep returning to the theme that astrology fails to deliver. But supposing it did deliver?

Researchers: Suppose that all the research ever done has got it wrong, and that we have a world where astrology works to the extent claimed in astrology books. Hunger and hardship have disappeared because economic trends and climate are predictable. Science has disappeared because horary astrology answers any question. So has competitive sport for the same reason. Cars and planes are hazard-free because assembly times conducive to accidents are routinely avoided. Crime, war, illness and divorce are unknown because predictable. Every person is empowered, self-actualised, spiritually enlightened, and knows their individual purpose and direction. Abuse of astrological knowledge is prevented by restricting it to those whose charts reveal due merit. This is astrology world. Now compare astrology world with the actual world. Bearing in mind that astrology has had two thousand years to get it right, can we conclude that it really does deliver? Probably not.

Q: How do astrologers generally react to the picture emerging from research?

Researchers: Most astrologers seem unaware of it. Those who are aware of it either: (1) dismiss it on the grounds that scientific research is irrelevant to astrology; or (2) admit its relevance but claim its methods are presently inadequate for unravelling astrology's secrets.

Re (1), the philosopher Thomas Kuhn noted that when an idea is in crisis, its supporters retreat behind a smokescreen of speculation that sounds good but is actually empty. This is precisely the situation with modern astrology. Rather than demonstrate their claims under artifact-free conditions, or specify what research would be relevant or how controversies and disagreements might be dealt with, astrologers retreat behind a smokescreen of speculation about the nature of truth, reality, perception, language, and so on. Talk yes, actual progress no.

Re (2), recall that the claims of astrology are grandiose, and that almost no area of human affairs (individual, collective, past, present, future) is supposed to be exempt. In other words we are supposed to believe simultaneously that astrology, like gravity, is writ most exceedingly large, while its influence is most exceedingly difficult to demonstrate. Scientists tend to part company with astrologers at this point. How can astrology be so difficult to demonstrate when astrologers are so readily convinced that it works?

Q: One answer might be as given by Stephen Arroyo in his 'Chart Interpretation Handbook' (CRCS, 1989; p.13). He says, "Statistical studies in astrology have been almost universally pointless [because] only experiments with living people in a clinical situation can fully show astrology's value and validity in its guidance, counselling and psychotherapy applications."

Researchers: Phrenologists said the same thing about an actually invalid phrenology. Arroyo seems unaware that "living people in a clinical situation" is precisely the situation where reasoning errors (Barnum, Dr Fox, hindsight, placebo, Polyanna, and so on) rage most out of control. In fact clinical studies of the kind he advocates have been made, but they have revealed nothing not explainable by reasoning errors and other artifacts. Indeed, scattered throughout the astrological literature are accounts by astrologers who had accidentally used the wrong chart during a client consultation. One of us (Smit) had the same experience, and another of us (Dean) deliberately used wrong charts. According to Arroyo, because "living people in a clinical situation" fully demonstrate astrology's validity, the error should have been instantly apparent. In fact nobody noticed. In Smit's case he had always been told that charts uniquely fitted their owners, so he was profoundly shocked—it showed that "astrology's validity" was effectively meaningless.

Q: Do you see any ways in which the scientific approach might be modified to increase the possibility of detecting genuine astrological effects?

Researchers: Increasing the sensitivity is straightforward—just increase the sample size. Alternatively we can increase the signal to be detected, say by testing only the best astrologers, or by selecting only extreme cases so they are unambiguous. But such approaches have already been well explored without success. In fact the variety and extent of studies to date is seldom appreciated, especially by astrologers who claim that the scientific approach is inadequate.

Q: How likely is it that the emerging picture will become more favourable to astrology?

Researchers: The totality of research results to date involves hundreds of diverse studies, some positive but mostly negative. Even the positive studies tend to be incommensurate with astrological claims. For example, a positive study in which astrologers scored 55% hits vs 50% expected by chance is incommensurate with the near-100% expected on the basis of what we read in astrology books. To overturn such a weight of negative evidence would require an avalanche of new studies where the results were consistently and dramatically positive. If Figure 2 is anything to go by, this is not going to happen. Nevertheless, could astrology deliver the necessary goods? For twenty-five years we have tried to find out. We have ransacked the literature and tested the most promising claims, both as astrologers and scientists. We have gathered our own data and analysed it using the most powerful methods available. We have looked at related areas in astronomy, philosophy, psychology, parapsychology, sociology, and statistics, in each case going back to the original academic literature, something that astrologers rarely do. We have lectured at conferences, run critical debates, issued challenges, and held prize competitions (all now closed) with prizes up to US $5000 for evidence in support of astrological claims. As far as we know nobody else has been as systematic or as thorough. The point is, if astrology could deliver the necessary goods then somewhere in all this it would be shining through. But we have found nothing that could not be explained by reasoning errors and other artifacts. Yes, a great way to spend twenty-five years!

Q: Were you disappointed?

Researchers: To some extent. But had we been working for a research institute, we would have been more than disappointed, we would have been fired, or at least diverted to more productive areas. Negative results means no grant money, little contribution to knowledge, little chance of publication, and no academic advancement. So nobody could have wanted positive results more than us. Which is not to say that negative findings are unimportant. For example, it is useful to know that eating lettuce does not send you mad. But to continue pursuing a topic with grave theoretical difficulties and grave lack of supporting evidence does seem rather futile.

But before we slash our wrists there is one beacon of hope. Many of these hundreds of negative studies would be instantly overturned if an astrologer could be found who delivered the goods under conditions where reasoning errors and other artifacts did not apply. In short, all it needs is one white crow. As the famous psychologist William James said in 1897, "If you wish to upset the law that all crows are black, you must not seek to show that no crows are; it is enough to prove one single crow to be white." Of course the research studies in astrology collectively cover a wider field than could be overturned by a single white crow, but it would be a good start.

For 25 years we have tried our best to find a white crow, as have those skeptic groups around the world who are currently offering a total of over one million dollars to anyone who can demonstrate genuine paranormal powers, astrology included, but without success. (For how to apply, visit the websites www.csicop.org and www.randi.org) There are many tens of thousands of astrologer crows but few seem willing to be proven white—and the few who have come forward have so far proven to be black. This might seem remarkable in view of the whiteness that shines out of astrology books, but such is the case. It might of course seem unremarkable to anyone familiar with phrenology.

Recently one of us (Smit) discovered a rare Dutch book describing a test of Leo Knegt (1882-1957), one of the Netherlands' most famous astrologers. Knegt was given the anonymous birth data of ten people and had to describe their character and circumstances. Because he was given no details whatever, this was far harder than a matching test—he had to describe each person from scratch. Unknown to Knegt, each person had a distinctive life, e.g. a university professor, a fantastic swindler, and an unsuccessful job-seeker, so to achieve a hit he would have to be very specific. And he was, ten times out of ten. For the swindler Knegt correctly predicted fraud and an unexpected scary end (it was actually suicide), and for the unsuccessful job-seeker he correctly predicted she would eventually find a job on a passenger ship. Not only was this the kind of specificity that many modern astrologers claim is impossible, it was achieved using only nine planets (the year was 1933 and Pluto had only just been discovered). Unfortunately the test had none of the features such as controls that we would consider essential today, so these results are difficult to assess. So we have only one option—we must try to repeat the test.

Q: And did you try?

Researchers: Yes. Smit compiled a new test using five of the ten cases for which Knegt had been successful. This new test asked astrologers to match case histories to birth data, a much easier task than the one given to Knegt even without the fewer number of charts. Furthermore, because Knegt had been successful, it could not be argued that the new test was poorly designed—the charts had clearly delivered the goods that astrologers want. If Knegt could succeed in such a difficult task, other astrologers should succeed in this much easier task using the same data. You could hardly get a fairer test!

Q: Sounds reasonable enough. What happened?

Researchers: In order to reach as large an audience as possible, the entire membership and council of the Astrological Association (over 1500 astrologers and students) were canvassed through the AA's newsletter 'Transit'. Only two astrologers responded, so readers of the smaller but more active international monthly 'Astrologers' Forum' were canvassed, which increased the total to 23. Their performance was poor (this is the result labelled 'Smit' in Figure 2) and their agreement was even slightly worse than expected by chance. Astrologers will have to do better than this if they are to stop high-profile skeptics concluding publicly that white crows do not exist, and that astrology has nothing to contribute to science or philosophy. So, to answer your original question: is it likely that the emerging picture will change? Don't ask us, ask astrologers about white crows. The ball is firmly in their court.

Q: The conclusion that astrology has nothing to contribute to science or philosophy would no doubt be disputed by astrologers.

Researchers: But go to any university library or large public library and look at modern works of science or philosophy. They almost never mention astrology. This is true even in the two fields closest to astrology, namely psychology and astronomy. Of the two dozen histories of psychology published since 1970, only two mention astrology, and even then only as an example of pseudo-science. No modern astronomical theory has been even slightly influenced by astrology. The reason is simple.

Q: Prejudice?

Researchers: No, track record. Astrology has been spectacularly unfruitful in guiding enquiry, mainly because it makes much less sense than existing theories. Which is why scientists and philosophers ignore astrology except for historical purposes. Nevertheless if astrology explained things for which there was no other conceivable explanation, or if it led to useful new discoveries such as new energies or channels of communication, they would immediately become interested.

Q: Perhaps we might look again at what you have defined as 'subjective astrology'. Could you give an example of research into this?

Researchers: In subjective astrology we are concerned with astrology as the language of images, metaphors and similes. The art form closest to astrology is poetry because both rely on words whereas music and pictures do not. Indeed, some astrologers hold that astrology is a form of poetry in disguise.

So our example involves poetry.

We can describe the best poetry quite simply. It is beautiful, it conveys the poet's passion and feeling, and it reveals inner meaning. The same is true of the best astrology. It is beautiful, it makes us care, and it reveals inner meaning. But note how subjective everything is. Who is to say what is beautiful, worthy of passion, and meaningful? But this is art, not science. Here we are concerned only with feeling. What matters is that our hearts are moved. Now the logical next step.

Could an understanding of poetry improve the practice of astrology? If poetry moves hearts better than prose does, could we improve a chart interpretation by writing it as a poem? These are the questions some of us looked at. The results were rather fruitful. For astrologers they suggested three useful things: (1) if your technique *feels* right, be it ever so humble, then for you it *is* right; (2) by the same token, it will not feel right for clients unless they share your particular sensitivities and understanding; (3) good poetry takes time. Before making an interpretation you should allow the chart to incubate in your unconscious, allowing its factors to translate spontaneously into poetry.

Q: What of those clients who come to an astrologer seeking straightforward answers to questions on health, wealth and romance? How would your poetry findings apply to them?

Researchers: Probably not at all, because this would no longer be subjective astrology. It would no doubt be okay if clients wanted only sympathy or spiritual uplift, but if they also wanted something factual then we are back to objective astrology and the dismal emerging picture. Actually your question uncovers a fundamental dilemma. Astrology seems unlikely to feel right unless astrologers and clients share a belief in objective astrology. Otherwise why bother with accurate charts? The same dilemma applied in phrenology. Phrenology worked because people believed (incorrectly) that it worked. If phrenologists had said (correctly) that phrenology uses interesting superstitions to stimulate self examination, or that phrenology is basically tea and sympathy, would clients have bothered?

Q: How would you resolve this dilemma?

Researchers: The dilemma is without doubt an agonising one. But it is one that only astrologers, not researchers, can resolve.

Credibility Problems

Q: What would you consider to be the most harmful things to astrology's credibility?

Researchers: We see five things as severely reducing astrology's credibility. First is the refusal to acknowledge the disconfirmation of claims. Perhaps the most disconfirmed claim in astrology is that of Sun-signs, yet the outpouring of fiction disguised as Sun-sign books seems unending.

Second is the dramatic disagreement on fundamentals such as which zodiac [works best], which house system if any, what planets once past the first seven, what aspects, what orbs, what methods of direction, and so on. Surely after several millenia there should be better agreement than this. There is not even agreement on how the fundamentals are supposed to work. In public it is asserted that the stars only incline and only acausally, but this conflicts with the conversation at any astrology conference—yes, I gesture a lot but that's because I'm a Gemini, or I have a strong Jupiter so I'm very religious, or we get on (or don't get on) because our Suns are in opposition, or Uranus always brings accidents, or Saturn is retrograde making financial markets unsettled. No acausal inclination here.

Third is the poor agreement between astrologers judging the same chart. For example, various astrologers have worked backwards from the life events of Ronald Reagan to produce over 30 different birth times spanning 15 hours, each one supposedly definitive according to the astrologer concerned. Even for a simple chart reading the agreement between astrologers is generally so poor that it is scarcely better than tossing a coin—a finding confirmed by more than two dozen studies (the mean correlation was 0.10), including those made by some of us. What price astrology if astrologers cannot even agree on what a chart means?

Fourth is the stagnation of astrology. When we look at psychology or sociology we find disciplines that have advanced because workers have been responsive to disconfirming evidence and alternative ideas. Their textbooks are packed with research studies and critical comparisons of competing theories, often with emphasis on areas needing investigation. Not so in astrology. Except in very rare cases, there is no critical evaluation of ideas and claims, no basing of theory on empirical results, and no mention of negative evidence except to explain it away. Instead astrology has stagnated into a continuing war between one untested idea and another. In 1973 the US astrologer Dr Zip Dobyns complained that, "Astrology is almost as confused as the earthly chaos it is supposed to clarify." Today it is even worse, which is hardly a sound basis for a profession or even a religion. Nevertheless astrology books still read as if they have the Rosetta stone for life on Earth.

Fifth, perhaps worst of all, is ignorance of existing research and of problems due to errors in human reasoning. This leads to making claims at variance with the evidence. Astrologers need to be more careful, which is nothing not already required of any ethical discipline. Our five points would of course be weakened to the extent that white crows could be found. They might disappear altogether if astrologers were to publicly define astrology as a religion, and then refrain (as priests do) from making claims that could be contradicted by scientific enquiry.

Q: What in the world of astrology do you see as helpful or beneficial to people?

Researchers: Good persons. A warm and sympathetic astrologer provides non-threatening therapy that is sometimes hard to come by, especially as no admission of some physical, mental, or moral weakness is required, as with a doctor or psychiatrist or priest.

Q: And what do you see as unhelpful or harmful?

Researchers: Bad persons. Donna Cunningham in her book 'An Astrological Guide to Self-Awareness' (CRCS, 1978) suggests we avoid the guru, the power-hungry, the astro-junkie, the totally negative, the totally positive, the prurient peeping tom, and the spotlight seeker.

Education and Critical Thinking

Q: Earlier you felt that the failure of astrologers to 'be careful' was one of their main faults. How might this be addressed?

Researchers: The single most important factor in helping astrologers be careful might be an improvement in their general education. This would be a necessary first step in correcting the five harmful influences on astrology's credibility that we talked about.

Q: And what do you think this improved general education for astrologers should include?

Researchers: To be adequately educated astrologers need to be informed about *all* aspects of applied astrology. Not just astrology but also related disciplines, not just counselling skills but also religion, philosophy, psychology, statistics (because astrology is probabilistic) and research methods. They need to be aware of the errors in reasoning to which they seem so abundantly prone. If they advocate subjective astrology then they need to refrain from making statements open to scientific challenge. If they advocate objective astrology then they need to be familiar with research results (all of them, not just the ones selected to support a particular view) and with informed criticisms of astrology (not just the nonsense put out by hostile debunkers). And before anyone starts to study any kind of astrology they need to acquire the critical thinking skills that today are part of any university course in the social sciences. Until they do such things, astrologers cannot expect to know what they are talking about.

Q: What do you mean by 'critical thinking skills'?

Researchers: Critical thinking is about evaluating evidence, judging conclusions, and considering alternatives. It gives teeth to rigour. Consider psychology, perhaps the single discipline nearest to astrology. In 1998 a survey of the 37 current introductory psychology texts found that 25 treated critical thinking in some detail, typically 1000-2000 words. This is in addition to the entire books that already exist on critical thinking. By contrast none of the hundreds of introductory astrology texts examined by us over the years give any hint that critical thinking even exists, even though it could hardly be more relevant to their implied invitation to 'test astrology for yourself'.

Modern Science and Astrology

Q: Are there developments in modern science which weaken the case against astrology as being intrinsically impossible?

Researchers: Nothing that we know of. If by astrology we mean the ideas found in astrology books, such as Saturn rising signifies an inhibited personality or adverse Mars transits incline to accidents, then in our opinion there are no developments in modern science that would support such ideas. But if by astrology we mean 'the way most astrologers behave', i.e. with no basing of theory on empirical results, no consideration of negative evidence except to explain it away, and no serious verification of a continuing profusion of claims, there would seem to be no developments in modern science, even in principle, that could possibly restore the feasibility of such sloppiness. Only a more disciplined approach by astrologers could succeed here.

Q: This seems dismissive. Astrologers have pointed to numerous developments that supposedly make astrology more plausible, such as fractals, interconnectedness, the theories of Bohm, Pribram, Sheldrake, and so on. Are these of no relevance?

Researchers: Even if science did turn out to be based on say interconnectedness, astrologers have not explained how this would support the idea that the heavens reflect what happens on Earth, let alone ideas such as Leos being generous. It is like saying astrology involves books, cooking involves books, therefore cooking makes astrology more plausible. Crucial steps in the argument are missing.

The theories are physicist David Bohm's idea of implicate order, where connections between things can exist independent of space and time; neuropsychologist Karl Pribram's idea of holographic order, where time and space are collapsed into a single frequency so that normal causality (which requires time and space for its operation) no longer applies; and plant physiologist Rupert Sheldrake's idea of morphic resonance, where the form of past systems has a cumulative effect on the form of subsequent similar systems. But astrologers do not erect charts by ignoring space and time or by collapsing them into a single frequency or by assuming they all have the same form. Indeed, the idea of morphic resonance suggests that, over the centuries, astrologies around the world should have become more similar, and astrological effects should have become more noticeable, but neither seems to be the case.

Claiming that such ideas make astrology more plausible, or that they explain why Leos are generous, is like claiming that rhubarb explains why airplanes fly. Until the steps in the argument are spelled out, it remains circular—astrology is made feasible by the kind of thing that, if it existed, would make astrology feasible. To bring support to astrology we need to know *exactly* how astrology is supported, but astrologers never tell us. Their arguments never even get started.

Q: There seems no doubt that various modern theories such as quantum mechanics are attempts to explain real phenomena, and that these phenomena do not fit within the Newtonian model, which is often blamed (or praised) for undermining belief in astrology. If a model that undermines astrology is flawed, surely the undermining is also flawed, which might conceivably restore feasibility to astrology?

Researchers: It does not follow. The discovery that quantum phenomena are real and undermine Newton's ideas does not necessarily restore the feasibility of astrology, just as the discovery that atoms are mostly empty space undermined Dalton's idea of oxygen but did not restore the feasibility of phlogiston. [Nor does] the undermining of one theory necessarily have any effect on the many other theories (in astronomy, in psychology, in medicine, in statistics) that are equally incompatible with astrology. As before, crucial steps in the argument are missing. In any case, how can any kind of theory restore feasibility to something for which there is no convincing evidence to start with? It is like asking for a theory to explain flying elephants.

Q: We ought not to omit a mention of Jung's synchronicity. In the past this has been the idea that astrologers have most often quoted in support of astrology. Is there anything you can say about it?

Researchers: Astrologers see synchronicity as a meaningful coincidence, but Jung saw it as more than that. Among other things he held that it was unlikely to occur unless the observer is experiencing strong archetypal emotions (see his 'Letters', 1976, volume 2, p.537). So it would require the chart reader to experience the most intense archetypal fear, anger, joy, sorrow, love, hatred, etc., in rapid succession. No reader or client could stand it. And even if they could, such intense emotions would impair their reasoning. So synchronicity is not the answer.

In 1931, before he invented synchonicity, Jung had his famous idea that "whatever is born or done in this moment of time has the quality of this moment of time," which of course seems perfectly matched to astrological claims. But there are problems—his idea implies that time quality is the same instantaneously throughout the universe, which is no help at all (light travels too slowly for us to ever know what that instantaneous condition is). So if time quality is to explain astrology, it has to be localised. In this case the relevance of the outer planets (even all the planets) might be denied, which presumably is not what astrologers have in mind. So time quality is probably not the answer either.

Complexity and Mind

Q: An alternative view is that it is not possible to talk about astrology as a single, coherent technique. Instead, each astrologer necessarily forges their own approach (e.g. by using midpoints or not), in which case there could be as many different astrologies as there are astrologers.

Researchers: To obtain a judgement from a given chart, astrologers have to juggle many factors at once, typically 40 for the traditional natal chart and 60 for an Ebertin midpoint chart. That's just for starters—a genuine whole chart is immeasurably more complex (see Figure 3). But our short-term memory cannot juggle more than about 5-9 chunks of information at a time, as is apparent whenever we try dialling an unfamiliar 10-digit telephone number. As a result the information content of the chart *always* exceeds our capacity to handle it. This means that astrologers cannot do what they say they do, namely juggle unaided every chart factor simultaneously. Instead they are forced to focus on whatever tiny subset of factors their experience or their teacher's experience has shown to 'work'. But the subset that 'works' is rarely the same from one astrologer to another. One astrologer may use factors such as midpoints or asteroids that the other rejects, which has led to the idea that every astrologer forges their own approach—and, of course, to the idea that astrology is even more mysterious (or perhaps even more problematic and implausible) than we might think. Exactly what are we talking about if every astrologer's definition of astrology is different?

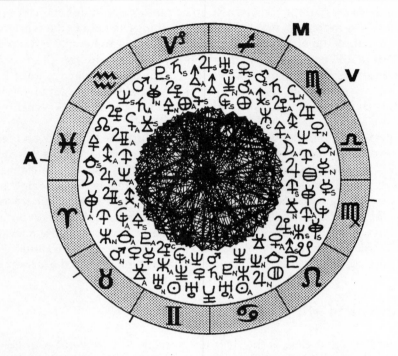

Figure 3. The superchart
Contains only those factors proposed and testified to by astrologers of some standing. With 20 words of delineation per sign position, aspect, etc., the result would be larger than the London or New York telephone directory (all you need is one client and you have enough work for the rest of your life, forecasts extra). But even this is a drop in the ocean compared to what a genuine whole chart would contain. Reproduced with permission from 'Recent Advances in Natal Astrology', p.35.

Q: Surely the situation is not unique to astrology?

Researchers: It applies quite generally where variables are numerous and ill-defined. For example, when people judge the aesthetic quality of artworks, the number of possible criteria is so large that they are forced to consider only a subset. But the subsets differ between persons and between occasions, leading to spectacular disagreement. Thus a given work may be top-rated by one and bottom-rated by another. Contrary to expectation, training in art reduces disagreement only slightly and may even increase it, so perhaps we should not be surprised by the disagreement among astrologers despite their training in astrology. But training in *art criticism* does tend to reduce disagreement, which suggests that training in *astrology criticism* (i.e. critical thinking) might have similar beneficial effects.

Q: But why should the complexity of the chart preclude the discovery and application of patterns at a relatively simple level—that of ten planets and twelve signs, for instance?

Researchers: The situation changes if we consider only a few isolated factors, or only factors consistent with the broad picture (which is whatever our favourite technique says it is), because our minds are then able to cope with the resulting simplicity. But there is a snag: everything is supposed to interact with everything else, so all we can observe are combinations, and even then (because the stars only incline, or because other factors were not considered) the outcomes might not be true to type. It would be like having a clock that might or might not be working, and trying to tell the time from just a few of its countless cogwheels. It could not be done. In short, we can cope with what tradition forbids, but we cannot cope with what tradition requires.

Q: Perhaps this is the source of much of the mystery, and the confusion, which surrounds astrology.

Researchers: But the mystery and confusion might be an illusion. As far as we know the perceived chart correspondences arise only through reasoning errors. So the different approaches confidently adopted by different astrologers are precisely equivalent to the different poses confidently adopted by Skinner's pigeons. (Their pose was whatever it was when food was first delivered into their individual feeding tray, which led them to believe their pose brought food, so they stayed with that pose, which then necessarily confirmed their belief even though the subsequent deliveries were actually at random, hence their confident but completely different poses.) That is, the diversity of approaches confidently adopted by astrologers is more plausibly explained by reasoning errors than by invoking mysteries. Again, because reasoning errors can lead astrologers to believe in correspondences that do not actually exist, we can hardly view the conflict between approaches as something special. Indeed, conflict would be predicted, just as the pigeons' differing poses would be predicted. Of course this explanation rather brutally de-mystifies the chart reading process, but the chips fall where they may.

Q: I imagine that what many astrologers will find surprising, and perhaps disappointing, about your approach is that there is no real debate about the nature of mind, the nature of reality, and the way in which we perceive reality.

Researchers: We find this hard to understand. First, our concern for reasoning errors is in effect precisely about such topics. Second, astrology books do not hedge their bets with such debates, so how are they suddenly relevant? Third, 'real debate' seems premature until astrology has been shown to work under conditions where reasoning errors are controlled. In short, what has mind/reality/perception to do with testing whether astrologers can pick correct charts from controls? How can it be relevant when astrologers give readings without worrying whether client and chart are real, or a figment of the mind, or a misperception?

Q: The same astrologers might say that astrology raises the most interesting questions about the nature of subject and object, the nature of perception, and the nature of truth and its relativity.

Researchers: We don't see how. If you check the psychological and philosophical literature you will find these questions are discussed at great length without any mention of astrology. And with good reason. Why should a process heavily prone to reasoning errors raise questions about the nature of truth? It is like claiming the nature of piano playing is questioned by wearing boxing gloves.

Q: Much of this discussion has been about 'objective astrology', as you have characterised it. But supposing that every astrologer in the world held up their hands tomorrow and said, "We admit it—astrology is an entirely subjective art." How would that affect your research?

Researchers: The research implications are then rather different. Subjective astrology is more like a religion, and researching it would be like researching a religion, where we examine its effects on people rather than its content. Research would focus not on the actual beliefs but on how people use them and are affected by them. For example, to study how astrological counselling works we could apply the same procedures used to study ordinary psychological counselling. The problem is that if you believe it is all foolish nonsense then by its own rules you are right. The implication is that subjective astrology should compete with other forms of counselling on an effectiveness scale determined by scientific investigation.

At the same time we should not make the mistake of treating astrology as if astrologers did not matter. For example, it is a common experience that clients (unless suffering from a genuine organic condition) prefer astrologers to psychiatrists because they find the former more caring, or more approachable, or more sympathetic to their religious views, and so on, all of which are attributes of the astrologer rather than of astrology. On this basis, whatever our views of astrology, if it encourages people to explore and express humane and spiritual values or to examine the problems of mankind's existence, if it does so in ways that are gentle and respectful or inspiring and uplifting, if in a chaotic world it provides individual retreat or support, if it helps provide a bridge between a person of wisdom and a person in need, then these qualities deserve study as much as any objective claim. Our respect for these qualities should not be diminished by our rejecting, at the same time, astrology as a source of scientific knowledge. There is more to astrology than being true or false.

Summary

Q: So why are you still interested in astrology? Why haven't you just given up hope and turned your backs on it?

Researchers: No matter what attitude we might have towards astrology, the experiences of astrologers and their clients are themselves fascinating, whether or not they prove to be astrological. Similarly, something that so many people believe in has to be worthy of study, whether or not the reasons prove to be astrological. Of course, study may not be easy or quick or financially rewarding, but with skill, care and knowledge we can do it. That is, if we want to—and surely we should. As for your second question, none of us has vested interests in astrology, so there are no particular results we could 'hope' for. If we do turn our backs on astrology, it will be because we have finished our researches, not because we have given up hope.

Q: So would you recommend anyone to take up astrological research?

Researchers: If the aim is to prove that astrological claims are true, the chance of a positive result strong enough to overturn the present predominantly negative evidence seems remote. In effect there is no good case for the investment of research dollars because the competition from other more profitable areas is simply too great. But as mentioned in our previous answer, the picture improves if the aim is no longer to prove astrology. The area remains worthy of study. Even so, students who hope it will open the door to research grants may be disappointed.

Q: One last question. For the benefit of readers who may feel overwhelmed, could you provide a summary of your position?

Researchers: Four things:

First—Astrology is no longer the mystery it used to be. Most of the important questions that can be asked now have answers that are generally consistent.

Second—The claim that astrology works implies that all non-astrological influences leading to the same result have been ruled out. Don't accept the first unless you can be sure of the second.

Third—Ask yourself if your kind of astrology needs to be true. If no, you are safe. If yes, you are on shaky ground, so ask yourself which alternative is the more likely: (1) that pervasive astrological influences exist that contradict known science (yet on whose nature astrologers spectacularly disagree); or (2) that the many known errors in human reasoning (of which most astrologers are spectacularly unaware) explain astrological beliefs.

Fourth—Whatever our views of astrology, they cannot deny its historical importance, and nor should they deny our open-mindedness to possible future discoveries in astrology and in extraterrestrial influences.

That ended the collective interview. I then asked each researcher for a personal view. The replies were as follows:

Dean: Readers' comments are most welcome. We want to hear from you. Send comments by email to rhsmit@smitpotze.demon.nl

Ertel: Despite our refuting astrology as a source of knowledge we should acknowledge the stimulating effect of the Gauquelins' prolific research. Although some of their purported discoveries have been disconfirmed there remains a core that has withstood my own and other researchers' independent tests. If this core cannot be explained by parental tampering of birth data, we would need some more demanding explanation, which, in my view, might eventually help to improve our understanding of mankind's place in the universe. Such understanding would differ considerably from astrology's historical intuitions. Rather, it would have to be consistent with existing astronomical knowledge and with models of cosmological evolution.

Mather: Astrology has been of major historical significance. The resistance so far to its disproof continues to pose a challenge.

Smit: Despite my changed views of astrology, I still cherish very fond memories of my dealings with my then fellow astrologers.

Kelly: On behalf of the group I would like to thank you for focussing on problematic areas that astrologers themselves tend to ignore. We hope your readers will explore these areas further. We also thank Geoffrey Dean for synthesising our diverse views into a mutually agreeable framework. The end result has been one of satisfaction to all of us.

Astrologers on the Status of Astrology

Astrologers are often able to dismiss criticisms of their craft as being based on ignorance of it. The rebuke from astrologer to critic—"Sir, I have studied it and you have not" (widely attributed to Sir Isaac Newton, though probably apocryphal)—is part of any self-respecting astrologer's collection of curt rejoinders, and is entirely reasonable in many situations. There are also, however, questions and doubts that are raised by people who have learned, practised and (for a time) been convinced by astrology; David Hamblin and some of the Researchers belong to this group, and the criticisms they raise have been covered in the last three chapters. What remains is to consider how astrologers view such criticisms (with a few links to parallels in other disciplines), before pondering possible conclusions on the status of astrology.

Natural and Judicial Astrology Revisited

This distinction, first touched upon in Chapter VIII, is fundamental to the matter in hand. The two terms can be defined, in a rough and ready way, like this:

Natural Astrology: astrology is seen as a set of scientifically quantifiable laws, which could (in theory at least) be coded into a computer program and produce accurate information about events in the world, characteristics of people and organisations, etc. Its reliability depends only on the correct techniques being applied and sufficient information being analysed.

Judicial Astrology: astrology is considered to be essentially law-less, working through a direct hook-up between astrologer and universe, which transcends categorisation or technique. This might be called magic. Its reliability depends on the quality of the astrologer's intuition.

In practice, most astrologers view what they do as existing somewhere between the extremes of 'natural' and 'judicial'—just as a footballer, or a musician, could consider that their performance depends upon a knowledge of the relevant techniques, plus a subjective quality that they might call 'inspiration'.

This distinction between natural and judicial astrology is what (for instance) Graeme Tobyn has in mind when he says "...I don't believe in objective astrology..." (Chapter VI) He doesn't accept that the act of reading a chart could ever be reduced to a sequence of operations in a computer program; the astrologer's intuition (for want of a better word) is a necessary part of the equation.

It needs to be stressed that this way of thinking about *how astrology works* is different from that employed by the Researchers when they discuss their categories of 'subjective' and 'objective' astrology. As they use them, these terms refer to the *information provided by astrology*. Hence objective astrology 'needs to be true', whilst subjective astrology 'does not need to be true'.

This, however, gives a misleading impression of astrologers (something that I am sure the Researchers would not want to do). To talk of an approach where chart readings 'do not have to be true', where 'we are concerned only with feeling' makes it sound as though some astrologers really think that way. Every astrologer I interviewed believes with some passion that their art can reveal genuine information about the world. Those who lose this conviction do not say, "Shame about that—I'll be a fantasy astrologer then." They stop practising astrology—as did David Hamblin, Geoffrey Dean, Arthur Mather and Rudolf Smit.

Perhaps the Researchers' suggestion that, even if astrology turns out not to be true, astrologers could still continue to practise 'subjective astrology' is grounded in the fond memories of using astrology that some of them have, and a consequent wish to avoid finding themselves in a position where they have to advise all astrologers to abandon their pernicious practices forthwith. The desire for tolerance may be admirable, but as they themselves acknowledge, "Astrology seems unlikely to feel right unless astrologers and clients share a belief in objective astrology"; hence it is cold comfort to suggest that disillusioned astrologers could spend their twilight years practising 'subjective astrology'.

Astrologers believe that they can get real information from the chart, and they need to believe this in order to motivate themselves to read charts. This means that the questions raised by scientists in the last two chapters could hardly be more significant for astrologers. For all that, an account of how they typically respond might begin by noting that eagerness for dialogue is not unanimous:

Q: Suppose someone suggests that all of these examples (where astrology seems to give accurate results) just represent the workings of chance. How would you answer?

John Frawley: I wouldn't bother.

Or, again:

Bernadette Brady: Personally I am not out to convert anybody. I am not one of these astrologers that does research to try and *prove* it to those scientists. I am not interested in that. That's not a valid exercise in my opinion. I am far more interested in doing research to actually learn how it works, so I can apply it in things.

Like Frawley and Brady, many astrologers regard scientific tests and research into astrology as (in one way or another) misguided, and therefore uninteresting. Of the membership of the UK's Astrological Association, only about 25% part with the £11 per year currently required for subscription to the journal 'Correlation', one of the main forums for the science/astrology dialogue. Many astrologers, it seems, do not believe in science.

This lack of interest is by no means universal, however, and there are also astrologers who feel that astrology could gain a great deal through dialogue with other disciplines.

Nicholas Campion: I would like to see more intelligent discussion of astrology. One of the reasons I'm focussing my PhD on contemporary astrology is that a lot of journalists phone up and ask if astrology is becoming more successful and more popular, and if so why. Most people assume that it is indeed becoming more popular, and people outside astrology will assume that the reason is that it is a replacement for religion. The churches are emptying, the theory runs, so people turn to Tarot, paganism, mother goddesses, and astrology, and so on. So one reason I'm doing the PhD is to look at those questions that have arisen out of journalistic interviews.

What I'm keen to do is to explain astrology, not defend it blindly. I don't want to be like politicians who unquestioningly follow the party line. I like to make sure that if astrology is criticised, it's criticised intelligently rather than unintelligently. I can't defend astrology uncritically, because in my mind I'm much too tangled up with all the complexities and complications of different positions on astrology. But I can explain it, and explain astrologers' positions, and also explain the anti-astrology position. So the approach I try and take is a neutral one, actually, of looking at both positions equally. I think that's fair enough, because the astrological position—if explained properly—is a lot stronger than it's usually represented. And the anti-astrology position contains a lot of flaws and weaknesses.

In Praise of Astrological Research

The remainder of this chapter will be an examination of what astrologers see as the 'flaws and weaknesses' in the 'anti-astrology position'. It is, perhaps, timely to note here that the distinction used over the last two chapters, between 'scientists' (or 'researchers') and 'astrologers', does not exist as an absolute; some scientists are also astrologers, and vice-versa. One such, Pat Harris, believes that many of the problems with research into astrology can be traced to inappropriate methods and/or a lack of astrological knowledge:

Pat Harris: On the subject of inter-relationships between astrologers and scientists (I am both): someone must learn someone else's language before there can be communication and understanding. Eventually, there is cross pollination. I have seen this at the Research Group for the Critical Study of Astrology (RGCSA*), recently installed at Southampton University, and created to facilitate this bringing together of the two communities (amongst other objectives). The word 'critical' in that title does not—here at least—mean 'subject to intensely negative destructive analysis'. It means unbiased rigorous analysis in order to facilitate a fuller understanding. Having mentioned analysis, it is necessary to distinguish two approaches:

---

* More details of the RGCSA will be found in Appendix 1.

1. The traditional method of data analysis, where you decide what you are looking for, then check your data to see if it is there.

2. The more modern approach (increasingly taught, in social science at any rate), of allowing your data to inform you. In this approach, you allow data to reveal its patterns and then interpret what those patterns represent *within the context of your study*. Pattern recognition is essential to good research in astrology. The Gauquelins did this, and it is an approach which is perfectly acceptable in modern scientific research*.

Many astrologers do become very defensive in the face of 'scientific scrutiny', but this may be largely due to the way the traditional method of analysis was mis-applied to astrology in the past. In the last decade (at the very least), research methods in the social sciences have changed greatly and become much more conducive to the kind of exploration which is needed to understand astrology and its apparent 'phenomena' better.

I take the point very seriously that you can design studies that will fail. But the real problem, from my point of view as a research astrologer in the social sciences, is that bad study designs are a product of laziness and/or ignorance, where researchers simply have not gained access to good research papers and do not properly understand the subject they are researching.

An example is the well-known case of a study undertaken to examine the incidence of kidney disease among patients with the Sun in the sign of Libra. The birthdates of 360 patients admitted to an area nephrology unit between August and October 1989 were studied for a significant correspondence between the number of patients admitted for kidney disease and incidence of Sun in the sign of Libra (Hughes, 1990). A chi-square test showed no significant association—"thus disproving the traditional astrologers' claims", the study concluded. The study was supported by four references: one of the references used to support the author's observation that "astrologers presume a link between the susceptibility of particular organs to disease and signs of the Zodiac" was taken from Margaret Hone's 'The Modern Text Book of Astrology', with specific reference to a table of suggested correspondences where the part of the body associated with Libra is shown as 'kidneys'. This table does not indicate kidney disease for those people born with the Sun in Libra; even later in the book (not cited by the author of the paper) where Hone suggests the predominantly Libran person is "usually healthy, but inclined to headaches and kidney trouble" she does not state that people with [just] the Sun in Libra are inclined to kidney trouble.

The researcher had not tracked down the extant research and literature, which suggested a correlation between *Saturn* (not the Sun) and certain configurations of Saturn in Libra with kidney disease (Dr. Davidson, 1973). The

---

* These two approaches are the hypothetico-deductive and inductive methods, widely known in the philosophy of social science. See, eg. 'Hypothetico-Deductive Method' (Johnson, 2000).

author excused his paucity of references by stating that, "The only recent papers to study astrology and illness were based upon psychiatric rather than physical morbidity." But as he was drawing his hypothesis from traditional astrology he would have done well to study the works of William Lilly and Nicholas Culpeper, two among many astrologers who wrote and researched on astrology in medical practice. I suspect that he did not do this because the material could not be accessed on the social science research databases. The outcome was that this researcher had taken a popularised unsubstantiated observation and wasted time, money and effort to pursue a useless hypothesis. The RGCSA aims to make good astrological research available to prevent this kind of ignorance from continuing.

So, I think it is very much a matter of going into the scientific community and sorting out its weaknesses in relation to astrological research, correcting it by education and then monitoring the results. This will stop much of the rubbish research that scientists get away with when trying to analyse astrological phenomena.

On the Limitations of Science

Another astrologer-scientist is Lee Lehman, who has a PhD in botany. I was keen to hear how her experience of training as a scientist had influenced her:

Q: Do you feel as though your scientific background gives you an edge that many astrologers don't have?

Lee Lehman: It has certainly changed the way that I approach astrology. There's a tremendous advantage to it in the sense that I have a very serious approach to research. I do like to see numbers, and I do like to look at populations. But the other thing is, I had reached a point with science of realising that there is very little that is done, using the scientific method, which can in any way represent ultimate truth. It's beyond some of the religious or philosophical questions that we astrologers normally think about. It simply becomes obvious, when you are on the inside doing the experiments, that there isn't an air-tight experiment. There just isn't.

For example, when I think back about ten years or so, when James Randi went after the homeopaths, he went into one of the laboratories and basically just trashed the thing. I remember reading about that in 'Science' magazine*. I realised that, had anyone applied that level of skepticism to any biology lab, any place on the globe, *the same thing would have happened*. It's just that 'real science' has certain rules of engagement, so that everybody suspends disbelief

---

* For the original article: Maddox, Randi & Stewart, 1988. For comments thereon: Pool, 1988; Bauer, 1994, p.58f.

around some critical issues. Since everybody operates that way, it's like this collective mask. But since astrology is outside the pale, they actually apply a different standard to us than they would do to themselves.

On the one hand, this gives me some real insights into why the so-called scientific approach to skepticism isn't appropriate for us. At the same time, it leaves me skeptical of our methods too, and so I like a little more in the way of a method than the statement 'it works for me'.

Q: Do you think it's possible for astrologers to talk with the scientific skeptics on their own terms, and if so what do you think astrology's strongest suit is?

Lee Lehman: I think a lot of the issue with the skeptics is that we, as a community, have been willing to cede too much to them. What we have is really a political issue, more than a knowledge issue or a philosophical issue.

Let me go back to what I meant when I said that any scientific experiment would be destroyed in the same way by that level of skepticism, because I think this then reflects on the answer to why the skeptical approach is—in my opinion—very insidious. Interestingly, it has had much more of an effect over here [in the UK] than it ever had in the States, because it just never had the level of influence in the States.

What I mean is, for example, when I was doing my post-doc, I was working at the Public Health Research Institute in New York City. I was doing very mundane work, working on protein synthesis in a particular virus that had been isolated from the East River in New York. Most of the people on my floor were doing similar kinds of protein and DNA or RNA analysis. The method of choice for doing these analyses was something called electrophoretic gel—which is simply a matrix in which you could separate out different nucleic acids or proteins using an electrical field. Then if you had made the isotopes radioactive to begin with, as we did, you could put a photographic plate on it and get results.

OK—sounds extremely cut and dried, sounds extremely uncontroversial. But the reality is that what everybody would do is this: run a hundred, two hundred, experiments that were pretty much clones of each other, then get one absolutely stunning result, and that one result would be published. The other 199 would never be mentioned. Everybody would take this as absolutely normal. Yet obviously, if you had had someone in there who was skeptical of the whole thing, they'd be saying, "You just threw out 199 experiments to take one!?" Obviously, this is an extreme double-standard.

This is why I say we've made a mistake in allowing too much criticism because what that period in the lab taught me is that had I stayed in science I would have been extremely dangerous. I learned that I could design any experiment to produce positive or negative results—almost at will; and that I could do this simply by the way I designed the experiment.

For example, if you are of a skeptical nature, it is extremely easy to design an astrological experiment that will fail. I saw several of these pop up at the old UK research conferences when I used to go to those, back in the '80s. There was one, for example—a study that was done on Pluto and the Moon. They were asking people ten questions such as, "Are you obsessive about [blank]?" That was the question. It was so stupid, because if you ask the Pluto-Moon person, they are going to say, "No! I'm not obsessive!" But if you ask their friends…! This is the issue of self-attribution. And this was designed by somebody who, in anybody else's experiment, would have been crying, "Foul! Self-attribution!" This is what I mean by different standards, this is what I mean by how to design an experiment to fail. That particular experiment, when it was analysed, failed. Well, duh! I looked at the sheet when it was being passed out and said, "This is going to fail."

So this is one side of it: you can very deliberately design an experiment to fail. The other side of it, however, is that I don't think many astrological statements should be approached statistically anyway. I think that one of the questions we don't stop to talk about is the whole issue of when the quantitative methods apply. Perfect case in point: horary. If somebody is asking me a question about [whether they'll get] married to somebody, they aren't interested in a statistical answer! They are interested in an absolute answer. I cannot take the rules of horary and simply boil them down to say, "Well, this chart had seven yeses and three nos, so that means that 70% of the time this will be a yes." I wouldn't be getting paid very well if that was my approach. So I think we do need to stop and ask these questions.

I think we can only ask these questions when there are enough of us in the astrological community who have the mathematical background to be able to ask the questions intelligently, so as to not be intimidated by a word like 'statistics'. Then we can really take the material and say, "OK, this is an interesting idea, this isn't an interesting idea." I think a lot of the quantitative studies that we can do, and should do, are more along the lines of giving us some insight into how something is working rather than making an absolute statement like, "Having this in the Gauquelin sector produces the following result." Because most of the time when you are working on a statistical level, you can't end up with that conclusion anyway because it isn't a valid statistical statement.

I guess I've always been a bit of a crier of "The emperor has no clothes!" I can remember when I was on my post-doc, I would do things like walk into labs where they were studying 'flu viruses and say, "So, how come everybody didn't get 'flu this year, when we were all exposed?" You'd get this little mantra about, "Well, people have different immunological capabilities…" I always knew that that was just a cop-out, just a way of saying, "We don't have a clue, so here's some jargon."

What was fascinating to me was that I couldn't see anyone else in the lab who was even interested in this. What this told me was that it's so easy for people to learn a procedure, a technology, a word, a concept—and then, you're in the 'in-group', whose rules are: "We of the 'in-group' can manipulate this stuff however we want, and whatever we say is true. And all of us will see it exactly the same way, and we will train you to see it that way. We're all going to share this viewpoint, that this is reality, and our viewpoint is right, and those on the outside don't see it this way because they haven't received the training."

It's a very insidious point of view, and in a sense I would call it cultic. This is no different from what people sometimes accuse religious cults of doing to their members. It's the same thing!

Q: Hmm, scientists as the new priesthood.

Lee Lehman: Oh yes, very much. Except that they're not encouraged to think of themselves that way… "We're just looking for the truth."

Two themes from Lee Lehman's comments are summarised below, before each is looked at in detail.

Open-Mindedness—a question about the impartiality of scientists in general terms; the suggestion that many scientists tend to be prejudiced against astrology, and therefore tend to see evidence against, rather than for, it.

Problems with Research into Astrology—an objection to the way in which scientific tests are designed. The argument is that research does not happen in an intellectual vacuum; experiments are designed by people, with views and opinions. Despite their best intentions, scientists inevitably tend to design experiments that prove what they want to prove. And what they want to prove is not, usually, astrology.

Open-Mindedness

Open-mindedness is, of course, a prerequisite for any examination into a subject such as astrology. A researcher who said, "I studied astrology, but my mind was made up beforehand" would not encourage us to take his findings seriously. An interesting perspective is to be found in this quotation from the Researchers:

Researchers: By forcing us to be neither believers nor disbelievers, astrology has helped us to be genuinely open-minded, so we can now enjoy more easily in other areas the benefits of being open-minded. In short, astrology has made us better able to observe the spirit of science, which ironically seems quite the opposite to its effect on astrologers.

Surely this may not be ironic: perhaps the study of an approach inimical to one's own always tends to stimulate clarity and openness of thought. This, I think, is something the philosopher of science Paul Feyerabend suggests in discussing the elusiveness of true 'open-mindedness'. He asks how it could be possible to "discover the kind of world we presuppose", and concludes: "The answer is clear: we cannot discover it from inside. We need an external standard of criticism, we need a set of alternative assumptions… we need a dream-world in order to discover the features of the real world we think we inhabit." (Feyerabend, 1998, p.22)

Some of the Researchers commented on how stimulating they found the 'cut and thrust' of our dialogue (unfortunately, much of the 'cut and thrust' had to be edited out in order to present their position within the confines of this book; the version to be published on the web may restore this). Perhaps more astrologers could benefit by honing their understanding of what they do by seeing it from the scientific angle. As Feyerabend suggests, exposure to a different worldview can open minds. The question remains to be asked: how long does an open mind remain open? It may be a little rash to assume that once opened, a mind will always remain open to everything…

"Having explicitly learned certain things, scientists and science have at the same time learned implicitly that other things are not so. We could then be truly open-minded only about things that we do not yet know about at all." This is how the scientist Henry H Bauer defines the problem. (Bauer, 1994, p.77.) He points out the contradiction of scientists being expected to deal in reliable, definite facts whilst simultaneously being completely open-minded about everything. As soon as we regard anything as definite, we have—to a certain extent—closed our minds on an alternative. Hence Bauer's conclusion: "The only truly open mind would have to be at the same time a truly empty one. Thus, even the assertion that science should be open-minded makes little sense." (ibid)

Two psychologists who investigated astrology certainly felt that they encountered a lack of open-mindedness in the scientific community: "Many of the people in the scientific establishment would have fitted well into the panel which condemned Galileo! We have become aware of this climate of censorship and intolerance… from remarks warning us that even criticising astrology in detail, and showing familiarity with its pronouncements, would undermine our scientific standing and reputation. So much for the religion of the open mind." (Eysenck and Nias, 1982, p.220)

No doubt there are many people of science who genuinely strive for open-mindedness, Yet even then, the struggle can be considerable, as this personal comment by Suitbert Ertel suggests: "What is wrong with us scientists who kept Gauquelin's claims, brought forward by him since 1955, stifled for four decades? I myself needed the span of 1975 to 1985 to overcome my disgust on imagining that some jelly superstition might have been confirmed by exact statistics." (Ertel & Irving, 1996, p.v) The point that Ertel goes on to make is: "I have come to realize that the Mars effect drama might be symptomatic. It might reflect the fallacy of a lurking pseudo-rationality shared by most members of our scientific institutions."

This 'lurking pseudo-rationality' is, it seems to me, pinned down by Bauer: "Humankind is reluctant to accept that all knowledge contains an irreducible, inherent element of uncertainty. Over the last few centuries, the authority of science came to supersede that of religion precisely because science seemed to offer more certain knowledge." (Bauer 1994, p.61.) In an echo of Lee Lehman's remarks, he concludes that, because of its quasi-religious status, there is a reluctance to accept that the scientific method is, ultimately, a myth. Such iconoclasm has become popular in the recent philosophy of science, with figures such as Feyerabend delighting to suggest that scientific progress has occurred, "Only because some thinkers either *decided* not to be bound by certain 'obvious' methodological rules, or because they *unwittingly broke* them." (Feyerabend, 1988, p.14)

To object to the neo-religious status of science is to consider that scientists overreach themselves by moving from an ability to predict what will happen in specific experiments to an overview of what is real and what is not in the world. This is a point that Robert Hand raised:

> **Robert Hand:** The scientific worldview has very little to do with science. Insofar as science is a set of models and theories designed to interpret and deal with phenomena, I have no quarrel with it at all. But when scientists generalise from that to a metaphysical position—usually very primitively— and say, "This is the only way it can be," that's when I think they go off the rails. But it says nothing about quantum mechanics, nuclear physics, laws of motion or biology or any of that. What astrology says is that some scientists— only some—generate a metaphysical viewpoint out of their perception of physics, which is incorrect.

The criticism of science and its assumptions, however, does nothing to support astrology unless it turns out that these assumptions somehow interfere with science's ability to assess astrological practice. Hence to the next point:

Problems with Research into Astrology

With the best will in the world, preconceptions may intrude into the way in which information is presented. For instance, compare the different spin which can be placed upon the same results:

"Thanks to Michel Gauquelin, astrologers now know that in principle astrology is justified." (West, 1991, p.318)

"(Gauquelin's) planetary effects, even though independently confirmed by us, are too tiny to be of the slightest practical value." (Researchers, Chapter X above)

The statements quoted do not strictly contradict one another; they simply reflect different interpretations of the same research. No matter how rigorous the procedures followed to collect research, it still has to be interpreted by people. I am reminded of Bauer's comment about the Loch Ness monster. He observed that people generally have a firm predisposition to believe in the monster or not—and that they are therefore attracted toward evidence that supports that belief/disbelief. In consequence, attitudes become entrenched and the difficulty of dialogue increases, all because (as he remarks),

"Having to say, 'we simply don't know,' is not particularly easy or pleasant." (Bauer, 1991 p.104). Much the same tends to happen with the Gauquelin findings: the findings show a link between planetary positions and human life, which is inconvenient for skeptics, but they also show no evidence to support the bulk of astrological technique, which is inconvenient for astrologers. In a situation where almost everyone wants a simple answer—either astrology works or it doesn't—the findings suggest that it both works and does not work. Which suits no-one very well.

In considering the role of interpretation in such a situation, it is interesting to note this observation from the Researchers, put forward as potentially invalidating the Gauquelin findings: "The Gauquelin data show evidence of manipulation by parents, for example there is a consistent deficit of births on the 13th, but if parents can manipulate dates then why not hours? In which case the Gauquelin findings might be due to parents, not planets."

As an aside, this illustrates a problem for the acceptance of any substantial astrological research: there will always be something that might have been mis-recorded.

But the main interest of the example is (it seems to me) as an illustration of how difficult it can be to avoid slipping an interpretation into research findings. To illustrate, suppose that there is no significant pattern in the data; then, parental interference might create one—just as, if there were no ripples on a pond, throwing a stone in would create a regular pattern of ripples. But if there actually was a significant pattern to begin with, any mis-recording of the data would be likely to obscure it—just as throwing a second rock into a pond interferes with the pattern of ripples created by the first.

Hence the 'manipulation of data by parents' issue could be used, with equal validity, as an argument for the findings being stronger than previously realised—their strength having been diluted by dirty data. My interest is not to argue this particular point, but rather to illustrate how malleable research findings can be. Our assumptions affect the way we interpret data, inclining us to see the answer (be it yes or no) that we believe should be there. Another illustration, in which evidence can be interpreted as for or against astrology, cropped up in the area of time twin research, and this will be found in Appendix 3.

Neo-Astrology or Neo-Science?

The last book that Michel Gauquelin wrote, 'Neo-Astrology', suggested that astrology as we know it was a crumbling ruin, and that the only way forward was to demolish and rebuild it in the light of research, so that a 'neo-astrology' could be raised up on a foundation of science. The converse of this view can be found amongst a few astrologers who follow developments within modern science. In their view it is classical science, not astrology, whose days are numbered; they argue that it is time to demolish and rebuild science on a basis of universal interconnection—the foundation on which astrology has always stood.

Bernadette Brady: I come from a scientific background—that's my bent, so I tend to try to understand the world through that kind of framework. I never understood why astrology worked, until the last ten years when Mandelbrot came onto the scene with his Mandelbrot sets; and then Chaos Theory came in. Now obviously this is a personal belief, but I'm now much more comfortable with astrology because it fits in very comfortably with the whole theory of fractals and Mandelbrot sets. A lot of orthodox science doesn't accept that, but once it does accept the connection with fractals and Mandelbrot sets, then it would be a real surprise if astrology *didn't* work!

If we take Bell's theorem, and link that to Mandelbrot and fractals, then really it has to work; there has to be an interconnectedness without scale in time or in size*.

It's not that I needed to know how it worked; I've got enough Pisces and 12th house in me to accept something on faith! I can believe my eyes, and I can believe the world around me—which supports astrology quite a lot. But I must admit that in the last ten years it has been quite comforting for the depths of my mind to play with fractals and Mandelbrot sets, and to recognise that it is in this ballpark that astrology lives.

I think that the whole concept of orthodox science as we know it is going to crumble. It might take fifty or a hundred years, but it is going to happen—because there are so many band-aids on it. You know how they once thought that the planets' orbits were circular—they had to be, because of the eight spheres. It was a whole worldview, which was a worldview of God as well; theological astronomy, really. If they weren't perfect circles then they couldn't have the eight spheres and the whole theology broke down. So there was tremendous resistance to changing the concept of the perfectly circular orbit. What they had, as you are well aware, were all these epicycles—band-aids, more and more band-aids! Life is simple, it's not complicated. So the whole thing disintegrated with Kepler† and the whole theology had to go, the whole worldview had to change to incorporate the ellipse.

That's where we are at with orthodox science now—there are many band-aids stuck on in order to make things fit. I think what is going to happen—fifty or a hundred years from now, I don't know the timing—is that the whole lot is going to collapse, and the major philosophy is going to be based on fractals and Mandelbrot theory—the interconnectedness of everything, and the cyclic nature of everything—and how things are reproducing at many levels without scale, time or size.

It is worth dwelling particularly on two themes in Bernadette Brady's comments: firstly, she provides a possible explanation for how astrology works and, secondly, raises further

---

* Bell's theorem (1964) predicts a non-causal interconnection between particles — subsequently proven experimentally (Gribbin, 1984, p215-228); Mandelbrot's pioneering work in fractals illustrates 'self-similarity'—the tendency for patterns to recur on different scales in the natural world (Gleick 1988, p115-7).
† Johannes Kepler, who demonstrated that the planets' orbits *are* elliptical.

criticisms of science's lack of internal coherence. Each will now be looked at...

Explanations of How Astrology Works

Many astrologers show little inclination to figure out *how* astrology might work in scientific terms. Of those who do, some work within the limits of classical physics, whilst others invoke modern physics. A noteworthy representative of the first school is Dr Percy Seymour, whose book, 'The Scientific Basis of Astrology', suggests that astrology can be explained in terms of electro-magnetic fields—with the Earth's magnetic field influencing electrical activity in the human nervous system, establishing basic predis-positions during gestation, and triggering these tendencies at certain times after birth. Dr Seymour suggests that, since the Earth's magnetic field is affected by planetary influences, the positions of the planets can be used as tools to understand an individual human being.

The model of *how* astrology works that Bernadette Brady proposes is firmly based on modern physics, and the fact that certain discoveries therein imply that everything is profoundly interconnected. This may be the first glimmer of a change in our worldview that would eventually see the idea of interconnection between people and planets as common sense. It would be possible to dwell on this point at greater length*; but so much in the new physics is strange, difficult or impossible to comprehend, that any intellectual structure built on it could—as Bernadette Brady pointed out—be no more than provisional. After the interview, she made the point that her comments here are no more than a working model of how astrology might work; she added that, whilst it may eventually prove to be inaccurate in its detail, still it is useful and necessary to work with such models in order to push our understanding of astrology forward.

Criticism of Science's Assumptions

Bernadette Brady's comments under this heading overlap somewhat with those of Lee Lehman and Henry Bauer. With the latter two, however, criticisms stemmed from practical and philosophical issues. Brady suggests that a fundamental weakness in the scientific edifice is being exposed by recent developments within science itself.

This weakness is that scientists generally operate within a conservative framework of belief, which holds that most of what there is to be discovered has been discovered, and the bits that have not will be discovered soon, through existing methodologies, and will fit into the existing framework. So scientists like Carl Sagan (writing in 1978) make giant claims: "This... is written just before... the answers to many of these vexing and awesome questions on origins and fates are pried loose from the

---

* Starting, perhaps with quotes such as these from scientists: "Everything in the universe, past, present and future, is connected to everything else, by a web of electromagnetic radiation that 'sees' everything at once." (Gribbin, 1984, p.191); "Human beings, though tiny on the cosmic scale, are integral parts of some huge picture..." (Barbour, 1999, p.334.)

cosmos… there is only one generation privileged to live through that unique transitional moment: that generation is ours." (quoted Bauer, 1994 p.75.) Henry H Bauer's comment is, "Thus, human beings, including scientists, do not function under continual awareness of humanity's fundamental ignorance; rather, they live under perpetual illusion of fundamental understanding." (ibid)

Human beings can see only a small part of the spectrum of electromagnetic energy, which extends from radio waves to gamma rays. Suppose that the human capacity to understand is similarly limited; it looks that way, when we try to make sense of quantum reality. Consider, for instance, the quantum experiment that shows that a radioactive particle can have both decayed and not decayed at the same instant; and the thought experiment built on this, which (to cut a long story short) suggests that a cat could be both alive and not alive at the same instant. Such states of affairs simply do not fit within our usual understanding of the world*.

Examples of strangeness at the quantum level could be multiplied, but these will suffice to establish a point. Recent discoveries in modern science fly in the face of our most basic assumptions about what is and is not possible, suggesting that the human mind's capacity to understand may be as limited as our ability to see.

It has already been remarked that scientists in the west today tend to have a faith in science as something that is leading humanity out of darkness and into light; out of ignorance and toward full understanding. One aspect of this belief is that it is assumed that the universe can be understood. Hence, when science looks at astrology there is usually an assumption (though this is never made explicit) that—if astrology is real, if it works—it should be possible to understand it and to quantify its operation. This assumption is so much taken for granted that it can be difficult even to see that it is there. But where does it come from?

Before Copernicus upset the cosmological applecart, man assumed that his place was at the physical centre of everything. In an analogous way, post-Copernican man has tended to assume that his place is at the intellectual centre of the universe, potentially able to see in all directions and to know everything. Historically, this can be traced to the Christian worldview, which conditioned the first classical scientists, and which has remained part of the scientific mindset ever since. This theme is fully developed in 'The Passion of the Western Mind' by Richard Tarnas, who suggests that the most powerful and enduring legacy of Scholastic/Christian philosophy may have been "the theologically founded but decidedly robust confidence that Man's God-given reason possessed the capacity, and the religious duty, to comprehend the natural world." (Tarnas, 1993, p.299.)

Western science was born in a Christian context; and although it has largely come to disown that background, it still carries within it certain assumptions—such as the assumption that Man has been (as it were) designed to fully understand the world, and that reality can be contained within an intellectual system. This attitude has come increasingly under attack in the last hundred years. When Nietzsche wrote, "The will to a system is a lack of integrity" (Nietzsche, 1968, p.25) at the end of the last century, his was a voice in the wilderness. But in this century the postmodern movement

* The reference is to the uncertainty principle; and to the thought experiment with a cat formulated by Erwin Schroedinger—see Gribbin 1984, esp. p.203ff.

(characterised by figures such as Foucault, Latour and Lyotard) has increasingly questioned the status of 'systems' such as the scientific method, arguing that it is impossible to generate value-free and context-independent universal truths, and suggesting that the pursuit of technological 'solutions' has led modern industrial societies to adopt catastrophic trajectories*.

The perception of science as a path to truth is under pressure, both internally—from discoveries in modern science—and externally, from thinkers who consider the claims of science. Many now agree with Wittgenstein: "It is not e.g. absurd to believe that the scientific and technological age is the beginning of the end for humanity, that the idea of Great Progress is a bedazzlement, along with the idea that the truth will ultimately be known; that there is nothing good or desirable about scientific knowledge and that humanity, in seeking it, is falling into a trap." (Wittgenstein, 1998, p.64e.)

When asked to evaluate the ways in which astrologers respond to research into their subject, the Researchers commented that, "Astrologers retreat behind a smokescreen of speculation about the nature of truth, reality, perception, language, and so on." They might wish to argue that something of that kind has just happened with our trawl through quantum physics and postmodern thought. It is questionable whether the massed critique of science's status from so many sides can be dismissed so easily, but this is something readers will evaluate for themselves; and in any case—a point already noted—criticisms of science (no matter how valid they may be) do nothing to prove astrology. So let us pursue the Researchers' argument on its own terms. In their follow-up point they ask us to:

"Recall that the claims of astrology are grandiose, and that almost no area of human affairs (individual, collective, past, present, future) is supposed to be exempt. In other words we are supposed to believe simultaneously that astrology, like gravity, is writ most exceedingly large, while its influence is most exceedingly difficult to demonstrate."

Is astrology like the law of gravity? Is there any reason to think that, if it exists at all, it will be found to operate with equal ubiquity? It is a huge claim, but is it one that all astrologers actually make? Before it is possible to evaluate this criticism of astrology further, it will be necessary to tease out an idea of what kind of thing astrologers see their subject as being; this happens in the next chapter.

---

* On this last point see particularly Bauman, 1989.

Chapter XII
What is Astrology – Science or Magic?

Astrology as Science

To decide whether astrology works, it is necessary to define how it is supposed to work; and to do that, we need to know what astrology is supposed to be in the first place. And so, in the wake of Chapter XI, we are brought at last to ask what astrology is. Is it the expression of some ubiquitous law—like the law of gravity? If it is, then the discovery of the mechanisms by which it works can only be a matter of time, and likewise it is inevitable that science will eventually recognise that astrology works and welcome it back to the faculty of respectable studies.

This is the perspective of some astrologers, including Pat Harris—whose research into the medical application of astrology was described in Chapter VI.

Q: Do you think that scientific research (if done properly) could potentially be used to validate all of astrology, or only a small amount?

Pat Harris: I believe that all things in the universe are comprehensible to us given enough time. I mean that history shows that what we do not understand in one age, we can fully master/control in another—certain forms of disease, the very nature of disease and infection itself and the control of certain types of disease such as polio and measles through vaccination programmes.

Superstition and magic evaporate in the face of knowledge that develops, over time, into wisdom (despite, in some cases, interim abuse of that knowledge). In fact, I think it inevitable that we will come to understand how and why astrology works eventually, when we have evolved scientifically to a level where we are equipped to recognise the processes behind apparently mysterious events.

Another advocate of astrology-as-science is Dennis Elwell, who (a propos of his predictions, covered in Chapter VII) commented:

Dennis Elwell: With so many predictions being ventured, worldwide, the chances are that somebody will get it right sometime. So you can't take any particular comfort when your turn comes around. The only merit is to be able to get it right consistently, because your methods are reliable, which means you can show everybody else how to get it right consistently. Given our pretensions, it is crazy that we cannot reach a consensus on what astrology says, rather than what this particular astrologer says. *We are here in the domain of testable science* [my italics]. Astrologers who insist that astrology is merely divination are indistinguishable from the Tarot readers and rune casters—my vision for the future of astrology is something altogether more tangible and objective.

Dennis Elwell and Pat Harris distinguish between 'science' on the one hand, and 'divination' (or 'magic') on the other. They consider astrology to be a science—with the rider that the partial state of our knowledge currently prevents it from being appreciated as such. This view of things is easy enough to understand (compared, that is, to the view of astrology as magic); astrology is like the law of gravity (or, perhaps, a combination of several such laws), so its workings can in principle be discerned and measured by humanity, and therefore—when or if that happens—it will be possible to formulate reliable and consistent techniques.

There is little more to add, *if* astrology is viewed in this way (as a long-lost cousin of gravity). Arguments in favour of astrology as a science will need to address criticisms of the kind raised by the Researchers in Chapters IX and X—either by presenting new data, or by criticising the methodology employed for testing, and suggesting more relevant techniques (as, for instance, Pat Harris does in Chapters VI and XI).

As the Researchers remark in Chapter X, investigation of parallels in the lives of time twins seems a most promising way of circumventing many of the problems encountered when research methods are applied to astrology. It is curious that relatively little work has been put into this topic. Appendix 3 contains contributions from Professor Peter Roberts and an astrologer who is the mother of twins; it would be good to think that these two different angles on time twin research might stimulate further investigation.

Astrology as Magic

The view that astrology is an objective, natural law (like gravity) is not the only way in which astrologers see their subject. The division of astrology into 'natural' and 'judicial' has been revisited since Nicholas Campion introduced it in Chapter XIII. The 'astrology-as-science' view is the view of natural astrology; the alternative to this approach is judicial astrology, also known as 'divinatory astrology'. To point up the difference between this and astrology-as-science, here are two quotations from Geoffrey Cornelius and Maggie Hyde, co-founders of the Company of Astrologers—a group that describes what it teaches as 'divinatory astrology':

Geoffrey Cornelius: In many ways I accept St Augustine's statement, where he attacks astrology and says, "When astrologers give answers that are true, it is not because of the technique, because there is nothing in that technique; it is from some other agency that the answer is true." I think there's a great perception in that particular line of criticism of astrology.

Symbolic perception appears to me to be a natural human faculty, or faculty of mind; and all the technical superstructures that then are built up around it advance that perception not one inch. It's like saying, "How can you improve your sight?" One sees, and everything we do around that might complicate the act of seeing.

Maggie Hyde: You have to practise your [astrological] work *as if* it were objective, and about other people and other things in the world, but every now and again that objective position is actually cut through by something else, by some other order of thing. If you notice it, you suddenly find that the symbols don't just address that objective thing in the world, but they address you and your relationship with it. Or—even more spooky in a way—they are talking, not about that thing in the world, but about you and where you are coming from, and what you are up to, in something else quite different in your life. I discuss this in detail, with examples, in 'Jung and Astrology'.

When symbols do that, I think you have to be open to the realisation that the symbols are dead things, and it's our own active imagination, read into them, that is the game of astrology... *almost all* the influential texts that we have had in this century, and our practice of astrology now, do not acknowledge this other order, *where the astrology is about your spiritual path*. The criticism of psychological astrology in my book is that it still assumes that the horoscope is a map of the psyche, but that I'm not going to find *my* psyche, or my latest love-affair, or my financial problems, in *your* map.

When that happens, there's a resistance to things being *shown* to you that are out of your control and that have sprung up. Who wants to feel that they're not master or mistress of the task at hand? So when it suddenly springs back on you, and shows you something you didn't realise you were doing, because you were unconscious of it, it's shocking. So of course people don't want to include that in the game.

With this, Maggie Hyde introduces one possible explanation for the resistance some astrologers feel to the 'judicial astrology' view. One motivation for taking up the subject (mentioned by Robert Zoller in second chapter) is a desire to become more powerful, to take control of one's life; it's not easy, then, to admit that the power and control one seeks is, ultimately, illusory. Several astrologers admitted to having resisted the recognition that they are not, finally, in control:

Christeen Skinner: There is always something that cannot be quantified, which is just not measurable. For me, with the work that I'm doing now, it is exasperating that I cannot tell you what that immeasurable thing is—I can't even find a word for it! But I have moved on to the point now where I can acknowledge that that thing exists. Until a couple of years ago I would have wanted to deny it altogether.

Robert Zoller: I've been bitten at one time or another by the same parasite that bites those people who think that astrology can be reduced to a mathematical science. I have to confess that, even now, there is something I find appealing about that idea. That which is appealing about it, I think, comes down to inflation—the idea that "I can do something without anybody else permitting me to do it, without subordinating myself to anybody or anything." It's the prelude to a song that goes to the tune, 'The Hell with Everybody Else'.

That attitude has existed for a long time, and it's the demon behind our science essentially. I think it always falls flat on its face, because there is a faculty of the human mind that is a kind of wild card. Maybe it's a faculty of more than the human mind; maybe a faculty of the way *being* operates as a whole. Maybe it's GK Chesterton's 'God as Anarchist'—he wrote a wonderful book called 'The Man Who Was Thursday', which is about a band of anarchists. A cop infiltrates this band, and finds out that it is run by some fat fellow who is always a step ahead of the game. The fat fellow turns out to be God. So GK Chesterton is portraying God as the ultimate anarchist. The justification for that point of view, in my opinion, is that although there are laws of the universe, sometimes for seemingly inexplicable reasons these laws don't work.

With this, an important distinction starts to emerge between divinatory astrology and the law of gravity. One of gravity's most charming features is its reliability. When you get up to go to work, you don't have to look out of the window to see whether gravity is working today or not. Yet exponents of divinatory astrology such as Maggie Hyde and Geoffrey Cornelius, and Robert Zoller (who defines his position as somewhere in the middle of the judicial-natural astrology divide) talk about astrology as something that cannot be *absolutely* relied on; as something whose working is, somehow, dependent on the observer, and which may even behave arbitrarily from time to time, as if to keep humanity's hubris in check.

This picture (of astrology as an art touched by divine anarchy) is not an easy thing to make any kind of sense of, but it is essential to an understanding of how many astrologers think about their subject. The next few pages will be devoted to the pursuit of that understanding. A good starting point might be the anthropic principle.

As Below, So Above

The anthropic principle* is a theory belonging to what some have dubbed 'postmodern cosmology'. There are variants of the theory; all of them link humanity to the universe in some way, and the bolder ones make such statements as these:
— That the universe is as it is so that humanity can exist
— That the universe exists because it is observed by intelligent observers

The theory is a subject of controversy in scientific circles—hardly surprising, since its conclusions can sound more theological than scientific. What is not disputed is that there is a major mystery at the core of this universe; the principle represents the 'best guess'

---

* See, e.g., Collins & Hawking, 1973; Newton, 1997, p.80-3.

of some scientists to resolve it. To the physicist, the mystery appears like this:

— Why is the strong nuclear force as strong as it is? (If it were weaker, stable nuclei would be rare and in consequence hydrogen would be the only element, making it impossible for life as we know it to evolve.)

— Why does gravity have precisely the strength that it has? (If it had been stronger or weaker, stars and galaxies would not have developed as they have and, again, life could not have evolved.)

The anthropic principle has, therefore, evolved as an attempt to answer the questions "Why are things the way they are?" and "Why do we exist?" The suggestion is that, somehow, there is an interaction, a reciprocity, between the universe and humanity. This principle is an essential foundation for the judicial astrology model. A useful next step in the attempt to characterise this elusive view of the world is to compare the 'postmodern cosmology' of the anthropic principle with a pre-modern cosmology that also attempted to answer the question "Why are things the way they are?" Robert Hand describes this as providing the philosophical ground for astrology:

> **Robert Hand:** I don't know whether you are aware of it—most people don't know the full statement at the beginning of the Emerald Tablet. It's usually cited as 'As above, so below.' The full statement goes:
> 'As it is above, so it is below;
> As it is below, so it is above;
> In order to accomplish the miracle of the one thing.'*

What that tells us is: we not only get created; we *create*. But it's not what psychologists would say—projections. *This stuff is really there.* In any meaningful definition of existence, that stuff is real. It's only if you narrow your definition of existence down to that which can be weighed and measured by laboratory instruments that [our creation] ceases being there. But by those criteria we cease being there also.

I think consciousness enters into a dialogue with the apparently external (it may be external, but I'm going to call it the apparently external) and creates, with that apparently external, a series of language systems. And these language systems, like the language you and I use with each other, begin to determine the experience of a phenomena. But it isn't quite the same as projecting, because the 'apparently external' has an equally powerful role in determining the nature of the language. What makes this different is, *there is no one correct language.* Just as you can say the same thing in French, German, English, Italian, Chinese, Japanese—more or less—you can say the same thing in different languages of this kind. These are what the Renaissance called 'natural languages'—the languages of nature. They would have thought they

---

* cf Copenhaver, 1992; for an historical overview of hermetic magic and philosophy, see Baigent & Leigh, 1997.

were wholly external. I would say that it arises out of this dialectic between consciousness within and consciousness without.

So that when we forcefully create, collectively, a construct, that construct becomes a part of the forming of our experience, and we get a feedback loop going. Now, can any construct be created? The answer is no, only some constructs can be created—maybe a large number, but it's finite. And these are determined: (a) by the structure of human consciousness; and (b) by the structure of nature—or 'the apparently external'.

Robert Hand's explanation of how astrology works implies that there can not be one uniquely right way of interpreting a chart; if astrology works at all, it works in multiple ways (though not, as he points out, an infinite number of ways). Different systems of astrology (such as western and Vedic) may therefore claim to be different fingers pointing at the same moon; and the complexity that can appear to astrology's critics as evidence against it, is—from this perspective—inevitable. Mike Harding makes a related point:

Mike Harding: I think astrology is infinitely complex, I think life is infinitely complex. If astrology claims to mirror life, then it will have life's complexity.

Astrology gives us a number of accounts of the human being. For me, astrology is very much a language; it can describe things that other languages can't do, it brings things together that for other people are completely separate. Astrology's usefulness is that it does bring things together, and does describe.

There isn't a language of any kind that can step outside of the world and perceive everything from some neutral position. I think that's a vanity, which some astrologers might have—I don't know. Some philosophies have had that vanity in the past, some therapies have had that vanity. But there isn't an objective position, we can't step outside our world and look at it. We can see pictures of it, and I think the different astrological techniques are better and worse *glimpses* of our world, taking in different points of reference—in just the same way, we may look at somebody's life, and they may talk about their waking experiences or they may talk about their dreams. The dreams are them, of course, in a different world—we're talking about different kinds of experiences. We can talk about parents and find fragmented examples of our self in their interactions, or we can talk about our world and see how we have adopted the values and the culture in which we live. So we get glimpses of our self in our world or in our parents or in our family, or in the ideas we have. The different techniques within astrology—looking at the natal chart of the country, or one's parents, or a relationship, or an aspect of our chart (like looking closely at midpoints or harmonic aspects)—all present different kinds of pictures of ourselves, and for me the value of it is whether somebody finds your picture useful at that particular time in their life.

We are interconnected; I think this is the central message of astrology. We are together with the world all the time. It may be hard, sometimes, to feel it—but I do think that's how it is, and we are all products of our collective background and culture, it's embedded in us.

Rituals and Reductionism

It is now time to revisit an objection to judicial astrology. In response to the suggestion that divinatory (or judicial) astrology might not be susceptible to scientific testing, the Researchers' comment was:

Researchers: [This] view is hard to understand. It is like saying we don't know how gravity works, therefore we cannot test the fall of apples. The issue is whether the astrology ritual works better than a control ritual, e.g. by providing new information or by improving self-esteem. Much is testable here.

Their point is that, even if astrology can not be reduced to a set of laws capable of being tested, if it works for individual astrologers then it should be possible to test it by getting individual astrologers to do whatever they do in a test situation, and then evaluate their results (this is the methodology of the Vernon Clark tests, for instance). Since such tests have been performed many times and have not produced convincing results, the conclusion still has to be drawn that astrology fails under circumstances where it would be expected to perform.

Does the case for a type of astrology that cannot be tested collapse at this point? In order to evaluate that, it will be useful to look into the implications of an interconnected universe (the kind of thing to which Robert Hand and Mike Harding refer) a little more. A useful way into this will be to consider reductionism.

Reductionism is the approach of explaining a thing by breaking it down into smaller units. This is a necessary step in many scientific procedures, but it is sometimes considered that, having found it to be useful in certain cases, science has taken it to be applicable in all cases. The objection to it was neatly put by PW Anderson: "The ability to reduce everything to simple fundamental laws does not imply the ability to start from those laws and reconstruct the universe." (Anderson, 1972, Norretranders, 1998 p.356.) I can analyse the atoms of my car forever, but this will not tell me why it won't start in the mornings; when a complex system functions, its functioning involves elements that cannot be understood in terms of the simple elements. The assumption that it should be possible to take astrology apart, investigate the parts and find out how it works, is sometimes seen as the start of astrology's loss of credibility in this scientific era:

Bernadette Brady: The big problem astrology has had is that it's the only 'science' (in inverted commas) that wouldn't go over to reductionism. You couldn't do it, because if you went over to orthodox science (I think of it more as reductionism)—well, it can't take it. The very centre standing stone of astrology is the interconnectedness of things, so it can't say that you are totally isolated and that's it. It can't!

There are several issues that could be discussed under the heading of reductionism; some have already been raised in the interview with the Researchers in Chapter XI—particularly those centred on the complexity of an astrological chart. Interesting as those issues may be, it may be more relevant to the matter in hand to consider a different form of reductionism—one that tends to be overlooked when evaluations of astrology are considered.

Since astrology is done by astrologers, to test and evaluate it without considering the mental state and motivation of the astrologer is reductionistic, insofar as it excludes an integral part of the system through which astrological interpretation is achieved—at least, in the 'judicial astrology' frame of reference.

When astrologers take part in tests to evaluate the validity of astrology, the question they are actually being asked is, "Does astrology work?" This is problematic for two reasons:

1. There is a logical paradox in asking astrology whether astrology works (to open the paradox, imagine receiving the answer 'no');

2. If the astrologer takes the question seriously, they doubt astrology whilst using astrology. The suggestion is that this doubt can, in itself, prevent astrology from working.

A parallel for the neo-Platonic philosopher would have been to question whether the gods existed. Iamblichus rejected the question: "…It is not proper to grant this, as if it might not be granted, nor to admit it as ambiguous… nor are we worthy thus to explore it, as if we had sufficient authority to approve or reject it. For we are comprehended in it…" (Taylor, 1997, p.23/Ch.3.)

The argument, applied to astrology, is this: astrology is possible because everything is interconnected. Since 'everything' must include the astrologer, it is inconsistent to imagine that their mental attitude (for instance the presence, or absence, of doubt) will not influence a reading. Under judicial astrology, the astrologer does not discern the workings of the cosmos in an objective way; they can gain insight into specific things and events, but cannot look on the universe from outside (as a creator God might) and report on how it all works—whether, for instance, astrology works or not. As Mike Harding observes, "There isn't a language of any kind that can step outside of the world and perceive everything from some neutral position." A similar point was made by the physicist Niels Bohr: "It is wrong to think that the task of physics is to find out how nature is. Physics concerns what we can say about nature." (quoted Norretranders, 1998, p.201.)

Another perspective can be found by analogy with the I Ching. The relevance of the Chinese 'Book of Changes' to judicial astrology emerged in discussion with Geoffrey Cornelius:

Q: Do you think it's useful to have a knowledge of I Ching and Tarot in addition to astrology?

Geoffrey Cornelius: Well I do, but I wouldn't want to get doctrinaire on this—I appreciate that people have many paths. Nevertheless, I don't know how you can arrive at the same perception of astrology unless you do have experience in the other main divinatory forms—especially the I Ching above all. Tarot will give you the practical understanding of divination; the I Ching will give you practical understanding of divination *and* will give an ethical and philosophical structure to take you some way deeper. That's my general view of it.

The attitude of the I Ching to being tested is given in hexagram 4: "…It is not I who seek the young fool; the young fool seeks me. At the first oracle I inform him. If he asks two or three times, it is importunity. If he importunes, I give him no information." (Wilhelm, 1951, p20-1.) It adds: "If mistrustful or unintelligent questioning is kept up, it serves only to annoy the teacher. He does well to ignore it in silence…" As on the previous page, the point emerges that questions based in doubt about that which one consults can not be valid.

The suggestion is that astrology (or the I Ching) has to be approached in the right spirit, as one would approach an honoured teacher. This is an approach that many astrologers have espoused. The 17th century English astrologer William Lilly, for instance, whose works are seen by many as a high-water mark in astrological excellence, advised the would-be astrologer: "Be thou humble, and let no natural knowledge, how profound and transcendent soever it be, elate thy mind to neglect that *divine Providence*… being confident, the more holy thou art, and more neer to God, the purer judgement thou shalt give. Beware of pride and self-conceit…" (Lilly, 1985, p.9.)

The Astrologer's Mind

Most of the astrologers I interviewed agreed that it is necessary to reduce pride and conceit in order for one's astrological work to be accurate and well-balanced:

Robert Zoller: One of the lessons that I've been learning in connection with astrology is the importance of humility, the importance of subordinating the individual will to a higher will. Which has not been an easy lesson for me, and I won't claim I've got it down yet; but I at least think that it's something that should be done. I recently had reason to go to a *santero* in New Jersey—a practitioner of *santeria*, an Afro-Cuban religion. You go to them with a problem, and they begin their analysis with certain questions, and then they get out their cowrie beads and do a divination.

At the beginning of the divination, and before every move in the divination, there is a prayer. Now contemporary occultism is quite capable of taking over the methods of the *santero* or any other traditional practitioner, keeping the strict technical aspects of what they do to arrive at their answers whilst, at the same time, excising the prayers. When a Moslem does this, and excises the pagan prayers of the *Ifa* from their geomancy—they don't leave it at that, they substitute the *Ifa* pagan prayers and sacrifices with Koranic verses and Koranic practices of some sort, which are regarded as being equivalent in some way to what they have excised. But when a contemporary westerner does the same thing, what they want to find if possible is a mathematical law that they can use instead of having any prayers at all. So they try to reduce the whole thing to binary mathematics, or to some sort of totally secular and scientific endeavour, which the individual human mind can do, *despite* the state of the individual operator.

First-hand experience of the way in which the state of the individual operator can affect astrological work was provided by John Frawley:

John Frawley: After my TV predictions, I found myself under pressure from various quarters to provide lucrative predictions, and did disastrously. It's only now, when these people have washed their hands of me and I can do it for fun again that I'm getting predictions right. It's a question of focus: like in tennis—if your focus is on hitting the ball, you'll do fine; if it's on lifting the trophy, you'll lose. So in astrology—the focus must be purely on the prediction, not on the consequences of that prediction.

Lilly's exhortation to be holy and humble may sound very different from John Frawley's approach of 'doing it for fun'. However, Robert Hand made a connection in his response to Lilly's words:

Robert Hand: Lilly put it in Christian terms: to be 'holy' is to be 'conscious'; and I don't just mean 'awake', either; it's a little more elaborate than that. The single greatest component of how I would describe 'being highly conscious' is that you have an accurate perspective on the relative significance of things. Because—to take a simple-minded example—people who are all hung up on earning money may exalt the earning of money to a status it's not entitled to. And consequently their lives may be made miserable by this. Now not all people who go out to earn money are made miserable. But, if you look at them, they are having a good time playing the game. My favourite comment along those lines came from a financial astrologer. He said, "The money isn't important—it's just a means of keeping score!" This is quite a different attitude than the one that makes money almost a god.

I believe that people who play life as a high-level game—I don't mean trivially, but who play life as the spontaneous, exuberant outpouring of energy along certain lines (whether they do it consciously or not) are going to be happy people. What these people who say that 'money is merely a way of keeping score' have done is restored the perspective. What's really fun is the game; the money is just a means of keeping the score!

I think all people who are happy in their lives do this at some level. I've stated many times that, if you define play or a game as an activity pursued for its own sake, rather than for the pursuit of something higher in a hierarchy, this is usually—in our culture—considered to be trivial and unimportant. What's important is work. And we define work as an activity that is pursued for the sake of something else—maybe higher, maybe not.

But at some point, unless you are going to have infinite regress, the answer to the question "Why is this happening?" has to be [to further] a *game*, which means that, at the top of all of this, is a colossal game—in the highest sense of the word. This is overtly stated in Hinduism as *Lila*. And playing games, therefore, is an emulation of the divine (in the highest sense of the word; I don't mean 'playing games' in the sense of tricking people and that kind of thing. I mean being a manifestation of divine energy, purely for the sake of being a manifestation of divine energy). One acts, not to get Brownie points with God, but one acts just simply as a pure manifestation of divine energy, playing. This is a very high activity. If you do it consciously, and you know what you are doing, it's even higher. But I think it's so good, that even if you are somewhat unconscious about it, you're still going to have a good time.

I'm not saying that we don't need discipline, that we don't need to work at all, because all good games require discipline. My favourite example is an athlete: he has to train.

That analogy is worth pursuing. It is now a commonplace in sport that training and technical ability are only part of the picture, and that sportspeople need to work on "performance-influencing factors such as under or over-motivation, self-doubt, lack of confidence, loss of motivation or fear"(Gyr, 1998). And John Frawley's comment, "If your focus is on hitting the ball, you'll do fine; if it's on lifting the trophy, you'll lose," has a clear parallel in Zen archery instruction: "The right art... is purposeless, aimless! The more obstinately you try to learn how to shoot the arrow for the sake of hitting the goal, the less you will succeed in the one and the further the other will recede..." (Herrigel, 1985, p.46).

The picture that emerges is that, so far as judicial astrology goes, it is more accurate to compare astrology to (say) archery than to the law of gravity; the involvement and attitude of the astrologer are key factors. This raises a practical question: if astrology is such a subtle skill, how—given the plethora of conflicting systems and techniques—is it possible for anyone to learn it in the first place? How is it possible for astrologers to teach what they have learned? The question had taxed a number of the astrologers I spoke with:

Robert Hand: One of the things that prevented 'Horoscope Synthesis'* from

* A book he had planned to write on how to interpret charts. 'Synthesis' is the process of deciding how the numerous, sometimes contradictory, influences in a chart will blend and manifest.

being written was realising how one does chart synthesis —*really*. You look at the chart, and you look at the chart [again], get familiar with all the components of the chart, and all of a sudden, bang! They come together. That's *not teachable*. It's an entirely intuitive process.

Lee Lehman: I realised that the teaching of astrology works when you, as the teacher, provide a field, or an environment, for your student to then be able to sweat; and that the sweating process is basically examples, examples, examples. It's only through actually working with charts that you get it. And I can't tell you whether a particular student will get it the first time, the hundredth time, the thousandth time. But if they consistently work the material, they *will* get it. There is information out there, there is history out there, there are citations, there are procedures, there are ideas that have come across and sources and all this other stuff. But ultimately, the synthesis is individual. And that is the art of astrology. You can't get to the art of astrology without mastering the technology of astrology; but ultimately, astrology done well is an art.

Mechanistic World, Organismic World

Nearly all of the astrologers I talked to contended that the art of astrology has to be built upon a firm grounding in technique; astrologers who consider that astrology is not 'objective' (not based on natural laws at all) still emphasise that the astrologer has to work *as if* they are applying objective laws. Looking from the outside, therefore, it is generally difficult to tell whether someone is a natural or judicial astrologer. The distinction may only come to the fore when astrologers are faced with scientific research into astrology, and discover that they have different expectations of it.

One more perspective can be figured into this consideration of judicial astrology—the characteristically optimistic view of Adrian Duncan:

Q: Do you really believe that astrology will experience a significant change of status in the next hundred years or so?

Adrian Duncan: I have chosen to believe that!

Q: How far do you see it going?

Adrian Duncan: I see it going pretty far. People will take it for granted that they are living their lives in harmony with planetary movements. I know there are a lot of good and bad [consequences of] that, but I think it's going to have a better result than the prevailing scientific/materialistic view, which is very unecological. The crucial thing with astrology, and the idea of being in harmony with nature, with the planets, is that it's ecological and therefore less harmful.

This is a point to dwell on. I alluded, in the previous chapter, to the criticisms of post-modern thinkers of the consequences for man and the planet of the technological/scientific drive to a "fully designed, fully controlled world." (Bauman, 1989, p.93.)

A vision of such a world was, strangely enough, provided by the Researchers in Chapter X when they discussed how things would be if astrology worked to the extent claimed in some astrology books: "Hunger and hardship have disappeared because economic trends and climate are predictable. Science has disappeared because horary astrology answers any question. So has competitive sport for the same reason. Cars and planes are hazard-free because assembly times conducive to accidents are routinely avoided. Crime, war, illness and divorce are unknown because predictable. Every person is empowered, self-actualised, spiritually enlightened, and knows their individual purpose and direction. Abuse of astrological knowledge is prevented by restricting it to those whose charts reveal due merit. This is astrology world."

This was, for sure, intended as no more than a light-hearted hint of the consequences of claims made in some astrology books. But what is of interest is that it might show how astrology *should* function, according to the conventional scientific view. In 'astrology world', astrological understanding is pictured as resulting in a dystopia similar to 'Brave New World', with all uncertainty, choice and challenge removed by astrology (instead of the drugs and genetic engineering used to the same end in Huxley's book). Let us consider why this should be significant for the present discussion.

In a talk he gave in 1984, the physicist David Bohm spoke of two worldviews. The 'mechanistic world view' says that the world is a machine, with stars, galaxies and so on built from atoms and molecules; each part independent, each blindly exerting forces on the other parts. "The ultimate implications of this view of universal order are, of course, that man is basically insignificant. What he does has meaning only in so far as he can give it meaning in his own eyes." (Bohm, 1985, p.2.)

The alternative is what he calls an 'organismic' worldview. Here, "The very nature of any part may be profoundly affected by changes of activity in other parts, and by the general state of the whole, and so the parts are basically internally related to each other as well as to the whole." (ibid p.3.) He points out that these two different perspectives have different consequences for the way in which we live, and that humanity is much more at home with an organismic view of life.

From these two views of the world, follow two ways of viewing astrology—as a natural resource of the world, to be investigated and (if possible) exploited to the hilt; or as a part of what we are, something to be respected, learned from and co-operated with. In the former view, astrology's role would be to control things and make life conform to a pattern imposed by humanity on a fundamentally chaotic, unintelligent world. That (I suggest) is the approach that underpins 'astrology world'.

The implications of the 'organismic' view are different. Based on the assumption that life is somehow intelligent, astrology is seen as a way to understand rather than to control. At an individual level, this means focussing more on changing one's understanding of what is happening than on changing what is happening. (Robert Hand describes this approach in Chapter V, in his comments on the 'contemplated Saturn'.) The implication here is that as we learn to co-operate with the universe at an individual level, so humanity will gradually come to see its collective relationship to the Earth (and its environs) as one of mutual dependency and involvement. Hence—to return to Adrian Duncan's point—the view of man as an interconnected part of the world, which supports judicial astrology, is ecological. This raises the interesting conundrum that, *even if astrology were not true*, a world in which people believed in astrology as part of an organismic universe might be qualitatively better than a world in which they did not.

What is Real?

In the last few pages the mechanism through which judicial astrology works has been edged around, alluded to in terms of reciprocity between human being and cosmos, defined as indefinable. The suggestion of the Researchers that, when under pressure, "astrologers retreat behind a smokescreen of speculation about the nature of truth, reality, perception, language, and so on" might be revisited at this point. Is this entire definition of judicial astrology simply an exercise in obfuscation, undertaken by astrologers to prevent their subject being seen for what it is?

Any judgement as to whether this explanation of astrology is a smokescreen, or a clue to a mysteriously interlinked world will be based on one's view of issues such as: what is real; how we acquire knowledge; and how our knowledge relates to reality. In other words, philosophical issues which are as old as philosophy itself.

A common reference point in considering such questions is Immanuel Kant's statement that "though all our knowledge begins with experience, it does not follow that it all arises out of experience." (Kant, 1929, p.41). Kant concluded that humanity was not in touch with reality as it actually is, but that everything we experience is pre-formatted, interpreted by the mind—primarily in terms of temporal, spatial and causal relationships. The universe may be timeless and acausal—an idea that finds some resonance in quantum theory—but design limitations in the standard human being prevent us from experiencing this. The mind processes the information it receives and presents us with a simplified version of things—so that, rather than our understanding being moulded by reality, the reality we experience is moulded by our understanding.

In her interview, Bernadette Brady referred to the world that rejects astrology as 'Flatland'; and the fable 'Flatland' (Abbott, 1953) provides an excellent way of thinking about this issue. In Edwin Abbott's tale, beings that exist in two dimensions (as lines, circles, squares and so on) find their world being intruded upon by three-dimensional beings. These intrusions are incomprehensible; as a sphere passes through Flatland, for instance, it appears to the inhabitants as a circle that expands, shrinks, and then disappears altogether. Their ability to make sense of the world is limited by the structure their minds impose upon experience.

It is possible that this describes our relation to astrology. Under the judicial model, astrology is not causal, not bound by the laws of time and space. If we, beings who experience all things in a framework of time, space and causality, encounter an order beyond them, it would be outside our frame of reference in the same way a three-dimensional solid is beyond the comprehension of two-dimensional beings. Under this view, astrology's incursions into our world would necessarily defy our attempts to interpret and understand them; it would be in the nature of astrology to be incomprehensible.

This can, of course, be rejected as a fifth-dimensional smokescreen. My point is not whether it is true or not, simply that it is philosophically consistent to suggest that astrology is beyond our understanding, but nonetheless real. Certainly, this raises more questions than it answers. But every attempt to pin astrology down with a definitive explanation runs into problems of some sort. For instance, to conclude that astrology is entirely illusory is to say that each of the cases where it appears to have worked (a few examples appeared in Chapters II–XII) were due to chance alone. That seems to show an amazing faith in what *chance* is capable of.

Many questions remain. The purpose of this book was not to arrive at final answers, but to question the views and assumptions usually encountered regarding astrology, so as to create a context within which informed discussion might take place. In conclusion, therefore, I make no apologies for not presenting a conclusion. As Joseph Joubert remarked (Jay, 1996, p.200), "It is better to debate a question without settling it than to settle a question without debating it."

Back to Zero

Look at the stars of the night sky and a sense of mystery and wonder can arise unbidden. The universe seems inscrutable, remote, yet somehow in communion. Or perhaps it seems like a lifeless void, punctuated by random objects on trajectories from the epicentre of the definitive accident, the Big Bang; a universe governed by chance, rather than intelligent design. Which view, in the end, is real? The stars remain enigmatic. We, who live out our lives under them, have to decide.

It is often assumed that astrology was created as an attempt to lend coherence to the ponderings of awe-struck star-gazers. If we, now, in considering astrologers and their craft, have stumbled upon paradoxes, enigmas and the sense of a timeless knowledge that manages to be alternately profound and implausible, that seems entirely fitting.

One of the many questions that remain is how, if astrology lies beyond the comprehension of the rational mind, it could fall within the ambit of human participation. One answer was hinted at by Adrian Duncan: "The astrologer who puts doubts about [astrology's] effectivity aside and embraces the hypothesis wholeheartedly is rewarded by this intelligent universe... it is in the nature of things that events normally confirm convictions." Under this view, those who believe in astrology find their belief supported by experience; those who doubt find their doubts confirmed. Astrology, then, would be both true and not true—the outcome being decided by the way in which the observer looks at it. In the end, perhaps the answer we find is really no more—and no less—than our own reflection.

POLO: ...Perhaps the terraces of this garden overlook only the lake of our mind...

KUBLAI: ...and however far our troubled enterprises as warriors and merchants may take us, we both harbour within ourselves this silent shade, this conversation of pauses, this evening that is always the same.

('Invisible Cities' by Italo Calvino; p.93)

For Further Information

Here, linking into and out of the book in different ways, are some additional resources:

Appendix 1: Information for anyone who wants to know more about people or groups.
Appendix 2: References to publications.
Appendix 3: Some further thoughts on the specific area of time twin research.
Appendix 4: A brief guide to the birth chart and for readers not familiar with astrological terminology, a glossary.

The book has an accompanying website:
> http://www.astrozero.btinternet.co.uk

This contains the following:

> Complete texts of selected interviews
> Additional articles and reviews
> Details of a CD-ROM with full versions of all the interviews from which this book was assembled
> Further discussion of the issues raised in this book
> News of future projects
> News of contributors and links to their sites

Contributions to the site are invited. These might take the form of: comments on any section(s) or individual(s) in this book; personal experiences of astrology; useful sources of information; and further ideas for the site.

Please contact me at:
> astrozero@btinternet.com

or write c/o the publisher:
> Flare Publications
> 29 Dolben Street
> London SE1 0UQ
> UK

Garry Phillipson

Biographies and Relevant Organisations

Part 1 of this appendix contains details of the people interviewed in the book; following this, some organisations are listed in Part 2. These groups (and people) are either connected with one of the interviewees, or are mentioned in the book, or are useful starting points for anyone wishing to get more information. The information here is, emphatically, limited. Anyone wishing to acquire a comprehensive listing of the different groups in astrology should approach one of the organisations, such as the Urania Trust, that co-ordinates details of groups and events in the astrological world.

Part 1: Biographies

Under 'Biographical Information', some or all of the following information is listed for each interviewee:

Date of interview

Birth data and Horoscope Wheel (where interviewees were willing for these to be included in the book. In the cases where the data were given during an interview, they are quoted verbatim. All birth charts are calculated in the tropical zodiac and Placidean house system)

Contact Details (where interviewees wished these to be included)

Brief biographical details (supplied by the interviewees in some cases; taken from websites, publications etc. where none were provided)

For Geoffrey Dean, Suitbert Ertel, Ivan Kelly, Arthur Mather or Rudolf Smit, please see the entry under 'Researchers'.

Bernadette Brady

Interview recorded:
31 May 1998

Website
www.bernadettebrady.com/

Birth Data
"I was born on 10th March 1950, and I was born about 11.13 pm (we always crib a few seconds, don't we?) in Adelaide. The time zone is nine and a half hours east. The latitude is 34.55 south, the longitude is 138.34 east."

Bernadette Brady is a professional consulting astrologer, co-principal of the Astro Logos astrological school in Australia (see 'Organisations') and is a member of the Council of the Astrological Guild of Educators (A.G.E). Her publications include: the astrological software package JigSaw (Astrolabe, USA and Esoteric Technologies, Australia); and her books 'The Eagle and the Lark: a Textbook of Predictive Astrology', (which has been translated into Portuguese, Russian and Dutch) and 'Brady's Book of Fixed Stars'. She has published many articles in the astrological community and has lectured worldwide.

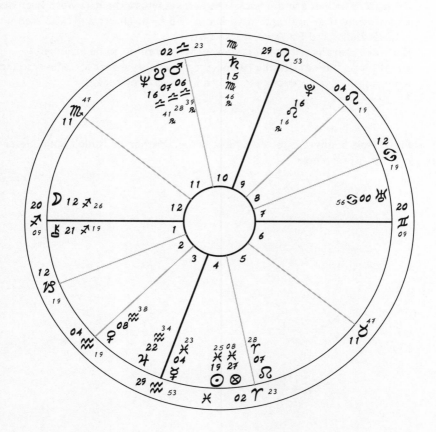

Nicholas Campion

Interview recorded:
27 March 1998

Website
www.NickCampion.com/

Birth Data
"4th March 1953, 10 minutes past midnight, in Bristol—20 Scorpio rising, 13 Pisces Sun and 18 Libra Moon."

Nicholas Campion is the author of 'An Introduction to the History of Astrology' (1982), 'Mundane Astrology', with Michael Baigent and Charles Harvey (1984), 'The Practical Astrologer' (1987), 'The Book of World Horoscopes' (1988), 'The Great Year' (1994), 'The New Astrology', with Steve Eddy (1999) and 'Astrology, History and Apocalypse' (2000). His next major work is 'Cosmos: A Cultural History of Astrology', to be published by London Books in 2001. He is the editor of 'Culture and Cosmos' (the academic journal on the history of astrology) and is currently pursuing research into the extent and nature of contemporary belief in astrology with the Study of Religions Department at Bath Spa University College, England. He is creating an online resource on the history of astrology—the website address is above.

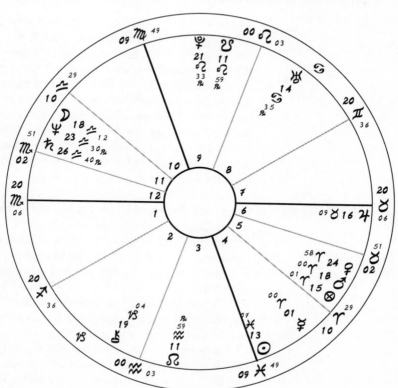

Geoffrey Cornelius

Interview recorded:
10 July 1998

Contact
as for
Company of Astrologers
(see 'Organisations')

Geoffrey Cornelius is a consultant astrologer with a background in philosophy and divination. He has been active in UK astrological education since the 1970s, and was one of the initiators of the Advisory Panel on Astrological Education (APAE). He is a past President of both the Astrological Lodge of the Theosophical Society and the Astrological Lodge of London, and a former editor of the quarterly journal 'Astrology'. In 1983 he co-founded the Company of Astrologers, with which he currently teaches and practises.

Rev. Pamela Crane

Interview recorded:
6 November 1997

Contact
Tel/Fax: 01795-532037

Birth Data
"My birth data are as follows: 19th January 1943 22h18 War Time (21h18 GMT) at Selly Oak, Birmingham UK (Source, my mother, who said it was 10h20 pm on the clock, which I have been able to rectify to 10h18 pm)."

Rev. Pamela Crane has been editor of the AA newsletter 'Transit'; Assistant Editor of 'The Astrological Journal'; has served on the Council of the Astrological Association; and was a founding member of The Advisory Panel on Astrological Education. After numerous articles have been published in (amongst others) 'The Astrological Journal', 'Astrology' and the 'CAO Times'. She has lectured to various groups including the AA and the Astrological Lodge of London, and has appeared on several TV programmes about astrology.

Since 1982, Reverend Crane has run the Pamela Crane College of Horoscopy to teach beginner, intermediate and advanced students by correspondence to a high standard, and to promote draconic astrology. In 1992, she was ordained to the Deaconate of the Liberal Catholic Church, TS. On 25th October 1992, "Inspiration led to discovery of the Nativity [birth chart] of Jesus, supported and confirmed by three years' painstaking work on Christian history with increasing verbal and symbolic help from Jesus, directly and through my own Guides." The work has grown into a book, 'The

Birth of Christ'.

Published papers: 'The Christian Astrologer'; 'The Birth of Christ'; 'Prime Movers'; 'Souls in Chains—Draconic Astrology and the Silent Twins'; 'Sympathy and Resonance—A Summary of Principles in Synastry'; 'Mars and Migraine (Interdimensional Astrology at Work)'; 'Associate Angles and the D.P.A.S.'; 'Interdimensional Astrology—A Summary of Principles'.

Books: 'Draconic Astrology'; 'Interdimensional Astrology (Revised)'; 'The Birth of Christ'; 'The Draconic Ephemeris'; 'The Draconic Chart' (revised edition, 1999).

Email Bulletin: Small World (newsletter, 1998 to date)

Constant aim: "To illumine human spiritual truths through astrology, and vice versa. Impossible (?) dream: To reconcile the Christian Churches and astrology; the Liberal Catholic Church, in which I currently serve as Deacon, is the only one, to my knowledge, which fully accepts the wisdom of astrological study and counsel."

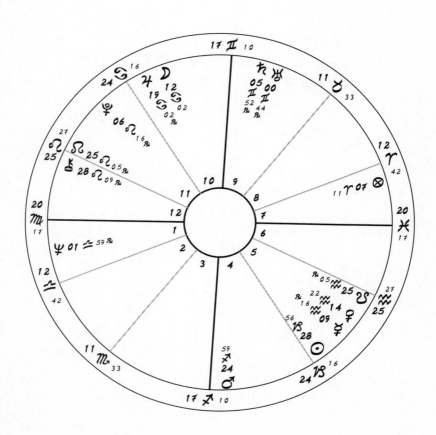

Martin Davis

Interview recorded:
23 November 1999

Contact
The Library Wing, Abbey
Saint Bathans House, Duns,
Berwickshire TD11 3TX,
Scotland
earthsearch@astral.demon.co.uk

Website
www.astral.demon.co.uk

Birth Data
10.58 am (CST), 7 September 1937, Saint Louis,
Missouri, USA (data from his book 'Astrolocality
Astrology').

In the course of his work as an engineer, business
consultant and sportsman, Martin Davis has travelled
widely and lived in many different countries. He is a
well known lecturer and practitioner in the area of
Astrolocality astrology and his enthusiasm for it has
encouraged many others to investigate the subject
further. Martin is currently the European
representative for Matrix astrological software.

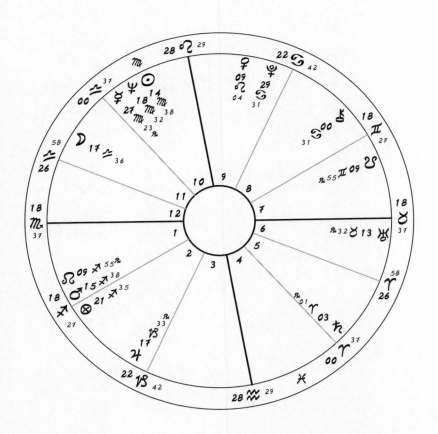

Adrian Duncan

Interview recorded:
13 March 1999

Website
www.world-of-wisdom.com

Birth Data
11.46 am (BST), 17 July 1949, York, England (data is in the World of Wisdom software program).

Adrian Duncan is a full-time astrologer working from his base in London. He is former president of the Copenhagen Astrology Society, having moved to Denmark aged thirty. He has spoken at astrological conferences from the USA to Holland, Norway and Sweden. His first book, 'Doing Time on Planet Earth', was published in 1987; the second, 'Astromancer —Creating Transformation via the Horoscope', is in progress. In the nineties he developed the World of Wisdom (aka 'WOW') chart interpretation software, which aims to make it possible for someone with no astrological knowledge to begin understanding their horoscope. Sales of WOW have now reached over 100,000 copies in 12 languages. The first program was followed, in 1998, by 'Astrology for Lovers'—a program that does for the relationship between two people (and their charts) what the original program did for an individual and their chart. In March 1998 Adrian returned to England to take up the position of Editor at 'The Astrological Journal'.

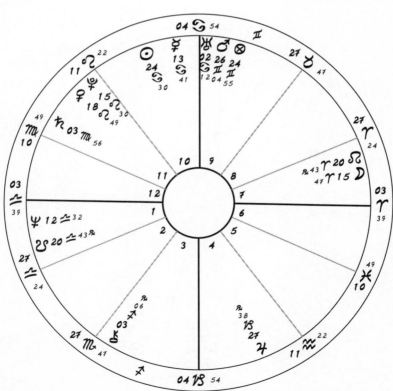

Dennis Elwell

Written reply despatched:
21 March 1999

Birth Data "My own time of birth has been rectified by myself from my parents' recollection that I was born late at night. As I came into the world the clock downstairs kept striking, and the irritated doctor asked for it to be stopped. Synchronistically, it announced the arrival of a noisy nuisance! I have settled for 11:44 pm (16 February 1930, Stourbridge)."

Dennis Elwell taught himself the astrological basics as a teenager, over 50 years ago—when few good books were available. At 23, he began contributing regularly to 'American Astrology'. This magazine did much to popularise the subject in the United States, and was a platform for the leading astrologers of the day. The connection continued for twenty years. Mr. Elwell began lecturing to astrologers worldwide in 1963, gaining a reputation as an original thinker and stimulating speaker. For most of his working life he was a newspaperman in his home town of Stourbridge, England, but his guiding passion throughout was the rehabilitation of astrology, and he was concerned to follow up any clue that might lead to further insights. The trail led to an interest in science on the one hand, and on the other to occultists like Gurdjieff and

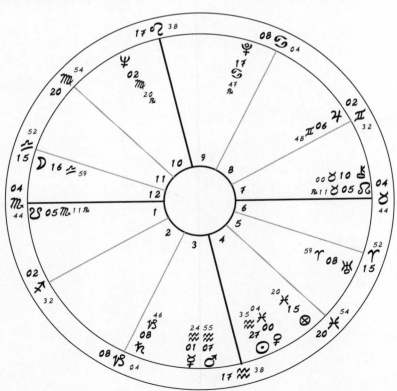

Rudolf Steiner. In recent years, realising its awesome potential, he has been saying to those who imagine that astrology is for amusement only: "Think again: all knowledge confers an advantage, and this material is positively dangerous." The author enjoys teaching, and has tutored his own correspondence course in advanced concepts and techniques. In 1987 Unwin Hyman published his first book, 'Cosmic Loom'. This was followed by a German edition, and in 1999, an enlarged and revised edition from the Urania Trust.

John Frawley

Interview recorded:
8 October 1997
A few case studies were
added in Jan and Feb 2000

Contact
j@apprentice.demon.co.uk

Website
www.apprentice.demon.co.uk

Birth Data
"16th May 1955, at twenty to one in the morning BST, in London."

John Frawley is a practitioner and teacher of the traditional techniques of astrology. He teaches the Apprenticeships in Horary, Electional and Traditional Natal Astrology. He is author of 'The Real Astrology', publisher/editor of 'The Astrologer's Apprentice' (an astrological magazine unlike any other), and writes widely in the astrological press.

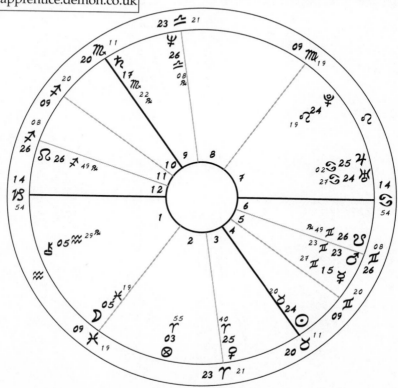

Adam Fronteras

Interview recorded:
20 October 1998

Contact
affronter@tlpplc.com

Birth Data
"11th March 1962, Eltham, 14.20. From my parents—they wanted me to hurry up because there was a rugby match due to start! In fact I believe it was 'between two and two-thirty', and was rectified by Bettina Lee."

Adam Fronteras is the current Chairman of the British Astrological and Psychic Society (BAPS—see 'Organisations'); he is a qualified astrologer and has been a BAPS Consultant for over 15 years in Astrology, Tarot and I-Ching. Adam is a regular contributor to magazines and newspapers; he appears frequently on television and radio, and has presented a series on astrology for Plymouth Sound Radio. He regularly lectures around the country and abroad. Adam has a syndicated horoscope column in a number of national newspapers and magazines. He operates his own premium rate telephone lines and was involved in the setting up and management of the Mystic Meg Live Psychic line. Adam is the author of the best seller 'The Tarot', published by Carlton Books in the UK and Stewart, Tabori and Chang in North America. 'The Tarot' sold out its first print run of over 35,000 copies in its first year of publication and received special promotion through Book Club Associates and 'Prediction' magazine.

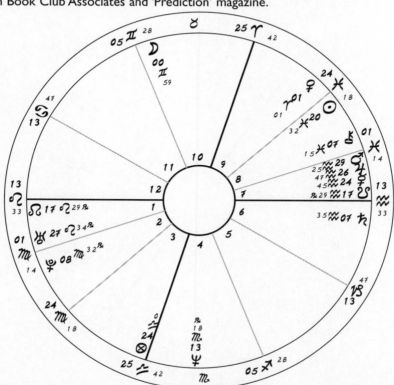

David Hamblin

Written reply despatched:
20 September 1999

Contact
11 Kensington Gardens,
Bath BA1 6LW
pigleystair@yahoo.co.uk

Birth Data
"I was born in Manchester at 9.50 p.m. BST on 8th
August 1935."

David Hamblin's 'Harmonic Charts' was published by
Aquarian Press in 1983.

Articles in 'The Astrological Journal':
'Hot and Cold Murder' (Winter 1973-74)
'The Teaching of Astrology' (Summer 1975)
'Isolated and Congested Suns' (Winter 1976-77)
'Jupiter in the Classroom' (Summer 1978 and
Summer 1981)
'The Need for Doubt and the Need for Wonder'
(Summer 1982)
'Astrological Reality and the Meaning of Number'
(Winter 1983-84)
'The Huber Approach: a Personal View' (July 1986)
'Harmonics and the Silent Twins' (June/July 1987).

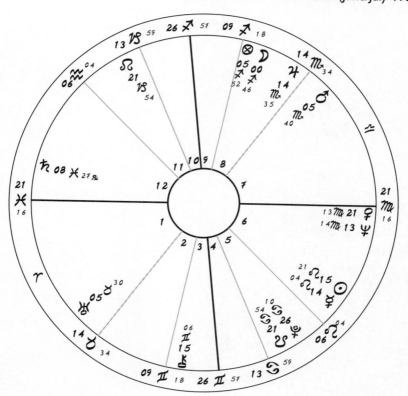

Robert Hand

Interview recorded:
7 September 1997

Contact
info@robhand.com

Website
www.robhand.com

Birth Data
19.30 (Eastern War Time), 5 December 1942, Plainfield, New Jersey, USA (taken from his book 'Planets in Transit').

Robert Hand graduated with honours in History from Brandeis University, and went on for graduate work at Princeton with 'History of Science'. He began an astrological practice in 1972 and as success came, he began travelling worldwide as a full time professional astrologer.

Robert Hand was known in his early career as the first practising astrologer to write astrology software for other astrologers. From this effort, he founded Astro-Graphics Services in 1979, which later became Astrolabe, Inc. In 1997 he established the 'Association for the Retrieval of Historical Astrological Texts' (ARHAT—see 'Organisations'), a formal archive, library and publishing company for preserving his work and findings. Robert Hand's library now houses the original texts and translations of over two dozen ancient and medieval astrologers. His books to date include:

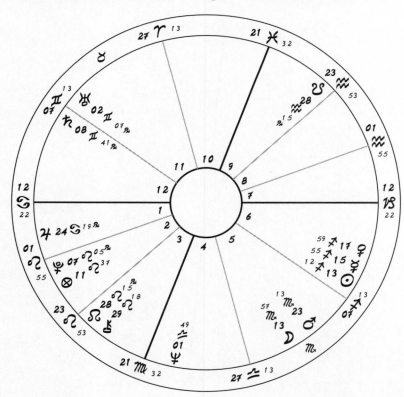

'Horoscope Symbols'; 'Planets in Transit'; 'Planets in Composite'; 'Planets in Youth'; 'Essays on Astrology' and 'Night and Day: Planetary Sect in Astrology'. He is chairman of the National Council for Geocosmic Research (NCGR) and is a patron of the Faculty of Astrological Studies. He lectures in conferences, seminars and workshops worldwide, and offers professional astrological services to astrologers and the general public.

Mike Harding

Interview recorded:
20 April 1999

Contact
mikeharding@ndirect.co.uk

Birth Data
"October 26th 1944, about 6.12pm (that's still wartime, so it's 5.12 GMT) and it's Croydon, which is 51.23N, 0.06W."

Mike Harding is an astrological consultant and a registered existential psychotherapist. A former chair of the Astrological Association and the Association of Professional Astrologers, he is now Chair of the Society for Existential Analysis, and Head of Pre-MA programmes at the School of Psychotherapy and Counselling at Regent's College, London (see 'Organisations'). He was for many years on the council of the Faculty for Astrological Studies, where he was also Director of

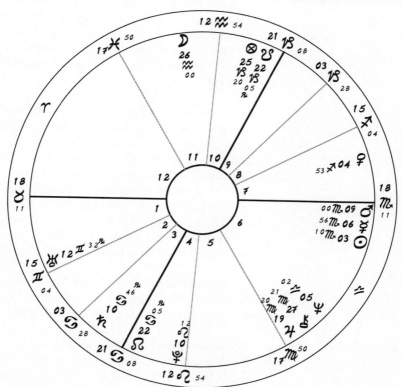

their two year 'Counselling Within Astrology' programme. He is currently on the Registration Board of the United Kingdom Council for Psychotherapy. The winner of the Astrological Association's 'The Truth of Astrology' prize (1997), he has written on many areas of technical and psychological astrology, particularly harmonics and midpoints, and is the author of 'Hymns to the Ancient Gods', and 'Working with Astrology' (with Charles Harvey). He is currently completing 'The Language of Time', which introduces the practice and philosophy of astrology to the general reader. As well as publishing in the area of astrology, he has published articles and run workshops on the experience of time, the philosophy of language, and the boundaries between philosophy and current psychoanalysis.

Pat Harris

Interview recorded:
4 May 1999

Contact
Tel: 01962 713134
harris@interalpha.co.uk

Birth Data
"20th May 1953, at 11.58 BST, Bradford in West Yorkshire. That's from a neighbour who witnessed my birth. She was a very spiritual person who felt it important to note the time of witnessing the arrival of another 'soul' on the earth."

Pat Harris created and took on the post of Public Relations Officer for the Faculty of Astrological Studies (FAS—see 'Organisations') in 1983, holding it until September 1999, as well as being a member of the FAS council during those years. She was a council member for the Astrological Association from 1982-83/84.

Pat was instrumental in setting up the Research Group for the Critical Study of Astrology (RGCSA) within the Faculty of Social Sciences at Southampton University (Professor Christopher Bagley is Group Convenor), with a view to paving the way for a Chair in astrology at the University. She was recently appointed as Administrative Assistant to the RGCSA, providing liaison between researchers in the astrological community and academics pursuing astrological research in universities.

Pat was appointed Editor for the Astrological Association research journal 'Correlation' in the summer of 1999 and is currently holding that office.

Her Diploma with the FAS was achieved in 1982; a Certificate in Counselling Skills in 1992; and she received her Master's Degree in Health Psychology at Southampton University in 1997.

Pat is currently studying for a PhD in the Applications of Astrology to Health Psychology, which should be completed in 2001/02. She has been invited to do a PhD on the strength of research done at MSc level, which looked at the effectiveness of astrological counselling in understanding coping strategies of chronic pain patients. Pat's PhD research involves looking at possible correlates between Jupiter and Saturn and success and failure, respectively, of infertility treatment.

Pat has been a part-time astrological consultant since qualifying in 1982 and a counselling astrologer since 1992. Seven of her articles have been published on Northern Ireland's peace process from 1992–1999 in 'The Astrological Journal', 'Realta' and 'The Dublin Astrologer'. Articles have also been published in 'Apollon' and 'Prediction' magazines.

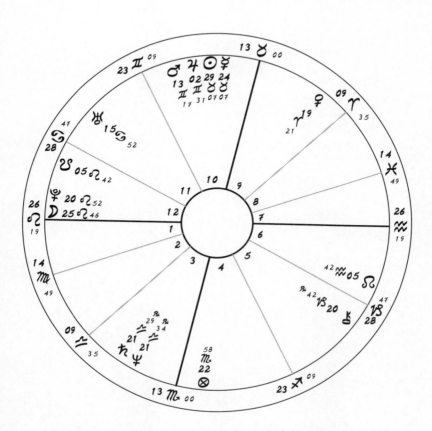

Robin Heath

Written reply despatched:
21 July 1998

Contact
Tel: 01239 613224
(office hours)
skyhenge@zetnet.co.uk

Birth Data
"I was born at Brockett Hall, Hitchin, Hertfordshire between 22:48 and 22:52 on the 8th May 1948."

Robin Heath has been practising astrology since 1973, and has been a professional astrologer since 1978. He is a member of the APA, has been editor of the AA Journal and is now a consultant editor for 'Correlation'. He has written for 'The Mountain Astrologer', 'Kindred Spirit', 'Chalice', 'Culture and Cosmos' and the 'NGCR Journal', in addition to the AA 'Journal', 'Realta' and the FAA 'Journal'.

He lectures to astrology groups and has run astrology classes for twenty years in addition to teaching on the Centre for Psychological Astrology course. He is a teacher with The Earth School (see 'Organisations') and has published several books. Those in print are 'Sun, Moon & Earth' (Wooden Books); 'Sun, Moon & Stonehenge' (Bluestone Press); and 'A Beginner's Guide to Stone Circles' (Hodder & Stoughton).

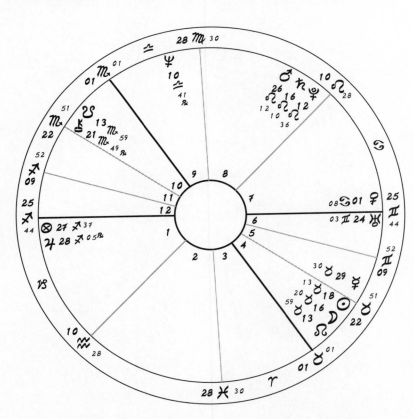

Maggie Hyde

Interview recorded:
10 July 1998

Contact
see Company of Astrologers

Maggie Hyde is a consultant astrologer with a particular interest in divination; she is also a leading writer of Sun-sign columns. In 1983 she co-founded the Company of Astrologers, with which she currently teaches and practises.

Warren Kenton

Interview recorded:
16 June 1999

Birth Data
"8.30 am, London (about a mile from Greenwich) 8th January 1933."

Educated at St. Martin's School of Art and the Royal Academy of Painting, Warren Kenton later worked in the theatre and as a graphic designer. He taught for a number of years at R.A.D.A. and the Architectural Association. He has published two novels and 14 other books, 11 of them on kabbalah, the Jewish mystical-philosophical tradition. These have been translated into 11 languages. He writes under his Hebrew name of Z'ev ben Shimon Halevi. His esoteric

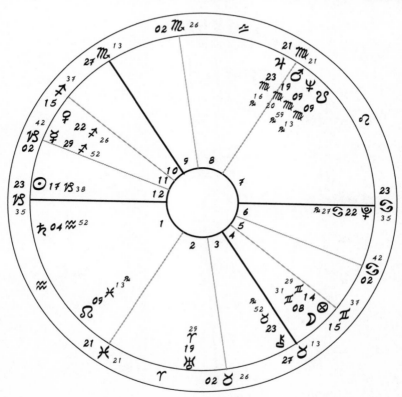

training began in 1958. He has lectured in Western and Eastern Europe, North, Central and South America and in Israel. He ran courses for many years for the Wrekin Trust and is a fellow of the Temenos Academy where he occasionally lectures. He has lectured at the Royal College of Art, the Theosophical Society, various rabbinic colleges and other institutions, including the Mystics and Scientists conference. His main work is with his Way of Kabbalah Workshops and The International Kabbalah Society, which held its first conference in Toledo, Spain. During nearly 40 years of research, writing and visiting ancient kabbalistic centres in Europe, North Africa and Israel, he has continued to be based in London, where he takes a core group. His books include 'The Anatomy of Fate (Astrology and Kabbalah)'; 'A Kabbalistic Universe'; and 'Psychology and Kabbalah'.

Lee Lehman

Interview recorded:
8 August 1999

Website
www.leelehman.com/

Birth Data
"9th September 1953, 4.45am, (that's rectified from a birth certificate of 4.35am) Wakefield, Nebraska."

Lee holds M.S. and Ph.D. degrees from Rutgers University. She has been Research Director of NCGR, and Treasurer and Program Chair of the United Astrology Congress (UAC). She is author of 'The Ultimate

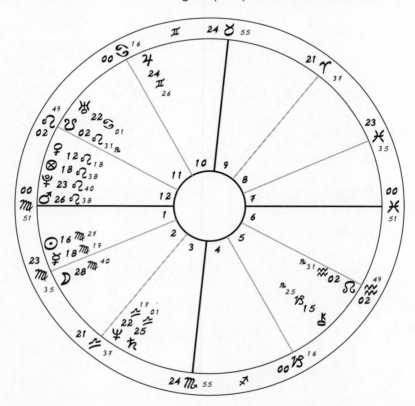

Asteroid Book' (1988), 'Essential Dignities' (1989), 'The Book of Rulerships' (1992), 'Classical Astrology for Modern Living' (1996), and a translation from the French of Papus' 'Astrology for Initiates'. Lee is busy working on her fifth book, 'The Martial Art of Horary Astrology'. She originated the Classical Studies course curriculum, which presently includes 6 regular courses. She teaches classes in Atlanta and Boston, and recurring classes in several other cities. In her spare time, she studies Chang-Hon style Tae Kwon Do. Along with Graham Dawson and Stephanie Johnson of Esoteric Technologies, Lee has created two software report writer programs written specifically for those interested in classical astrology: Solar Writer/Medicus, for medical questions and decumbitures; and Solar Writer/Classical, for natal delineation in the matter-of-fact style of the Renaissance astrologer.

Maurice McCann	**Birth Data**
Interview recorded: 5 February 1998	"23 December 1938, 1.20 am, Belfast."

Maurice McCann

Interview recorded:
5 February 1998

Contact
mcmcann@compuserve.com

Website
http://ourworld.compuserve.com/homepages/mcmcann

Birth Data
"23 December 1938, 1.20 am, Belfast."

Maurice McCann has been an astrologer for 25 years, of which the last 20 have been spent as a professional working astrologer. He has a Diploma in Higher Education on the History of Astrology for the English Civil War period as well as a BA (Hons)

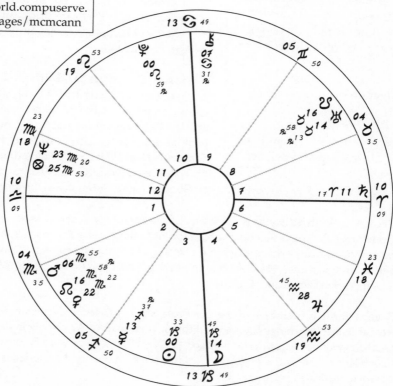

degree in the same subject. He has been, at various times, Chair of the Astrological Lodge of London, and its treasurer; a co-director of the Meonen School of Horary Astrology; and is currently editor of 'Réalta', the journal of the Irish Astrological Association. He was co-author of 'Eclipses' published in 1989 by Aquarian Press with Derek Appleby, and is the author of 'The Void of Course Moon' published in 1997 by Tara Astrological Publications. He is also creator of Tara–Horary Astrology. He has also researched and written widely on astrology generally. He is a regular contributor to a wide variety of international astrological journals and his essays have appeared in several anthologies on the subject. He has also lectured in many countries including Russia, Canada, USA, Australia, Norway, Denmark, Belgium, Italy, as well as in his native Ireland and the UK.

The Researchers

Interview arrived at by email conference; first questions sent out on 9 February 1999, final amendments to interview as it appears in this book received on 12 March 2000

Contact
rhsmit@smitpotze.demon.nl

Website
www.smitpotze.demon.nl/Astrology-and-Science

Dr Geoffrey Dean and **Arthur Mather** are compilers of 'Recent Advances in Natal Astrology: A Critical Review 1900-1976', the first book-length critical review of scientific research into astrology, and collaborators (since 1975) on critical articles, debates, surveys, and prize competitions for research into astrology. Dean is a freelance technical writer and editor living in Perth, Western Australia. Mather is in charge of technical training projects in Livingston, Scotland.

Professor Emeritus Dr Suitbert Ertel is the world's leading investigator of Gauquelin planetary effects, on which he has authored many scientific articles, including a bibliography of Gauquelin's publications. He has also co-authored the book 'The Tenacious Mars Effect' with Kenneth Irving. Before his retirement, Dr. Ertel was Professor of Psychology at Georg-August University in Göttingen, Germany.

Professor Ivan W Kelly is Chairman of the Astrology Subcommittee of the US-based Committee for the Scientific Investigation of Claims of the Paranormal, and author or co-author of many critical works on astrology, human judgement, and alleged lunar effects on behaviour. He is Professor of Educational Psychology at the University of Saskatchewan, Saskatoon, Canada.

Rudolf Smit is secretary of the late Professor H J Eysenck's Committee for Objective Research into Astrology, founding editor of what is now 'Astrologie in Onderzoek' (Astrology under Scrutiny), and editor (1992-1999) of the research journal 'Correlation'. He is the editor and translator of one of the Netherlands' leading scientific institutes.

Professor
Peter Roberts

Written reply despatched:
11 February 2000

Peter Roberts is a research scientist, and visiting professor in Systems at City University, London and the Open University. He is author of 'The Message of Astrology', and co-author, with Helen Greengrass, of 'The Astrology of Time Twins'.

Christeen Skinner

Interviews recorded:
15 January 1996
11 April 1996
13 July 1999

Website
www.horoscopes.co.uk

Birth Data
"5 October 1951, 19.20 BST, Edinburgh."

Christeen Skinner calculated her first chart in 1967. During the 1980s, she qualified with the Faculty of Astrological Studies in London, sitting their examinations as an external candidate. She specialises in the study of planetary cycles and their relationship to economic affairs. Her practice in London attracts business clients seeking to understand their own birth charts as well as the likely developments in world

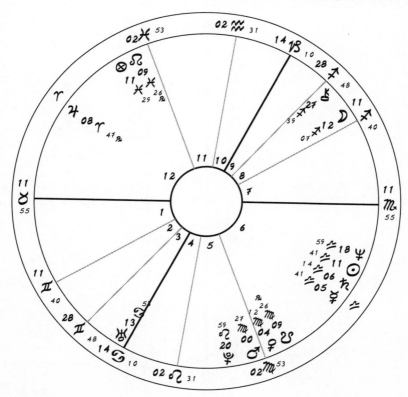

affairs as interpreted through planetary cycles. Christeen is also a teacher and lecturer in more general aspects of astrology. She has appeared on radio and television in the UK, USA, Germany, Norway, Finland, Japan and Eire and gave a notably correct financial forecast on the BBC's 'Heart of the Matter' programme. She has been Chair of the Astrological Association of Great Britain, a Trustee of the Urania Trust and was on the Council of the Faculty of Astrological Studies for nine years. She also produces her own monthly newsletter, 'Cycles', covering social, political and financial world affairs. Her first book, 'Money Signs', was published in 1998 by Hodder & Stoughton, and more books are currently in preparation.

Komilla Sutton

Interview recorded:
21 April 1998

Contact
as for BAVA
(see 'Organisations')

Birth Data
"15 August 1953, 9.00 pm, Jullundur in India (just north of Delhi, south of Amritsar)."

Komilla Sutton is co-founder of the British Association for Vedic Astrology (BAVA), and runs Vedic astrology beginner's groups in London and Romsey (Hampshire), as well as a correspondence course. Her first book is 'Essentials of Vedic Astrology', published in 1999.

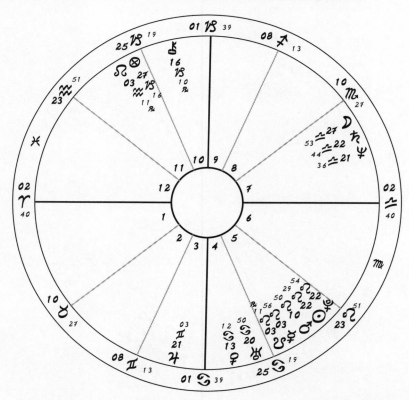

Graeme Tobyn

Interview recorded:
8 March 1999

Contact
Tel: 01432-279653
also via the Company of
Astrologers (see
'Organisations')

Graeme Tobyn is a medical herbalist in private practice with over two years' experience of working in the NHS, a clinical tutor on BSc courses in herbal medicine, a professional astrologer and a translator of Medieval and Renaissance Latin astrological texts. His publications include 'Culpeper's Medicine' (Element, 1997). Consultations are available in Hereford, Cheltenham and London.

Noel Tyl

Interview recorded:
25 May 1996

Website
www.noeltyl.com

Birth Data
3.57p.m. EST, 31 December 1936, West Chester, PA, USA (from Tyl who quotes his birth certificate in 'Prediction in Astrology', Llewellyn, 1991, p. 67).

Noel Tyl estimates that he must have interpreted around 20,000 charts during his career in astrology.

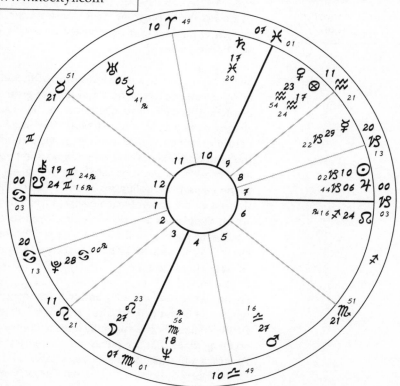

His twenty-four textbooks have been a major influence for two generations—see in particular his professional, 1000-page manual 'Synthesis & Counseling in Astrology'. He is a graduate of Harvard University in Social Relations (Psychology, Sociology, and Anthropology). He lectures constantly throughout 16 countries and maintains a formidable list of clients, both individual and corporate, from all over the world. His office and home are in Fountain Hills, a suburb of Phoenix, Arizona. In May, 1998, Tyl was honoured at the United Astrology Congress, the world convention for astrology, receiving the Regulus Award for establishing and maintaining professional image in the field. He has also been designated Director Principal of Milley Dome/Johannesburg, a 42,000 square feet ($7.5 million) domed edifice now under construction in South Africa as the Noel Tyl Learning Centre for Astrology and New Age Exploration. Noel Tyl was a co-founder of AFAN (Association for Astrological Networking), and has just retired from the position of Presiding Officer after eleven years. He also designed, and runs, his Master's Degree Certification Course in Astrology—a correspondence course comprising 19 lessons and a final exam.

Shelley von Strunckel

Interview recorded:
10 June 1999

Birth Data
"My chart absolutely declares what I do! 15th July 1946, 4.42pm, Hollywood (not Los Angeles), California. With Neptune right smack on the midheaven, and Uranus right smack on the descendant, exactly."

Shelley von Strunckel is best known to the public for bringing respect to her field and for her ground-breaking approach to its presentation. She had already been a consulting astrologer for fifteen years before creating the first ever astrological column in the London 'Sunday Times' newspaper eight years ago. In addition she uses astrology to analyse people in the news, from politicians to movie stars. She has devised a new style of astrological journalism in which the planets and signs are employed to create a revealing thumbnail sketch of high profile and intriguing subjects; these have appeared in the 'Sunday Times' and 'W'.

Shelley writes daily, weekly and monthly columns, which she began in 1991, then sharing a byline with Patric Walker. These currently appear in newspapers and magazines that are published in America, Europe, Australia and Asia; these include, notably, 'The South China Morning Post', 'The Bombay Times', French and English 'Vogue' and, in America, 'W' magazine. Shelley's columns can also be accessed via the internet on www. handbag. com and, in 2001, from her own website. She is a frequent and popular guest on radio and television. Her appearances include: leading the news on the BBC TV World Service, 'Kilroy', shows on ABC and NBC in America, ITV and Channel 9 (Australia) news, as well as many debates and discussion shows.

Shelley was born and raised in Hollywood, with a British nanny, which enabled her effortlessly to blend the traditional with the new. From her late teens she pursued studies of various philosophies as well as studying astrology; her formal training, however, was in retailing and merchandising with the renowned Federated Department Store chain. Whilst working in the fashion business, she attended the University of California Evening School, studying the psychology of trends and cycles. Finally, she made the move into a more sensible line of work, and became a consulting astrologer. Within two years she was lecturing on the subject in India with her client base emcompassing New York, to London and her native Los Angeles. She is married to a barrister and has homes in London and New York.

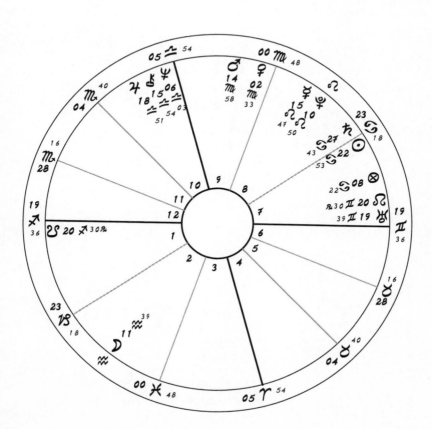

Robert Zoller

Interview recorded:
5 September 1998

Birth Data

8.59 am (EST), 25th January 1947, Mount Vernon, NY, USA (Source: chart used in talk, 'Medieval Delineations & Predictive Techniques', presented by Robert Zoller on 4th September 1998 as part of the annual AA Conference).

Robert Zoller is a medievalist, Latinist, student and practitioner of medieval astrology and occult philosophy. He learned his Latin at the Summer Latin Institute at the City University Graduate Center in 1974 and received his training in Medieval Studies at the Institute for Medieval and Renaissance Studies at CCNY in 1977. He is the author of 'Lost Key to Prediction: The Arabic Parts in Astrology' (Inner Traditions, NY 1980), 'On the Fifth House' (Ixion Press, 1992), 'Fate, Free Will and Astrologyy (Ixion Press,1992) and 'Tools and Techniques of the Medieval Astrologers' (Ixion Press, 1994). For the Latin Track of Project Hindsight he translated Al-Kindi's 'On the Stellar Rays', 'Liber Hermetis' and part of the Second Tractates of Guido Bonatti's 13th century work 'Liber Astronomiae'.

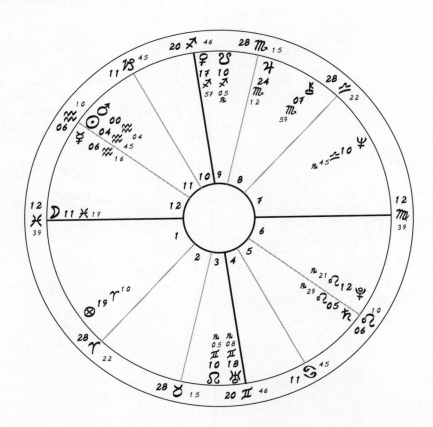

Mr Zoller has also translated Bonatti's instructions on how to wage war astrologically from the Sixth Tractate of 'Liber Astronomiae'. These dicta were published in 'Astrological Quarterly', the periodical of The Astrological Lodge of London (Vol 62 No3, 63, Nos 1-3).

He has contributed numerous articles to a variety of astrological periodicals. Mr. Zoller has taught astrology, Hermetic Philosophy and other related subjects for over 15 years and is the Principal of the Medieval Astrology Correspondence Course. He is co-founder of the Mid-Hudson Chapter of the National Council of Geocosmic Research. He has an extensive background in the Western, Nordic and Indian Esoteric Traditions. In 1998, Robert was honored by the Federation of Australian Astrologers by being awarded their Southern Cross International Award given to the overseas astrologer who has done the most to further astrology in Australia.

Part 2: Organisations

Association for the Retrieval of Historical Astrological Texts (ARHAT)
PO Box 2008, Reston, VA 21095, USA; http://www.RobHand.com

Translates and publishes classical and medieval astrological texts.

Association of Professional Astrologers (APA)
Secretary, Box No. AJI, 80 High Street, Wargrave, Berks RG10 8DE
Tel: 01189 404424

Organisation provides support for professional astrologers.

Astrological Lodge of London (ALL)
50 Gloucester Place, London W1H

A registered charity founded in 1915, and from which many of the UK's current astrological groups have sprung. It holds weekly meetings, seminars, and publishes the 'Astrological Quarterly'.

Astro Logos
PO Box 216, Welland, South Australia, Australia 5007
Email: bnbrady@chariot.net.au

Website: http://www.bernadettebrady.com/astlog.HTM

Astro Logos is one of Australia's most successful astrological training centres. Located in Adelaide it offers a wide range of opportunities to both the new student and the professional astrologer. Courses are provided through lectures and workshops to both attending students and students from around the world studying through open learning.

Astrological Association (AA)

Unit 168, Lee Valley Technopark, Tottenham Hale, London N17 9LN
Tel: 020-8880-4848
Email: astrological.association@zetnet.com
Website: http://www.astrologer.com/aanet

Publishes 'The Astrological Journal' and 'Transit' newsletter bi-monthly, and 'Correlation', the journal of scientific research into astrology, every six months. Its conference, at the beginning of September each year, is a major event in the international astrological calendar.

British Association for Vedic Astrology (BAVA)

2 Tee Court, Romsey, Hants SO51 8GY
Tel: 01794-524178

Promotes and co-ordinates Vedic astrology activities in the UK.

British Astrological and Psychic Society (BAPS)

Robert Denholm House, Bletchingley Road, Nutfield, Redhill, Surrey RH1 4HW
Tel: 07071-780796
Email: BAPS@tlpplc.com

Primarily for those interested in a variety of esoteric studies, e.g. palmistry, numerology, and clairvoyance as well as astrology. Runs training courses in astrology and Tarot, publishes a quarterly journal, 'The Mercury', and maintains a list of approved consultants in various disciplines.

Centre for Psychological Astrology (CPA)

BCM Box 1815, London, N1 1LY
Email: cpalondon@aol.com
Website: http://www.astrologer.com/cpa

Focusses particularly on astrology in relationship to depth psychology; provides courses, seminars, the magazine 'Apollon', and books from the CPA Press.

Committee for the Scientific Investigation of Claims of the Paranormal (CSICOP)
Box 703, Amherst, NY, 14226, USA
716-636-1425
Website: http://www.csicop.org/
Email: info@csicop.org

A non-profit organisation that encourages the critical investigation of paranormal and fringe-science claims. 'The Skeptical Inquirer' is its official journal.

The Company of Astrologers
PO Box 3001, London, N1 1LY
Tel: 01227 362427
E-mail: admin@coa.org.uk
Website: http://www.hubcom.com/coa

The Company of Astrologers was founded in 1983 to promote the practice of astrology as a way of insight and self-knowledge. To this end, the Company offers a full teaching programme, and a forum for the sharing of astrology. Provides a 'Foundation Programme', giving a grounding in astrological basics, and more advanced courses that focus on the understanding of astrology as divination. Also offers other studies in divination, especially Tarot and the I Ching. The Company of Astrologers is a private limited company. Its shareholders receive no dividends; any profit is used to further the educational work of the Company. The Company of Astrologers is a full Member of APAE (The Advisory Panel on Astrological Education).

Continuum (Angel Thompson)
1809 Washington Way, Venice, CA 90291, USA
Email: forcntnuum@aol.com
Website: http://www.starIQ.com/continuum

Ralph and Lahni DeAmicis—see 'Space and Time'

The Earth School
6 Borough Road, Kingston upon Thames, KT2 6BD, England
Tel: 020-8549-1307

The Earth School offers a comprehensive programme of study which leads to the development of practical skills combined with spiritual awareness, enabling students to live and work better on and with the Earth. It provides a synthesis of ancient and modern wisdoms, placing traditional studies alongside modern concerns such as the environment, bodywork and healing.

Faculty of Astrological Studies (FAS)
54 High Street, Orpington, Kent BR6 0QJ, UK
Tel: 07000-790143
Email: info@astrology.org.uk
Website: http://www.astrology.org.uk

Established in 1948; provides classes, courses and qualifications—its Diploma (DFAstrolS) is one of the main qualifications in the world of astrology.

International Society of Astrological Research, Inc (ISAR)
PO Box 38613, Los Angeles, CA90038.
Tel: 805-525-0461

Publishes a quarterly journal, 'KOSMOS', and hosts a biennial research conference amongst other activities.

James Randi Educational Foundation
201 S.E. 12th St (E Davie Blvd), Fort Lauderdale, FL 33316-1815, USA
Tel: 954-467-1112
Email: jref@randi.org
Website: http://www.randi.org

A non-profit organisation founded in 1996 to promote critical thinking about paranormal and supernatural ideas. The Foundation offers a $1,000,000 prize to anyone who can "demonstrate any psychic, supernatural or paranormal ability of any kind under mutually agreed upon scientific conditions."

National Council for Geocosmic Research (NCGR)
PO Box 38866, Los Angeles, CA 90038.
Tel: 818-761-6433
Email: montra@earthlink.net
Website: http://www.geocosmic.org

Dedicated to astrological education and research; has over 3000 members in 26 countries, with many 'Special Interest Groups' for research into specific areas of interest (e.g. asteroids).

Project Hindsight
532 Washington Street, Cumberland, MD21502, USA
Website: http://projecthindsight-tghp.com

Translates and publishes classical and medieval astrological texts.

Research Group for the Critical Study of Astrology (RGCSA)

Professor Christopher Bagley, Department of Social Work Studies, University of Southampton , Highfield, Southampton, SO17 1BJ, UK.
Email: cb5@socsci.soton.ac.uk

The RGCSA exists to promote critical research in astrology, i.e., exploring astrology in order to achieve a fuller understanding of the discipline in broad fields of interest, for example, within the social sciences and the arts. It is also intended to forge links between academics in all fields who are interested in researching astrology related to their special interest and astrologers of high standards who are specialists in identical or complementary research fields.

Students who are interested in registering for MPhil degrees with a view to doing research in astrology are invited to contact the RGCSA Director, Professor Christopher Bagley for details about how the RGCSA may be able to help them. Students must have a demonstrably high standard of knowledge in astrology and/or professional qualifications which attest to this.

School of Psychotherapy & Counselling

Regent's College
Inner Circle
Regent's Park
London
NW1 4NS
Tel: 020 7487 7406
Email: spc@regents.ac.uk
Website: www.spc.ac.uk

The School offers pre-professional, academic and professional training in existential-phenome-nological, psychodynamic, and integrative psychotherapy.

Space and Time (Ralph and Lahni DeAmicis)

Website: http://www.spaceandtime.com

Angel Thompson – see 'Continuum'

Urania Trust (UT)

BCM Urania, London, WC1N 3XX
Tel: 020-7700-0639
urania@globalnet.co.uk

http://www.urania.org

A registered charity that acts as an information service to promote serious astrological study in many ways; their yearbook is a particularly useful source of information about the world of astrology.

Bibliography

This appendix again falls naturally into two parts. The first is the main bibliography; this contains works referred to in the text, some works by the interviewees (this is by no means exhaustive), and a few other works by authors who are mentioned in the text.

Part 2 is an annotated list of books which evaluate astrology from scientific perspectives; this was supplied by the Researchers as an adjunct to their interview, and it seemed best to reproduce it intact.

For anyone who has found one aspect or another of this book interesting and wonders where to look next, I can make a few recommendations—these are, of course, entirely personal:

    1. For a concise overview of astrology, its different guises and the issues it raise: *Astrology for Beginners* by Cornelius, Hyde & Webster.

    2. For an introduction to how to calculate and interpret charts: *Teach Yourself Astrology* by Jeff Mayo.

    3. For the philosophy behind astrology, Geoffrey Cornelius's *The Moment of Astrology*, and Dennis Elwell's *Cosmic Loom*—and let me acknowledge, with thanks, my debt to both for their influence on many of the ideas between these covers.

    4. For the arguments in favour of astrology's validity, and an account of some of the arguments between astrologers and skeptics: *The Case For Astrology* by John Anthony West.

    5. For the case of scientists/skeptics against astrology, Chapters IX and X of this book are (I think) the most concise formulation generally available. If you have read those chapters and want more, see the bibliography provided by the Researchers in Part 2 of this Appendix.

Part 1: Books Quoted or Alluded to

Abbott, Edwin A. *Flatland*. New York: Dover, 1953.

Anderson, P.W. *More is Different*. 'Science' 177, 1972.

Appleby, Derek & McCann, Maurice. *Eclipses*. Wellingborough: Aquarian Press, 1989.

Arroyo, Stephen. *Chart Interpretation Handbook*. Reno: CRCS, 1989.

Baigent, Michael. *The Natal Chart of Communist Russia*. 'The Astrological Journal' Vol 22 No.3, Summer 1980 p.173.

Baigent, Michael; Harvey, Charles; Campion, Nicholas. *Mundane Astrology*. London:

Aquarian/Harper Collins, 1992 (2nd edition, revised & expanded; original was 1984).

Baigent, Michael; Leigh, Richard. *The Elixir and the Stone—The Tradition of Magic and Alchemy*. London: Penguin Books, 1997.

Barbour, Julian. *The End of Time*. London: Weidenfeld & Nicholson, 1999.

Barton, Tamsyn. *Ancient Astrology*. London: Routledge, 1994.

Bauer, Henry H. *The Enigma of Loch Ness: Making Sense of a Mystery*. Stirling: Johnston & Bacon, 1991.

Bauer, Henry H. *Scientific Literacy and the Myth of the Scientific Method*. Urbana & Chicago: University of Illinois Press, 1992.

Bauman, Zygmunt. *Modernity and the Holocaust*. Oxford: Polity, 1989.

Bohm, David. *Unfolding Meaning: a Weekend of Dialogue with David Bohm*. London: Routledge, 1985.

Bonatti, Guido. *Liber Astronomiae*. Part is translated in Zoller 1980. For the original: *Guidonis Bonati Forliviensis Mathematici de Astronomia Tractatus X universum quod iudiciariam rationem, aeris tempestatum attinet, comprehendentes*. Basel, 1550.

Bonatus, Guido. *The Astrologer's Guide*. Tr. Henry Coley. London: Regulus Publishing Company, 1986.

Brady, Bernadette. *The Eagle and the Lark, A Textbook of Predictive Astrology*. New York: Samuel Weiser, 1992.

Brady, Bernadette. *Brady's Book of Fixed Stars*. New York: Samuel Weiser, 1998.

Calvino, Italo. *Invisible Cities*. London: Secker & Warburg, 1974.

Cassidy, Lawrence. *The Believing Christian as a Dedicated Astrologer*. 'The Astrological Quarterly', Vol. 64 No. 3 (Summer 1994), pp.3-13.

Chesterton, G.K. *The Man Who Was Thursday*. New York: Dodd, Mead & Co, 1935.

Cicero. Tr. W.A. Falconer. *On Divination*. London, 1929.

Collins, C.B. & Hawking, S.W. *Why is the Universe Isotropic?* 'Astrophysical Journal', 180. 1973.

Cook, Peter L. *The Astrology of Some Recent Earthquakes*. 'The Astrological Journal', Vol 42 No.1, Jan/Feb 2000

Copenhaver, Brian P. *Hermetica*. Cambridge: Cambridge University Press, 1992.

Cornelius, Geoffrey. *The Moment of Astrology*. London: Arkana/Penguin, 1994.

Cornelius, Geoffrey; Hyde, Maggie; Webster, Chris. *Astrology for Beginners*. Cambridge: Icon Books, 1995.

Cornell, Dr. H L. *Encyclopaedia of Medical Astrology*. Los Angeles: Cornell Publishing, 1933.

'Correlation'. Six-monthly 'Journal of Research into Astrology', published by the Astrological Association (see Appendix 1, part 2).

Cozzi, Steve. *Planets in Locality*. Tempe, AZ: AFA Publications, 1997.

Culpeper, Nicholas. *Culpeper's Herbal & English Physician*. London, 1652 (see also Tobyn).

Curry, Patrick. *Prophecy and Power*. London: Polity Press, 1989.

Curry, Patrick. *A Confusion of Prophets*. London: Collins & Brown, 1992.

Davidson, William M (Dr). *Planetary Symptoms of Disease and the Confirming Symptoms*. Lecture III of the series of nine special lectures on medical astrology and health. (Published by: Astrological Bureau, 5 Old Quaker Hill Road, Monroe, N.Y. 10950 USA) New York: Astrological Bureau, 1973 (2nd edition).

Davis, Martin. *Astrolocality Astrology*. Bournemouth: The Wessex Astrologer, 1999.

Dawkins, Richard. *The Real Romance in the Stars*. Article in the Independent on Sunday, 31 December 1995; republished in the Astrological Association Journal, Vol 38 No.3, May/June 1996 with 4 additional footnotes from Professor Dawkins and a critique by Nicholas Campion.

Dean G, Mather A, & 52 others. *Recent Advances in Natal Astrology: A Critical Review 1900-1976*. Perth, Western Australia: Analogic, 1977.

Duncan, Adrian. *Is Astrology Reality?* http://wow.world-of-wisdom.com/articlereality.htm

Elwell, Dennis. *Cosmic Loom*. London: Unwin Hyman. 1987 Second (revised & enlarged) edition: London: Urania Trust, 1999.

Elwell, Dennis. *How Far Can the Future be Predicted?* The Astrological Journal, Vol XXIX

No. 6 p.263, 1987a.

Ertel, Suitbert; Irving, Kenneth. *The Tenacious Mars Effect*. London: Urania Trust, 1996.

Eysenck, H.J and Nias, D.K.B. *Astrology: Science or Superstition*. London: Maurice Temple, 1982.

Feyerabend, Paul. *Against Method* (revised ed.) London: Verso, 1988.

Ficino, Marsilio. Tr. C. Boer. *The Book of Life*. Irving: Spring Publications, 1980.

Fortune, Dion. *Psychic Self-Defence*. London: Aquarian, 1988.

Gauquelin, Michel. *Cosmic Influences on Human Behaviour*. New York: Stein & Day, 1973.

Gauquelin, Michel. *Neo-Astrology*. London: Penguin, 1991.

Gleick, James. *Chaos*. London: Abacus, 1988.

Greene, Liz. *The Outer Planets & Their Cycles*. Reno: CRCS Publications, 1983.

Gribbin, John. *In Search of Schroedinger's Cat*. London: Wildwood, 1984.

Gyr, Peter. *Getting Players to Take Psychological Responsibility*. Fifa Magazine. February 1998.

Hamblin, David. *The Need for Doubt and the Need for Wonder*. 'Journal of the Astrological Association', Vol. XXIV No.3 (Summer), p.152, 1982.

Hamblin, David. *Harmonic Charts*. Wellingborough: Aquarian, 1983.

Hand, Robert. *Planets in Transit*. Rockport, MA: Para Research, 1976.

Hand, Robert. *Horoscope Symbols*. Rockport, MA: Para Research, 1981.

Harding, Michael. *Hymns to the Ancient Gods*. London: Arkana/Penguin, 1992.

Heath, Robin. *Sun, Moon & Earth*. Wooden Books, 1999.

Heath, Robin. Sun, Moon & Stonehenge. Bluestone Press, 1998.

Heath, Robin. *A Beginner's Guide to Stone Circles*. London: Hodder & Stoughton, 1999.

Herrigel, Eugen. *Zen in the Art of Archery*. London: Arkana/Penguin, 1985.

Hone, Margaret E. *The Modern Textbook of Astrology*. London: Lowe & Brydon, 1951.

Hughes, Stephen. *Nephrology and Astrology—is there a link?* 'British Journal of Clinical Practice', Vol 44 no.7 p278, 1990.

Huxley, Aldous. *Brave New World*. London: Chatto & Windus, 1932.

Hyde, Maggie. *Jung and Astrology*. London: Aquarian Press, 1992.

Jackson, Eve 1986. *Jupiter: An Astrologer's Guide*. Wellingborough: Aquarian Press, 1986.

Jay, A. *Oxford Dictionary of Political Quotations*. Oxford: Oxford University Press, 1996.

Johnson, Alan G. *The Blackwell Dictionary of Sociology*. Oxford: Blackwell, 1995, 2000.

Kant, Immanuel. Tr. Kemp-Smith, Norman. *Immanuel Kant's Critique of Pure Reason*. London: Macmillan Press, 1929.

Kenton, Warren. *The Anatomy of Fate*. London: Rider & Company, 1978.

Kornfield, Jack. *A Path With Heart*. London: Rider & Company, 1995.

Leo, Alan. *Astrology for All*. London, LN Fowler, 1921.

Levi-Strauss, Claude. *Myth and Meaning*. London: Routledge & Kegan Paul, 1978.

Lewis, Jim with Irving, Kenneth. *The Psychology of Astro*Carto*Graphy*. London: Arkana/Penguin, 1997.

Lilly, William. *Christian Astrology*. 1647. Reprinted London: Regulus, 1985.

Llewellyn's 1993 Moon Sign Book.

Maddox, John; Randi, James; Stewart, Walter W. *'High-Dilution' Experiments a Delusion*. 'Nature' 334, 1988.

Mayo, Jeff. *Teach Yourself Astrology*. London: Hodder & Stoughton, 1964 (note: a revised version of the book has recently been introduced and it is now under the names of Jeff Mayo and Christine Ramsdale).

McCann, Maurice. *The Void of Course Moon*. London: Tara Astrological Publications, 1997.

Millard, Margaret. *In Vitro Fertilisation*. 'The Astrological Association Journal' Vol.35, No.6 Nov/Dec 1993.

Morin de Villefranche, Jean Baptist. *Astrologia Gallica*. Paris, 1661.

Newton, Roger G. *The Truth of Science*. Cambridge, Mass: Harvard University Press, 1997.

Nietzsche, Friedrich. Tr. Hollingdale, R.J. *Twilight of the Idols*. Harmondsworth: Penguin, 1968.

Norretranders, Tor. *The User Illusion*. New York: Viking Penguin, 1998.

Parker, Derek & Parker, Julia. *The Compleat Astrologer*. Mitchell Beazley, 1971.

Pool, Robert. *Unbelievable Results Spark a Controversy*. 'Science' 241, 1988.

Quigley, Joan. *What Does Joan Say?* New York: Birch Lane Press, 1990.

Roberts, Peter. *The Message of Astrology*. Wellingborough. Aquarian Press, 1990.

Roberts, Peter & Greengrass, Helen. *The Astrology of Time Twins*. Edinburgh: The Pentland Press, 1994.

Roman Catholic Church. *Catechism*. The catechism can be downloaded from the Christus Rex Web Site: www.christusrex.org/www1/CDHN/

Rudhyar, Dane. *The Astrology of Personality*. New York: Doubleday, 1970.

Sasportas, Howard. *The Twelve Houses*. Wellingborough: Aquarian Press, 1985.

Seymour, Percy. *The Scientific Basis of Astrology*. New York: St Martin's Press, 1997.

Skinner, Christeen. *Money Signs*. London: Hodder & Stoughton, 1998.

Sutton, Komilla. *Essentials of Vedic Astrology*. Bournemouth: Wessex Astrologer, 1999.

Tarnas, Richard. *The Passion of the Western Mind*. New York: Ballantine, 1993.

Taylor, Thomas. *Iamblichus on the Mysteries*. San Diego: Wizards Bookshelf, 1997.

Tobyn, Graeme. *Culpeper's Medicine*. Shaftesbury, Element Books, 1997 (see also: Culpeper).

Tyl, Noel. *Synthesis & Counselling in Astrology*. St Paul: Llewellyn Publications, 1994.

Tyl, Noel. *Predictions for a New Millenium*. St Paul: Llewellyn Publications, 1996.

West, John Anthony. *The Case for Astrology*. London: Viking, 1991.

Wilhelm, Richard. Tr. Barnes, Cary F. *The I Ching*. London: Routledge & Kegan Paul, 1951.

Wittgenstein, Ludwig. Tr. Winch, Peter. *Culture and Value*. Oxford: Blackwell, 1998.

Zoller, Robert. *The Arabic Parts in Astrology*. Rochester: Inner Traditions, 1980.

Part 2: Annotated List of Some Books Critical of Astrology (comments by the Researchers)

Ankerberg J & Weldon J (1989). *Astrology: Do the Heavens Rule Our Destiny?* Harvest House, Eugene OR 97402, 334 pages with 356 references but no index.
Very readable critique by Bible scholars who have done their homework (the Christian perspective does not intrude). Many useful quotes, all referenced to the exact page.

Benski C et al (1996). *The Mars Effect: A French test of over 1000 sports champions.* Prometheus Books, Amherst NY, 157 pages but no index.
Includes a critical commentary by JW Nienhuys.

Boyd A (1996). *Dangerous Obsessions: Teenagers and the Occult.* Marshall Pickering, London, 250 pages with 350 references.
Surveys over 500 young people in Britain and finds that dabbling in the occult can lead to trauma and abuse. Astrology (pages 20-26) is no exception.

Cazeau CJ & Scott SD (1979). *Exploring the Unknown: Great Mysteries Reexamined.* Plenum Press, New York.
Astrology is addressed on pages 225-237.

Correlation (1994 on). *Crucial issues in astrology research: Is the scientific approach relevant to astrology?* 1994, 13(1), 10-53.
Some philosophical problems of astrology 1995, 14(2), 32-44. Theories of astrology including Jung's synchronicity 1996, 15(1), 17-52. Astrology and human judgement (cognitive and perceptual biases) 1998, 17(2), 24-71. All items are amply referenced. The first is a unique peer commentary involving 22 astrologers and 11 scientists modelled on the peer commentaries in the journal Behavioral and Brain Sciences. Back copies of Correlation can be purchased from The Astrological Association,

Lee Valley Technopark, Tottenham Vale, London N17 9LN. Telephone (020) 8880-4848. http://www.astrologer.com/aanet/index.html

Couttie B (1988). *Forbidden Knowledge: The Paranormal Paradox.* Lutterworth Press, Cambridge UK.
        Astrology is on pages 68-72 (mostly lunar effects) and pages 73-79.

Culver RG & Ianna PA (1988). *Astrology: True or False? A Scientific Evaluation.* Prometheus Books, Buffalo NY, 228 pages with over 200 references.
        Minor update of the original 1979 version. A clear and very readable critique by astronomers. Much useful information including test results, a classic survey of astrological prediction, and ten tests issued as a challenge to astrologers (no volunteers to date), but lacking the psychological perspective of Eysenck & Nias (1982). Concludes that astrology is neither scientifically sound nor scientifically useful.

Dean G, Mather A, & 52 others (1977). *Recent Advances in Natal Astrology: A Critical Review 1900-1976.* Analogic, Perth Western Australia, 608 pages with 1010 references.
        Out of print but several copies are held by the library of the Astrological Association. Much is now very dated, and most of the positive findings have subsequently been overturned. All the important studies are in Eysenck & Nias (1982).

Dean G (1992). *'Does astrology need to be true?'* In Frazier K (ed). *The Hundredth Monkey and other paradigms of the paranormal.* Prometheus Books, Buffalo NY, pages 279-319 with 126 references.
        The answer to the title question is no.

Dean GA, Kelly IW, Saklofske DH, & Furnham A (1992). *Graphology and Human Judgment.* In Beyerstein BL & DF (eds). *The Write Stuff: Evaluations of Graphology.* Prometheus Books, Buffalo NY, pages 342-396 with 175 references.
        The arguments apply equally to astrology. On pages 163-200 with 45 references is a most useful discussion by BL Beyerstein of sympathetic magic, again very relevant to astrology.

Dean G, Mather A & Kelly IW (1996). *'Astrology'* in Stein G (ed) *Encyclopedia of the Paranormal.* Prometheus Books, Buffalo NY, pages 47-99 with 15 general references.
        Presently the most recent scientific survey in print covering history, popularity, arguments for and against, conceptual problems, controlled tests, effect size comparisons, problems of birth chart interpretation, how belief in astrology arises, role of human

judgement biases, and the future of astrology. At US $149.95 the encyclopedia is affordable only by libraries.

Dean GA, Nias DKB, & French CC (1997). *'Graphology, astrology, and parapsychology'*. In Nyborg H (ed). *The Scientific Study of Human Nature: Tribute to Hans J. Eysenck at Eighty*. Pergamon, Oxford, pages 511-542 with 124 references.
   Surveys Eysenck's contributions to paranormal research.

Dean M (1980). *The Astrology Game*. Beaufort, New York, 360 pages with nearly 200 references.
   About one fifth is a useful critique of the pop astrology industry. The rest, now dated, tries to establish evidence for astrology. Predicts (wrongly) that a new astrology is being born.

Eisler R (1946). *The Royal Art of Astrology*. Michael Joseph, London, 296 pages but no index.
   Mostly historical. A critique of British newspaper horoscopes and their writers is on pages 19-25.

Ertel S & Irving K (1996). *The Tenacious Mars Effect*. Urania Trust, London.
   Among other things it highlights the often dubious methods used by skeptics to discredit Gauquelin's uncomfortable findings.

Eysenck HJ & Nias DKB (1982). *Astrology: Science or Superstition?* St Martin's Press, New York, 244 pages with 230 references.
   Also in Penguin paperback but out of print. Best single source on research up to 1982 and possibly the easiest to obtain in public libraries. Clear, sympathetic and very readable critique by psychologists. Concludes that everything is negative except the Gauquelin results. Now somewhat dated but still valid, its later research tends to be even more negative.

Gallant RA (1974). *Astrology: Sense or Nonsense?* Doubleday, Garden City NY, 201 pages with glossary and index but no references.

Gauquelin M (1979). *Dreams and Illusions of Astrology*. Prometheus Books, Buffalo NY, 158 pages with 125 references and notes but no index.
   Originally published in French 1969. Mostly a survey of Gauquelin's early non-positive results. Concludes that "since the most painstaking studies have shown the

inanity of horoscopes, there should be a strong rising up against this exploitation of public credulity" (p.158).

Gauquelin M (1983). *The Truth about Astrology*. Basil Blackwell, London, 202 pages.
    The title was imposed by the publisher. Published in the USA as Birthtimes by St Martin's Press, New York. Although the best single source on the Gauquelin work, it includes little on non-Gauquelin work and, of course, nothing on the important later developments. Also in Hutchinson paperback 1984. Details of sources occupy 15 pages.

Gauquelin M (1988). *Written in the Stars*. Aquarian, Wellingborough UK, 256 pages with 70 references.
    A translation of excerpts from earlier French works with an overview and brief update to 1988.

Hines T (1988). *Pseudoscience and the Paranormal: A Critical Examination of the Evidence*. Prometheus Books, Buffalo NY. Astrology (along with lunar effects and biorhythms) is on pages 141-164.

Kelly IW, Culver R, & Loptson P (1989). *'Arguments of the astrologers'*. In Biswas SK, Malik DCV, & Vishveshwara CV (eds). *Cosmic Perspectives*. Cambridge University Press, New York, pages 207-231.

Kelly IW, Dean GA, & Saklofske DH (1990). *'Astrology: A Critical Review'*. In Grim P (ed). *Philosophy of Science and the Occult*. State University of New York, Albany NY, pages 51-81 with 78 references.

Leahey TH & Leahey GE (1983). *Psychology's Occult Doubles: Psychology and the Problem of Pseudoscience*. Nelson-Hall, Chicago.
    Astrology is discussed on pages 32-42 with 8 references.

Martens R & Trachet T (1998). *Making Sense of Astrology*. Prometheus Books, Amherst NY, 276 pages.
    A readable survey by two prominent but often uninformed Belgian skeptics.

Neher A (1990). *The Psychology of Transcendence*, second edition. Dover, New York.
    Astrology is on pages 229-243 and 310-311 with many references. On pages

313-322 is a review of the anti-science arguments used by occultists and others untrained in scientific method.

Parker D (1970). *The Question of Astrology: A Personal Investigation.* Eyre & Spottiswoode, London, 254 pages.

    Articulate, much useful inside information and social observations covering numerous countries.

Pottenger M ed (1995). *Astrological Research Methods Volume 1.* ISAR, PO Box 38613, Los Angeles CA 90038-8613, 466 pages.

    Not a critique but included here because it is the only available anthology of articles on research methods. Unfortunately there are frequent opposing views that are left unresolved, and there is no mention of human reasoning errors. But the authors include scientists as well as astrologers, quite a few articles convey the scientific spirit, and in general the anthology represents a major advance in astrological thinking.

Sladek J (1974). *The New Apocrypha: A Guide to Strange Science and Occult Beliefs.* Stein and Day, New York.

    Astrology is presented on pages 157-166.

Standen A (1977). *Forget Your Sun Sign: An Outline of Antiastrology.* Legacy Publishing, Baton Rouge LA, 135 pages with 33 references.

Stewart JV (1996). *Astrology: What's really in the stars.* Prometheus Books, Buffalo NY, 156 pages 194 references.

    First two-thirds looks at early sources, including Babylonian omen tablets (many photographs), the ancient Greeks, and Ptolemy. The rest is sketchy and lacking in detail.

Thomen AA (1938). *Doctors Don't Believe It.* Dent, London.

    Astrology is discussed on pages 283-290. The book is described by Lord Horder in his Introduction as the first critical work on health superstitions for nearly 300 years.

Appendix 3
Time Twin Research

The purpose of this appendix is two-fold:

      1. The point emerges (in Chapter X) that research into time twins is very well-suited to evaluating astrology. Relatively little work has so far been done in this area, and since it proved possible during a late stage of this book's preparation to talk to two people who have interesting contributions (from quite different perspectives), these are presented here for their intrinsic interest and also in the hope that they may inspire further research.

      2. The point is made in Chapter XI that the interpretation of data can lead to quite different conclusions. The presentation of time twin research by the Researchers is a case in point, as emerges in Peter Roberts's comments.

The Interpretation of Roberts & Greengrass

In Chapter X, the Researchers say:

"Roberts and Greengrass, in their 'The Astrology of Time Twins' (Roberts & Greengrass, 1994), collected a total of 128 people born on six dates, but they found no clear parallels in personality scores, appearance, handwriting, names, interests, occupation, or life events. The strong similarities predicted by astrology were simply not there."

I asked Professor Peter Roberts (co-author of the book in question) whether he agreed with this assessment:

> **Peter Roberts:** In 'The Astrology of Time Twins' Helen Greengrass and I set out to establish whether pairs of people born close together in time resembled each other more than pairs whose birth times were separated by long intervals. What we found was interesting, because there was no overall effect applying to time twins. (Indeed, as Dean has remarked, there have been so many time twins born within the last century that numerous close resemblances would have been noticed long since.) Instead, we found a small but important group of 'close resemblers'—and these occurred more frequently among pairs born close together than for those born far apart. French et al have tried to discredit this finding by arguing that an inappropriate statistical test was applied. However, it emerges that they want to test a different model and therefore propose a different test procedure. This follows a syllogism:
>
>   Astrology is all about pink elephants
>   Roberts and Greengrass found no pink elephants
>   There are no pink elephants
>   Astrology is rubbish

We found brown elephants. The model proposed in 'The Message of Astrology' and elsewhere works on the basis that only a small proportion of the general population have personality traits, preferred occupations etc. corresponding to their natal charts. Toonder and West ('The Case for Astrology'; Penguin Books, 1973*) found several quite remarkable cases of strongly resembling time twins. Similarly, Gauquelin obtained his outstanding results for professionals only by selecting those at the very top (i.e. increasing the proportion of those likely to correspond to their astrological indicators).

More recently, there has been research on personality traits published in 'Correlation' and this too supports the thesis of a small but significant group whose traits correspond to their astrological indicators.

As with the Gauquelin example quoted in Chapter XI, significantly different interpretations are derived from the same basic data: "No clear parallels"; or "A small but important group of 'close resemblers.'" As with that case there is no contradiction, simply a choice to emphasise one facet or another of the study. The significance of twins for astrological research, together with the fact that surprisingly little work has been done in the area, has already been touched upon in the interview with the Researchers.

Having discovered an astrologer who has twins of her own, I managed to record a brief interview and this—offering an experiential rather than statistical perspective on the matter—follows. In order not to infringe anyone's privacy, the astrologer appears as 'Anon' and the names of the twins have been changed.

Experience of Raising Twins

Q: You were saying that your twins are now 25?

Anon: They're girls, fraternal twins, and not identical. Their birth date is 6 February 1975; they were born 16 minutes apart: one was born at 11.55 (midday) and the other at 12.11. They both have Gemini rising, which is interesting from a twins point of view, and they have Moon on the descendant—also interesting from a twin point of view, in the sense of having a built-in mirror.

I did a lot of work on their charts when they were relatively small, when I was doing quite a lot of local group lecturing. While there are no huge differences—all the signs come up the same, the Moons are the same sign, the Ascendants are the same sign and so on—the 16 minute difference shifts the Ascendant by four degrees, so one has 17 Gemini rising, and the other has 21 Gemini. This means that the aspects to the angles come up with slight differences in exactitude. For instance, the first twin (Polly) has an exact trine between her Ascendant and her Sun. The second one (Kristin) has an exact

* West, 1991, included in Appendix 2, is an updated version of this book.

trine between Mercury and her Ascendant.

In that sense, you can differentiate them as being the Solar twin (the older one) and the Mercury twin (the one who picks a line and adapts). That is one way I've looked at them.

Q: Do you feel that really works well as a way of distinguishing them?

Anon: Yes. They looked very much alike for fraternal twins with many people thinking they could be identical. But there were tiny differences in birth weight (one ounce between them), tiny differences in height as children, and these things make a huge difference with twins. I think that, astrologically, you can say the same: that although the base chart, looked at casually, looks very similar, it's the very slight differences that distinguish them. In the work that's been done on twins, the point often comes up that when twins grow up together, they need to (as it were) live out their differences in order to establish their identity.

I find it fascinating; I also feel slightly guilty that I haven't done more! Here I am, with built-in research material and although I do have notes, which I've used in lectures, I feel that if I'd been more diligent I could have observed more along the way. But a lot of it's in my head.

Q: Have there been events where you can see that something happens to one twin, and then to the other one a little later, as transits and progressions become exact?

Anon: Yes, there have been. Off the top of my head I can't summon anything up, but I think with children it's very difficult to decide what events are important. For instance, when Kristin (as a four year old) fell off a playground slide, hit her head and was concussed for a week—I don't think I documented all that stuff well enough.

Let's take something more recent. Here they are, aged 25. Kristin, the second twin, had been hunting for her own flat for near on two years. She had fallen foul of the housing market and had had lots of problems. Eventually, after various failures, she did go through with a flat just before Christmas, and completed—within a few weeks of Polly's flat going through. Now Polly hadn't even thought of getting one for most of that time, and had very recently decided to go for it, and really speeded through the whole process. Yet they completed on flats within a couple of weeks of one another.

Also, the recent eclipse (5 February 2000) was on the day before their birthday, with Uranus conjunct Sun and Moon. They are both having relationship stuff at the moment—major things in terms of their partners, whom they have been with in fairly stable relationships for several years. The twins are both feeling—surprise, surprise—constricted by their partners, who think they are in relationships for life; the twins, on the other hand, are trying to establish their independence. Just what you would imagine, in fact, for any self-respecting Aquarian with Gemini rising and Sagittarius Moon!

But again, the timing is quite extraordinary. Both relationships have been very stable, and this has popped out of the blue—for both of them, simultaneously. But then you might expect some kind of disruptions for anyone born near to the eclipse date.

Q: It has struck me that a problem in looking at events in the lives of time twins is that you aren't necessarily going to get literally the same event happening to them.

Anon: No, you aren't, and it's a general problem across astrology: you are going to get something symbolically appropriate, which could be a totally different event. An astrologer can see how it is appropriate, how it fits with the planetary pattern at the time. The individual perspective also has to be taken into account—what one person thinks is important won't necessarily be so for somebody else. It's very difficult to measure.

Q: Some ground-rules would be needed for a proper study of twins. A Mars transit could mean taking part in a sport, or being wounded with a sharp piece of metal.

Anon: Absolutely.

Q: How useful has astrology been in bringing up your children?

Anon: I think astrology is incredibly helpful, right across the board, for any parent. It helps you to treat your children as individuals, rather than as projections of your own wish-fulfilment, or as simply members of a family. You tend to see them as unique.

With twins particularly, it will help you to spot the differences. While you would expect, say, a pair of Cancerian twins to have a more symbiotic, nurturing or dependent relationship, you wouldn't expect Aquarian twins to. Bearing this in mind, we made a decision not to send them to the same school at the age of eight. They went to different schools, and I think that worked very well; in their teens they became great mates, and they now have a lot of friends in common. Giving them that space, treating them as individuals, probably made it possible for them to come back together through their own choice.

We had very interesting set-ups in their adolescence. When they were around 15 or 16, they were going out with a pair of boys who were also friends—and who were themselves both Gemini. I've got some lovely astrology around that, the synastry between the four charts.

Q: Were you able to help them in a vocational direction?

Anon: No, beyond being there to discuss with them whatever they felt like talking about... but then, I've got Uranus rising in my chart, and I try not to steer anyone anyway! My feeling is that they will find it in their own time. In fact Polly, the older one, is now doing psychology—which I think is a fairly appropriate thing for an Aquarian. Kristin is not in any particular niche as yet.

A propos of the Mercury thing—the elder, what I call the Solar twin, was bright enough and went to a fairly academic girls' school. The younger one was diagnosed as dyslexic. She's left-handed, and wrote backwards and upside-down. We went through the usual middle-class things of sending her to an educational psychologist, and so on and so forth, I don't think there was actually anything wrong there at all. I think it's the Laingian* thing: children do whatever they do in order to make the family cohere (or whatever they are trying to do). Kristin's definitely non-academic; and while she's bright, she simply can't cope with exams and the normal academic set-up. And yet she is incredibly Mercurial; you really can't measure intelligence.

Q: Any other thoughts on astrological parallels?

Anon: There was a man that I might have married—I was virtually engaged to him for a long time, and then we broke up and I married my husband. I had one child, then the twins as my second and third children; this other man (who I didn't marry) had his first child within three hours of my twins. So we've actually got biological twins plus a time twin. And the fact that this child was born so close to my twins, to a man who I might actually have married... what astrological conclusions could one draw from that, about the time when they were born?

---

* That is, as described by the therapist R D Laing.

Glossary; The Astrological Chart

Part 1 - Glossary

The explanations and definitions here are extremely basic; they are provided for non-astrologers reading this book, who want to follow what is being talked about in technical passages. Readers who feel they belong in this category are recommended to read through Part 2 of this appendix, 'The Astrological Chart', to establish some basic points of reference.

AA – Astrological Association; see Appendix 1, part 2 for details.

Age of Aquarius – see 'Aquarian Age.'

Angle(s) – see 'Angular'; 'Ascendant'; 'Midheaven'.

Angular – when a planet is close to the Ascendant, Descendant, Midheaven or IC—otherwise known as the four 'angles' of the chart. This is considered to make the planet concerned strong, and also to involve it particularly with the symbolism of the angle concerned.

APA – Association of Professional Astrologers; see Appendix 1, part 2 for details.

Applying – as in, e.g., 'Moon applying'—a planet is in an aspect to another planet or point in a chart, and is moving closer to make that aspect exact. An aspect which is becoming closer in this way is often considered stronger than one which is waning.

Aquarian Age – there are 'ages' of 2,160 years per sign, based on long-term astronomical movements; we are currently in the transition between the age of Pisces and the Age of Aquarius, but there is little agreement as to when the change should be regarded as complete. The phrase is sometimes used as a shorthand expression for 'a golden age of brotherly love which is just around the corner'.

Arabian Parts – points in the chart derived by, e.g., adding the position (in degrees, starting from zero degrees of Aries) of two planets and subtracting the position of a third. Considered (by some) significant indicators on various issues—from friendship to journeys by water.

Ascendant – the zodiacal sign that is crossed by the horizon on the left (more correctly, 'in the east') of a birth chart. Generally considered an important indicator of personality. The point where the horizon crosses the zodiac on the other side is the descendant, symbolic of one-to-one relationships of all kinds. See 'The Astrological Chart' below.

Aspect – a particular type of geometric relationship between planets etc in the chart; see 'The Astrological Chart' in the following section for more.

Asteroids – bits of rock in orbit around the Earth, between the orbits of Mars and Jupiter. There are more than 7,000 of them. Some astrologers use a few of the major ones in interpretation; a smaller number use them all (at least, all the ones which have been named).

Astro*carto*graphy – see 'Astrolocality'.

Astrolocality – generic term (introduced by Martin Davis), which embraces all techniques for applying astrological information to physical territory—particularly Astro*carto*graphy and Local Space.

Athla (also the Circle of Athla) – arrangement of 'Houses' (q.v.) starting from the Part of Fortune instead of the Ascendant.

BAPS – British Astrological and Psychic Society; see Appendix 1, part 2 for details.

Battle astrology – system of astrological analysis developed by medieval astrologers to predict the outcome of battles.

Birth chart – an astrological chart drawn up for the moment a being, organisation, or whatever, is born; see 'The Astrological Chart', above.

Chart – will usually mean 'Birth Chart' (q.v.); could also be a chart of 'Directions' (q.v.), or an astrolocality map (q.v.).

Conjunction – an 'Aspect' (q.v.) of zero degrees, more or less; if two planets are 'in conjunction' they are very close together in the chart and will influence each other very directly.

Converse (directions) – directions that are applied backwards (in zodiacal order or calendar time) to the conventional approach, on the basis that the past reveals information about the future.

Culminates (as in, 'Moon culminates'). When a planet arrives at the Midheaven (q.v.) it is said to culminate. Before that point it is said to rise; afterwards, to decrease. This is considered to increase its strength.

Cusp – as in, 'cusp of the sign'. The exact point at which one zodiacal sign (see 'Zodiac') finishes and the next begins.

Cycles – as in, e.g., 'Jupiter cycles'. Repetitive patterns of planetary movement: e.g. Jupiter orbits the Sun in 11.86 years; Jupiter and Saturn form a conjunction approximately every twenty years; the Jupiter-Saturn conjunctions occur in zodiacal signs of the same element (q.v.) for approximately 240 years. Planetary cycles of this type are seen as significant by astrologers, giving information about the evolution (or degeneration) of people, countries etc.

Decumbiture (chart) – chart drawn up for the moment a person takes to their sick-bed, or contacts an astrologer about their illness, which is used to diagnose the illness and prescribe a cure.

Descendant – see 'Ascendant'.

Directions – generic term which embraces all the techniques used by astrologers to gain information about how things develop for a given birth chart. The most straightforward such technique is to look at transits—where the actual movements of the planets for a particular week (say) are compared to the birth chart, giving information about trends and (possible) events for the entity that owns the birth chart. The method of progressions is to use a symbolic measure of time—e.g., to take the movements of the planets over a day as representing trends for a year, so that an individual's forty-sixth year would be represented by the planet's motions between day 45 and day 46 after birth (this is one out of many methods of secondary progression). Solar arc directions represent a variation on the theme, where the motion of the progressed Sun is added to each planet. There are many variations on the basic themes mentioned here, and any given astrologer is likely to use two or more in combination.

Draconic chart – a chart in which the zodiac is based on the Sun/Moon relationship; planets remain in the same place relative to one another, but (almost always) they will be in different signs of the zodiac to the 'Tropical' chart (q.v.).

Dwads – divisions of 2.5°, which divide a sign of the zodiac into 12 segments, thereby creating a mini-zodiac within each sign, used to get additional information and fine-tuning after looking at the birth chart.

Eclipse – eclipses are generally seen as powerful and significant, though the precise significance of any given eclipse will depend on the other planetary positions at the time, and the way in which the whole configuration connects to the chart of particular individuals and countries. A 'solar eclipse' means that the Moon blocks out light from the Sun; a 'lunar eclipse' means that the Earth comes between Moon and Sun, preventing light from getting to the Moon.

Eighth – see 'House(s)'.

Ephemeris – book (or software) that lists planetary positions, etc.

Exaltation – a planet's exaltation is a sign where it is (so to speak) happy and at ease, like an honoured guest; exaltation increases a planet's strength. (See also 'Honour').

Harmonics – an approach in which charts are analysed in terms of a particular number—e.g. applying the number 5 to a chart gives the '5th harmonic'. Harmonic charts can reveal relationships between planets which are not evident from the birth chart on its own.

Geo, geocentric chart – a chart drawn up with the Earth at the centre; this is usually assumed to be the case, but may need to be stated explicitly when an astrologer also works with heliocentric charts.

Helio, Heliocentric chart – a chart drawn up from the perspective of the Sun, rather than (as is usual) the Earth. Cf 'Geocentric'.

Honour – a planet is said to have honour in a particular sign (or in the house which is ruled by that sign) if it fulfils various conditions; the most straightforward is rulership (see ruled by…) but there are several other possibilities including exaltation (q.v.). The subtleties of astrological honour and rulership are too intricate to go into here, but they give a wide range of possible strengths and nuances of relationship to the factors in a chart.

Horary – system where a chart is drawn up for the moment a question is asked (e.g. 'where is my lost key?'); it is considered that the astrologer can get the answer from the chart. In general usage, 'horary' often means 'a horary chart'.

House(s) – there are (usually) twelve houses in the astrological chart, identified as first, second, third, etc.—see 'The Astrological Chart' (following section) for more. Sometimes referred to simply as 'the twelfth', 'my eighth', etc.

House systems – different systems for calculating the houses in the chart, usually named after their creators—e.g., Placidus, Regiomontanus, Koch. The methods and differences in such approaches are too complex to go into here. Different astrologers favour different systems. See also 'House(s)'.

IC – see 'Midheaven'.

I Ching – Chinese oracle, consulted by casting yarrow stalks or throwing coins to arrive at an arrangement of six lines called a hexagram.

In aspect – see 'Aspect'.

In conjunction – see 'Conjunction'.

Judicial Astrology – half of a two-part distinction that was intended to segregate natural, understandable phenomena from those that defy logic and may, in former times, have been attributed to the devil. Judicial astrology is 'supernatural'—depending for its efficacy on the astrologer's intuition and not capable of being fully understood in terms of scientific laws or logical procedures. Judicial astrology is often characterised as being more akin to the I Ching or Tarot than to a scientific discipline. See also 'Natural Astrology'.

Jupiter cycles – see 'Cycles'.

Jyotish – means 'astrology', specifically the form which is indigenous to India.

Kabbalah – ancient system of esoteric knowledge in the Judaic tradition.

Lines – as in, 'Neptune lines', etc; lines of planetary influence mapped out on the surface of the Earth using 'Astrolocality' techniques (q.v.).

Local Space – see 'Astrolocality'.

Lunar eclipse – see 'Eclipse'.

MC – see 'Midheaven'.

Meridian – another term for 'Midheaven' (q.v.).

Midheaven – also known as the MC (from Medium Coeli, Latin for 'middle of the skies'). Usually the cusp of the tenth house, it is said to represent one's career, aspirations (and more). The opposite point in the chart, the IC (Imum Coeli) relates to home issues (and so on) in a chart.

Midpoint – a point half-way between two planets (etc.) in a chart; used (by some) as a significant factor that links the principles of the two factors involved. 'Midpoints' can also be used in the sense of, 'a chart showing midpoints'.

Natal Chart – 'Birth chart' (q.v.).

Natural Astrology – one half of a two-part distinction that was intended to segregate natural, understandable phenomena from those that appear 'supernatural'. Natural astrology comprises those parts of the subject that can (in theory at least) be measured by rational, scientific methods. This would include astronomical influences (Sun spots, for instance) on weather and agriculture. The Gauquelin findings—showing a statistical tendency for planetary position to correlate with career—would also fall under the heading 'natural astrology'. See also 'Judicial Astrology'.

Noon chart – a chart drawn up for noon, usually because a precise birth time is not available.

Opposition – an aspect of about 180°; when used in the form, eg. "I had been going through my Uranus opposition", it refers to a transit of Uranus to a position 180° away from its position in the birth chart. In this sense, a Uranus opposition occurs around the age of 42 and signifies a time of evaluation in the life, of looking back on youth and ahead to old age and thinking, "My God! What have I done!"

Outer Planets – the three planets that are furthest from the Earth, and which therefore were the last to be discovered: Uranus, Neptune and Pluto.

Part of Fortune – one of the 'Arabian Parts'.

Planetary aspects – see 'Aspect'.

Progressed – see 'Directions'.

Quincunx – an aspect of 150°.

Relocation chart – a birth chart that is drawn up as if the chartee had been born somewhere else. Most commonly used to see how someone is influenced by a major change of location. This starts shading into 'Astrolocality' (q.v.).

Retrograde – as in, e.g., 'Mercury retrograde'. As seen from the Earth, the planets sometimes appear to pause in their normal motion through the zodiacal signs and move backwards a little way; a planet which is doing this is retrograde. Being retrograde is considered to affect a planet's functioning—the influence is generally considered adverse, so that e.g. many astrologers expect communication (ruled by Mercury) to be problematic when that planet is retrograde.

Return – as in, e.g., 'Saturn return'. The time when a planet returns to the point it occupied in the birth chart. The period around a return is seen as significant; the most notorious example is the Saturn return, which occurs for the first time around the age of 29. For the individual this is seen as a time for facing up to reality in one's life, a process that is often accompanied by frustration and difficulties in the short term. The 'Solar return' occurs once a year, on or near the birth date, and is often used as a blueprint for trends in the year ahead.

Rises, Rising – as in, e.g., 'Libra rising' or 'Mars rises'—a sign, or planet, in the first house (said to make it more influential).

Ruled by... – Planets are seen as having dominion over zodiacal signs, other planets, and people through various systems of rulership (astrologers use differing systems). At the simplest level, someone with (e.g.) Mercury in Sagittarius might say that Mercury is ruled by Jupiter, since Jupiter rules Sagittarius; if Jupiter is considered to rule the entire chart, by e.g. ruling the ascendant (there are also many more complicated ways of evaluating the chart's ruler) then someone might say 'I am ruled by Jupiter'. When a planet 'rules' it is considered to have particular significance in characterising the way in which the entity ruled will function—e.g., Jupiter is associated with generosity and wisdom (amongst other qualities), so these would be expected to be predominating concerns for the planet or person ruled by Jupiter.

Ruler – see 'Ruled by...'

Saturn Return – see 'Return'.

Secondary converse – see 'Converse' and 'Directions'.

Secondary progressed – see 'Directions'.

Sidereal – literally 'of the stars'; the sidereal zodiac is based on the positions of the constellations. This is the one used in Vedic astrology; some western astrologers also use it, either instead of the tropical zodiac, or in addition. For contrast, cf 'Tropical'.

Sign – see 'Zodiac'.

Solar arc – a type of 'Direction' (q.v.).

Solar eclipse – see 'Eclipse'.

Solar return – see 'Return'.

Square – an aspect of 90°; when used as in (e.g.) 'my Pluto square', it refers to a transit of Pluto to square its position in the birth chart; this particular transit can signify a time of regeneration, born out of destruction and power struggles.

Star-signs – same thing as 'Sun-signs' (q.v.)

Strong (as in, e.g., 'Strong Saturn') – a planet (etc) which, due to its placement by sign, house, and/or aspect, is particularly powerful in a chart.

Sun-signs – see 'The Astrological Chart' below, and Chapter III.

Tarot – cards used for divination.

Transits – see 'Directions'.

Tropical – as in, e.g., 'basic tropical pattern'; the tropical zodiac is the one commonly used in the west, and derived from the motion of the Sun rather than from the constellations. Hence, 'basic tropical pattern' means a chart using the tropical zodiac—i.e. the one which most western astrologers would generally use. Cf 'Sidereal'.

T-square – a combination of three aspects (an opposition and two squares) that form a right-angled triangle in the chart, indicating particular tensions, challenges, abilities etc.

Twelfth – see 'House(s)'.

Uranus in Cancer – as in, 'the Uranus in Cancer bunch'; people born in the approximate period of seven years when Uranus was in Cancer (most recently 1949-56). Since Uranus is iconoclastic and Cancer relates to home and family, this is a short-hand way of referring to the tendency for people of that generation to be independent, single parents, etc.

Uranus opposition – see 'Opposition'.

Vedic astrologer – a practitioner of the Indian tradition of astrology.

Zodiac – the circle comprised of 12 signs: Aries, Taurus, Gemini, Cancer, Leo, Virgo, Libra, Scorpio, Sagittarius, Capricorn, Aquarius, Pisces; see 'The Astrological Chart' below for more.

Part 2 - The Astrological Chart

There is frequent reference to 'charts' in this book; here is a basic introduction to the astrological chart.

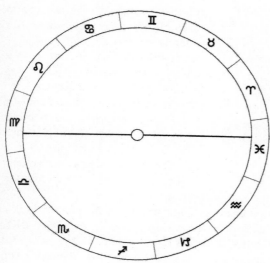

(Left) The Earth is the small circle in the middle; its horizon is the horizontal line, and the twelve signs of the zodiac are in the outer circle. The zodiac itself is derived either from the annual motion of the Sun (the tropical zodiac) or from the positions of the stars (the sidereal zodiac). Different traditions and astrologers favour one or the other; as a generalisation, astrologers in India use the sidereal whilst westerners use the tropical zodiac. Each sign has particular qualities and meanings. The point where the horizon touches the zodiac on the left is called 'the ascendant', and on the right it is 'the descendant'.

(Right) The 'ascendant/descendant' axis has been augmented (and there are many different systems for doing this) to create twelve segments—the twelve 'houses'. Counting anti-clockwise from the first segment under the horizon on the left side, they are identified as 'first house', 'second house' and so on. Each house has particular meanings and areas of life associated with it.

The Earth's orbit means that the signs of the zodiac appear to move; in 24 hours, they rotate through 360°, giving twelve different signs on the ascendant every day.

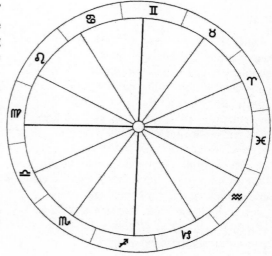

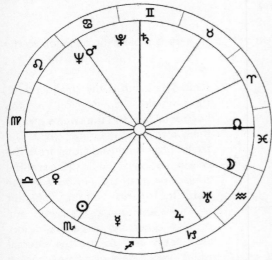

(Left) Now the planets have been added (in fact, what are shown here are ten planets and the north node of the Moon—in addition to the basic ten planets, there are many points, planetoids, asteroids, Arabian parts etc. which any given astrologer might include in a chart).

In a (loosely) similar way to the zodiacal signs, each planet has particular qualities and meanings—for instance, Mercury signifies (amongst other things) language, the nervous system, and transport. Note that each planet is in a particular sign, and a particular house; these placements influence the expression of the planet's energy, creating a huge number of permutations amongst different charts.

The planets move at vastly different speeds. The most swiftly-moving, the Moon, takes a little over 27 days to go through all twelve zodiacal signs. The slowest, Pluto, takes 248 years. One consequence of this is that it would take forever for the complete pattern of a chart to recur, and hence almost every chart is significantly different. (The exceptions to this rule are the 'time twins' discussed in Chapter X and Appendix 3—though even in such cases it is rare to get identical charts.)

Remember also that, owing to the Earth's rotation, the planets move through all twelve houses in 24 hours—further increasing the complexity of the chart. This, incidentally, is why astrologers are always keen to get a precise time for an event; even a difference of five minutes will change the chart.

(Right) The planets also interact with one another in different ways. The simplest type of interaction is geometric: if planets are roughly 120° apart, for instance, this yields information about how they will interact. The angle of 120° is an 'aspect'; astrologers use a variety of aspects. Other techniques (such as harmonics and midpoints) yield information about how each pair of planets will interact, regardless of whether or not there is a conventional aspect between them.

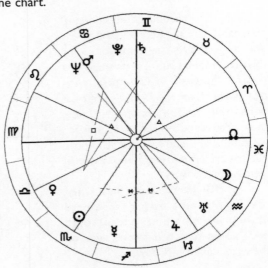

Sun-Sign Astrology and the Birth Chart

The account so far starts to explain the kinds of things that astrologers look at when they cast a chart—whether it be for the birth of a person, a company, or a question.

The approach of Sun-sign astrology is significantly different. It begins by taking the sign in which someone's Sun is placed (Taurus, say) as representative of them in a general way (this is what we mean when we say 'I'm a Taurus' or whatever; that is the sign the Sun was in at birth). To see what might be said to Taureans, the Sun-sign astrologer might rotate the zodiacal wheel so that the sign of Taurus begins at the ascendant. The positions of planets in the corresponding houses, and their mutual interactions over a period (day, week, month, year—whatever period the astrologer chooses to look at), are then interpreted.

Index

Please note: all general entries have astrological connections, for instance, 'Media' refers to the media's attitude towards, and interactions with, astrology and astrologers. The word 'astrology' itself is therefore used sparingly to avoid redundancy. Pages in which a subject is defined are in **bold**. In addition, pages in which interviewees are quoted directly, rather than referred to, are in **bold**.

Saturn return	28, **252**
School of Psychotherapy & Counselling	96n
Science and Scientists	21, 89, 124–166 *passim*
	Characterised as a quasi-religious group 174, 175, 176, 180
	(see also 'Modern Science', 'Research')
Seley's Adaptation Syndrome	85
Sex	98
Seymour, Dr. Percy	179
Sheldrake, Rupert	160
Sikhism	25
Simplicity	
— see 'Complexity and Simplicity'	
Skinner, Christeen	**11, 15**, 16, 20, 40, **44–48**, 49, 50–51, **52–53**, **63–64**, **108**, **184**, 219–220
Sleep	92–93, 98
Smit, Rudolf	
— see 'Researchers'	
Soviet Union	35 (see also 'Russia')
Speer, Richard	149
Spencer, Neil	42n
Spirituality	33–34, 74, 75–77, 111, 112–113, 184, 190–192
Sports Astrology	55–61
Sports Psychology	192
Stock Market	24, 45, 54
Stonehenge	
— see 'Megaliths'	
Sun-sign astrology	25–26, 27–43, 125, 145, **257** (see also 'Totem')
Surgery	82
Susskind, David	13
Sutton, Komilla	**24–25, 66–68, 69–70**, 108, 220
Synchronicity	160–161
Synthesis (of a chart)	161–163, 192–193
Tara (software program)	110n
Tarnas, Richard	180
Tarot	12, 19, 100, 183, 189, **253**
Telephone Services	34–35, 40–41
Television	
— see 'Media'	
Thedossiou, Katina	104
Theosophical Society, The	29
Therapy	62–64, 94–97, 113, 120–121, 123, 155, 157, 159

About the Author

Garry Phillipson graduated from the University of East Anglia in 1976, with honours in Philosophy. By that point, he had grown disillusioned with traditional western philosophy, and consequently began an exploration of other paths and systems. The ones that proved to have the most enduring appeal were astrology and Buddhist philosophy.

Whilst this internal search went on, his external circumstances fluctuated regularly. The next ten years saw him working as: a carer in sheltered accommodation for the elderly, a lorry loader, an executive officer in a major bank, a bingo hall attendant, a computer operator, and a member of Part Form—the techno/dada band from Liverpool.

In 1986 Garry decided to devote time exclusively to the study of Buddhist philosophy and meditation, ordaining as a monk with the Aukana Trust (with whom he had been studying since 1983). He left the monastery in 1993, but remains actively involved with the Trust—as a trustee (the organisation is a registered charity), and as a meditation teacher and organiser of the Trust's London Group. He now works as Resources Manager for a London-based software company.

'Astrology in the Year Zero' resulted from Garry's continued study of astrology—in particular, from his investigation of the philosophy and assumptions that underpin the subject. His articles and lectures have appeared under the aegis of groups including the Astrological Association of Great Britain, the Company of Astrologers, the Urania Trust, the Standing Conference on Organizational Symbolism, The Mountain Astrologer, and Ascella.

THE DRACONIC CHART   by Rev. Pamela Crane

From the recognised authority comes the long-awaited revision of a pioneering masterwork

The fruit of 22 years' study and experience, Pamela Crane's important work is now available in a new, enlarged and revised edition. This trail-blazing volume unravels the history of the Draconic Zodiac and its meaning in the natal chart, synastry, forecasting, rectification and even horary, using a host of well-known examples.

The Draconic Chart is an extremely important element in a lucid, multi-layered system in which each zodiac expresses a distinctly different facet of human experience.

This book focuses on the interaction between the familiar Tropical chart—describing the conditions of your current life—and the Draconic, with its deep insight into your life meaning: driving principles, spiritual purpose, vocation, and karma.

All this as well as a documenting of Pamela Crane's own impassioned journey from her first apprenticeship to the discovery of the horoscope of Christ's Nativity.

Reviews:

"Fascinating and thought provoking. A well researched and stimulating work... destined to become a classic"
— Graham Bates

"Pamela Crane was one of the first to realise that since the cosmos itself is multidimensional, a genuine astrology must likewise operate on many levels, each amplifying the others. I admire her persuasive enthusiasm, as she demonstrates how planetary configurations can be beneficially translated into another zodiac altogether"
— Dennis Elwell

"An essential addition to the bookshelf of every astrologer"
— *The Kabbalist Magazine*

"[it] presents a well-thought-out complementary approach to Tropical and Vedic astrology"
— *Dell Horoscope*

"Pamela Crane is an extraordinary astrologer... a remarkable book and a unique contribution to astrology; those who are curious about astrology's far-reaching potential will welcome it"
— *The Mountain Astrologer*

"This is much more than some how-to textbook. It is also interwoven with the story of a very personal spiritual odyssey told with humour, self-deprecation and imagination... a glimpse too, into the modus operandi of a dedicated astrologer"
— *The Astrological Journal*

"If you are seriously interested in the subject, I promise that this book will open your eyes as never before... [it is] something special"
— *The Square*

"For the student of astrology and the counsellor, it opens a door to a world of a different level which can throw light on our journey"
— Marian Davison

ISBN: 0 9530261 4 0
RRP: £16.99; $30

Flare 'Pioneers' Series
Extent: 278 pages

UK edition: comb-bound
Format: 297x210mm

SHORTHAND OF THE SOUL
The Quotable Horoscope by David Hayward

Bridging the gap between astrology and literature

An inspirational collection of over 2000 quotations with astrological references, providing an invaluable tool for professional astrologers and students.

This is a unique anthology embracing every aspect of life. From professional creeds to personal reflections, you'll find David Hayward's collection amusing, provocative and enlightening. It stands solidly as a well-researched and intelligently compiled book of quotations and has a full index and list of keywords.

Reviews:

"This collection of thoughtful and, at times, zany quips and quotes is a real delight... a pleasure to read and to reference using the index to look up authors and sources"   — Sidney Sheldon

"A gift with words helps to reveal analysis creatively and memorably. In *Shorthand of the Soul*, David Hayward demonstrates both gifts admirably"   — Noel Tyl

"The terse and succinct phrases often hit more closely to the heart of the definition than complex pages of text"   — Lois Rodden

"Here we are entertainingly introduced to the zodiac signs as complexes of meaning, twelve different but equally valid philosophies, different ideals, different ways of looking and of being. And here too, is confirmation that whatever lies behind our human reality, it does not lack humour!"   — Dennis Elwell

"This is a unique book... David likens his book to an 'ADR' or an Astro-Desk Reference. He intends the book to help both the astrologer and the client relate to the various astrological energies through something other than traditional keywords. While keywords lend one insight into the meanings of the astrological symbols, the quotes, he feels, bring an added dimension into the understanding of these symbols... The book should be a worthwhile addition to your library. It gives a fresh and new view to images which embody the astrological paradigm"   — Michael Munkasey, *NCGR Journal*

"What an icebreaker it is, at the beginning of an astrological consultation, to hand a new client the copy of a brief phrase written by Shakespeare, Emerson or Gandhi... If you are going to have an astrology book sitting on your coffee table, this is the one!... Pick it up at anytime and get a lift, experience a deep thought or laugh until your sides split"   — Jeani Lewis, *Aspects* magazine

ISBN: 0 9530261 2 4
RRP: £12.99; $19.95

Flare 'Astro-Links' Series
Extent: 256 pages

Paperback
Format: 228x152mm

BRITISH ENTERTAINERS The Astrological Profiles by Frank C. Clifford

Which celebrities share your Sun, Moon or Ascendant sign?
What are the astrological spotlights on entertainment?
Which planets, signs and houses are vital to success as a performer?

This best-selling and acclaimed work combines astrology with the concise biographies of over 700 prominent personalities from the worlds of film, theatre, TV, comedy and music. It also uncovers the prime indicators of performing talent in birth charts. All data are meticulously researched and classified.

It is the reference book for researchers and astrologers wishing to explore correlations between life events & character and planetary placements & cycles.

It is an ideal companion for starwatchers and fans of the famous wanting to know the major life events of their favourite celebrities. Discover the real personalities of the famous, whilst examining the astrological stars behind the stars. Don't miss out on the reference book astrologers rely upon before, during and after talk shows, comedies, concerts and drama series!

Reviews:

"For those into CelebrityWatch, this has a deeper fascination than 'Hello!' magazine and all those chat shows. It's a chance to see the bones beneath the masks and the make up... original, stylish and beautiful"
— *Astrological Journal*

"A 'must' for data collectors"
— AFA

"Nicely written and the book is well-presented and well-organized"
— Kenneth Irving, *American Astrology*

"Well thought out, laid out and put together... not only is the data reliable but the profiles are well-written and fun to read"
— Marion March, *Aspects* magazine

"For data collectors... this is a must-buy"
— *Dell Horoscope*

"I could review this in three words: 'Buy this book' but I am more inclined to do it in four: 'Buy this book now'... a comprehensive astro-guide to British entertainment"
— John Frawley, *The Astrologer's Apprentice*

"...a snappy, accessible introduction"
— Neil Spencer, *The Observer*

"[the book] is a 'must' if the ennui of frosty nights is to be kept at bay"
— *Astrological Quarterly*

"For those who want to learn astrology, (this book) can be a teaching manual as well... accurate data collections are the best teaching tools available"
— Dana Holliday, as quoted in the introduction

ISBN: 0 9530261 1 8
RRP: £9.99; $15

Flare 'Astro-Profiles' Series
Extent: 224 pages

Paperback
Format: 212x148

THE SUN SIGN READER   by Joan Revill

What astrology reveals about authors, books and fictional characters

From a renowned astrology writer comes the ultimate astrological birthday book of fictional events and people for every day of the year.

Drawing from literature, radio and television, *The Sun Sign Reader* is an indispensable and entertaining cocktail of birthdays and event dates. It breathes new life into numerous classics, contemporary texts and forgotten works.

Find out if there are similarities between those born under the same Sun sign, and build up an understanding of the zodiac by meeting various characters and authors.

A stimulating introduction to hundreds of authors and their works, *The Sun Sign Reader* is a perfect gift for every book lover and a sure way to excite a student's interest in literature.

Enjoy Joan Revill's inimitable English style, humorous observations and incisive assessments of over 400 characters, writers and events.

Meet Agatha Christie, Jane Austen, Ruth Rendell, Robert Burns, Virginia Woolf, James Joyce, Sylvia Plath, Anita Loos, Charles Baudelaire, Jeffrey Archer, Terry Pratchett, Ian Fleming, J.D. Salinger, J.R.R. Tolkien, Catherine Cookson, Margaret Mitchell, Marcel Proust, Margaret Atwood, Ernest Hemingway, Carl Jung, William Shakespeare, Dorothy Parker, Fay Weldon, Bram Stoker, Muriel Spark, Truman Capote, Oscar Wilde, George Eliot, Mark Twain, Chris Carter.... and their famous creations.

Reviews:

"The Sun Sign Reader is a fascinating insight. Lots of research has gone into this book and I'm sure readers will feel that it deserves a space on their bookshelves where it can easily be found and delved into many, many times"
— Carole Golder

"Was Tarzan a winging Sagittarius? Did Sherlock Holmes owe his powers to Jupiter? Is poor Bridget Jones really stuck on the cusp of Pisces and Aries? The Sun Sign Reader is a gleeful romp through the birthdays of fiction's heroes, with thoughtful stop-offs to ponder the horoscopes of their creators. How can authors as different as Charles Dickens, Jules Verne and William Burroughs all be typically Aquarian? Joan Revill knows"
— Neil Spencer, astrologer to *The Observer*

"The Sun Sign Reader will remain glued to your fingers from the moment you pick it up. No bookworm should be without it"
— Jane Struthers, astrologer to *The Sun*

ISBN: 0 9530261 3 2   Flare 'Astro-Profiles' Series   Paperback
RRP: £9.99; $15.99   Extent: 224 pages   Format: 216x138mm

For books, popular discounted titles, consultations and giveaways, check out our updated website at: **www.flareUK.com**

Bookstores and internet bookshops stock most Flare titles, but if you wish to keep informed of our special offers and new books as they become available, please write to us at: Flare Publications, 29 Dolben Street, London SE1 0UQ, England or call: +44 (0) 20 7 922 1123; or email to: info@flareuk.com